HEADWAY

STUDENT'S BOOK **ELEMENTARY**

Liz & John Soars

D1718448

Oxford University Press

STUDENT'S BOOK

WORKBOOK

STUDENT'S BOOK

WORKBOOK

5

UNIT 1

am/is/are – Possessive adjectives – Spelling

Hello!

PRESENTATION (1)

T 1a Read and listen.

A Hello. My name's Jenny. What's your name?
B Anna.
A Where are you from, Anna?
B I'm from New York.

> ⚠️
> name's = name is
> what's = what is
> I'm = I am

Practice

1 Writing and listening

Complete the conversation.

A Hello. My _____ Thomas.
   What's _____ name?
B Johann.
A _____ are you from, Johann?
B _____ from Berlin.
   Where _____ you from?
A _____ _____ Oxford.

T 1b Listen and check.

2 Speaking

Stand up!
Talk to the students in the class.

> Hello! My name's _____ .
> What's your name?

> Anna.

> Where are you
> from, Anna?

> I'm from _____ .

PRESENTATION (2)

Read about Manuel.

My name's Manuel Garcia and I'm a doctor. I'm thirty.
I'm married and I have two children. I live in a house in Seville
in the south of Spain. I want to learn English for my job.

Practice

schreiben
im eigen
Namen

1 Writing and listening

Complete the text about Mayumi.

Ich Machtend ein dorive ein

My name's Mayumi Kimura and I'm ~~are~~ **student.**
technische controler
I ~~am~~ nineteen years old. I'm not married. I have two
brothers and a sister. I lev in a flat in *Berlin* Osaka, Japan.
I want to learn English because it's an international
language

T2 Listen and check.

2 Writing and speaking

Write about you. Then read it to the class.

PRESENTATION (3)

1 **T3** Look at the stress marks. Practise saying the countries.

	●●	●●	●●●
France	England	Brazil	Germany
Spain	Egypt	Japan	Mexico
Greece	Russia		Hungary
			Italy

2 Look at the photographs and read the words.

¡Buenos días!

This is Manuel.
He's from Spain.

Konnichiwa!

This is Mayumi.
She's from Japan.

Hello!
Hello!

This is Mike and Rosie.
They're from England.

He's = He is
They're = They are

3 Write where the people are from. Choose one of the countries in Exercise 1.

Bonjour!

This is Jean-Paul.
his from France

Guten Tag!

This is Johann.
his from Germany

Salem ala gaum!

This is Fatima.
his from Egypt

Buongiorno!

This is Paola.
his from Italy

Hairetai!

This is Christina.
his from Brasil

This is Clara and Bruno.

_____

This is Ivan.

his from Russia
(Rascha)

This is Pablo.

his from Mexico

This is János and Irén.

his from Hungar

Practice

1 Speaking

1 Work in pairs.
Ask and answer questions about the people in the photographs.

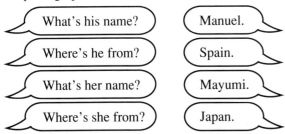

What's his name?	Manuel.
Where's he from?	Spain.
What's her name?	Mayumi.
Where's she from?	Japan.

2 Ask and answer the same questions about the students in the class.

2 Listening and pronunciation

T4 Tick (✔) the sentence you hear.

1 a She's from Spain.
  b He's from Spain.
2 a I'm sixteen.
  b I'm sixty.
3 a His name's Pat.
  b Her name's Pat.
4 a They're from Britain.
  b They're from Brazil.
5 a Where's she from?
  b Where's he from?
6 a He's a teacher in France.
  b His teacher in France.

3 Grammar

Put *am*, *is*, *are*, *his*, or *her* into the gaps.

Example
My name __is__ Anna.

a Where _____ you from?

b I _____ from Italy.

c 'What's _____ name?' 'Peter.'

d Christina _____ twenty-nine years old.

e Mike and Rosie _____ from London.

f Clara _____ married.

g 'What's _____ name?' 'Mayumi.'

h He _____ a doctor.

i I have a daughter. _____ name's Kate.

j János and Irén _____ married. They have a son.

4 Choosing the correct sentence

One sentence has a mistake. Choose the correct sentence.
Put ✔ and ✗.

Examples
His from Greece. ✗   She's a teacher. ✔
He's from Greece. ✔   She's teacher. ✗

1 a Where she from?
  b Where's she from?
2 a What's her name?
  b What's she's name?
3 a I'm a student.
  b I'm student.
4 a She is twenty-nine years old.
  b She has twenty-nine years old.
5 a I live in flat.
  b I live in a flat.
6 a I have two sisters.
  b I have two sister.
7 a They from Japan.
  b They're from Japan.
8 a He's a doctor.
  b His a doctor.
9 a He's name's Bruno.
  b His name's Bruno.
10 a Her surname is Smith.
  b Her surname it's Smith.

● LISTENING AND SPEAKING

Hello and goodbye

1 Write the conversations in the correct order.

a Fine, thank you. And you?
   I'm OK, thanks.
   Hello, Mary. How are you?

   A _____

   B _____

   A _____

b Not bad, thanks. And you?
   Very well. How are the
      children?
   Hi, Dave! How are you?
   They're fine.

   A _____

   B _____

   A _____

   B _____

c Goodbye, Anne. Have a
      nice evening.
   Thanks, Chris. See you
      tomorrow!
   Goodbye, Chris.

   A _____

   B _____

   A _____

T5 Listen and check.

2 Stand up! Have conversations with other students.

10

● VOCABULARY AND PRONUNCIATION

1 Using a bilingual dictionary

Look at the extract from the *Oxford Italian Minidictionary*.

the word in English   the part of speech
                               (*n.* = noun)

apple /æpl/ *n.* mela *f.*

the pronunciation   the word in Italian

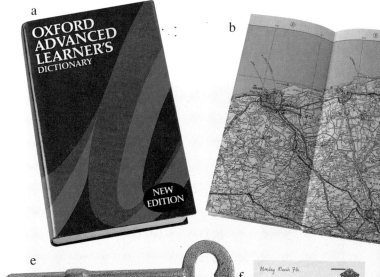

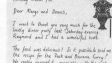

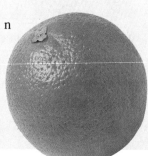

2 What's this in English?

1 Use your dictionary and match a word in the box with an object in the photographs.

Example
a *It's a dictionary.*

	● •	● ••	•• ●
a stamp a bag a map ⌐ a key	an apple a postcard a ticket a notebook an orange a letter a suitcase - *Kafer*	a dictionary an envelope a newspaper *Kafer*	a magazine

2 **T6** Look at the stress marks (● •). Listen and practise saying the words.

3 Look at the words.

an apple	*an* envelope
an orange	*a* bag
a ticket	*an* English book

When is it *a*? When is it *an*?

What are the letters *a*, *e*, *i*, *o*, and *u*?

3 A vocabulary notebook

Buy a notebook and write the new words in it. Translate the words.
This is an Italian student's notebook. Look at how she writes the stress marks.

● EVERYDAY ENGLISH

Spelling

1 **T 7a** Listen to the letters of the alphabet.
Practise saying them.

/eɪ/	a h j k
/i:/	b c d e g p t v
/e/	f l m n s x z
/aɪ/	i y
/əʊ/	o
/u:/	q u w
/ɑ:/	r

2 **T 7b** Listen to the alphabet song. Sing it!

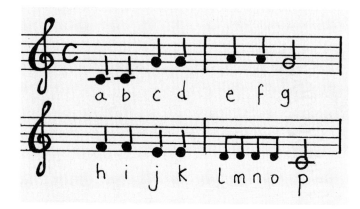

3 **T 7c** Listen and write the words you hear.

4 **T 7d** Read and listen to the conversation.

A How do you spell your first name?
B J - A - M - E - S.
A How do you spell your surname?
B H - A - double R - I - S - O - N.
A James Harrison.
B That's right.

In pairs, ask the same questions. Write the answers.

> How do you spell your first name?

> How do you spell your surname?

5 Ask and answer questions about things in the room.

> What's this in English? > A dictionary.

> How do you spell it? > D-I-C-T-I-O-N-A-R-Y.

> What's this in English? > I don't know.

GRAMMAR SUMMARY

Verb *to be*

Positive

I	am	
He She It	is	from England.
We You They	are	

I'm	=	I am
He's	=	He is
She's	=	She is
It's	=	It is
We're	=	We are
You're	=	You are
They're	=	They are

Question

	am	I	
Where	is	he she it	from?
	are	we you they	

I'm 20

I'm 20.   NOT ~~I'm 20 years.~~
I'm 20 years old.   ~~I have 20 years.~~

Possessive adjectives

What's	my your his her	name?
This is	its our your their	house.

What's = What is

a/an

It's a	ticket. dictionary. magazine.

We use *an* before a vowel.

It's an	apple. envelope. English dictionary.

Prepositions

Where are you **from**?
I live **in** a flat **in** Paris.
What's this **in** English?

Study the Word List for this unit on page 123.

UNIT 2

Questions and negatives – Possessive *'s* – Prices – *Can I have ...?*

People

PRESENTATION (1)

Questions and negatives

1 **T8** Write the numbers and phone numbers you hear.

2 Read about Mary Hopkins.

SURNAME	HOPKINS
FIRST NAME	MARY
COUNTRY	England
JOB	Journalist
ADDRESS	35, North Street, Bristol
PHONE NUMBER	0272 478 2209
AGE	23
MARRIED?	No

3 Complete the questions.

a What's **her** surname? Hopkins.

b _What_ her first name? Mary.

c _Where does_ she _live_ England.

d _Whats her_ job? She's a journalist.

e What's _her adrs_? 35 North Street, Bristol.

f _What her_ phone number? 0272 478 2209.

g How old _is she_? Twenty-three.

h Is she _marrivied_ No, she isn't.

T9 Listen and check. Practise saying the questions and answers.

4 Ask your teacher questions about Mary's brother.

> What's his first name?

Practice

1 Speaking

1 Student A Look at the information on this page.
 Student B Look at the information from your teacher.

Ask and answer questions to complete the information.

SURNAME	PETERS
FIRST NAME	
COUNTRY	Scotland
JOB	
ADDRESS	62, Church Street, Glasgow
PHONE NUMBER	
AGE	47
MARRIED?	

2 Ask your teacher the same questions.

> What's your name?   Rosa Gonzalez.

> Are you married?   Yes, I am./No, I'm not.

3 Look at the form from your teacher. Stand up! Ask two other students questions to complete the form about them. Answer questions about you.

4 Tell the class about one of the students.

> Her name's Anne-Marie. She's from Strasbourg.

13

2 Negatives and short answers

> **!**
>
> 1 Look at the negative forms.
>   She **isn't** married.
>   You **aren't** English.
>   But: I**'m not** a doctor.   NOT ~~I amn't~~ a doctor.
>
> 2 Look at the short answers to Yes/No questions.
>   Is Mary English?   **Yes, she is.** (she = Mary)
>   Is her surname Atkins?   **No, it isn't.** (it = surname)
>   Are you a doctor?   **No, I'm not.**

1 Ask and answer Yes/No questions about Mary and Martin.

About Mary

Example
French? German? English?

> Is she French?   No, she isn't.
> Is she German?   No, she isn't.
> Is she English? Yes, she is.

a a doctor? a teacher? a journalist?
b eighteen? twenty-one? twenty-three?

About Martin

c Smith? Jones? Peters?
d American? English? Scottish?
e a taxi driver? a shop assistant? a policeman?

2 Ask Yes/No questions about the students in the class.

> Juan, are you married?   No, I'm not.
> Is Maria a student?   Yes, she is.

3 Grammar

Make true sentences!

a We _____ in class.

b It _____ Monday today.

c I _____ at home.

d The teacher's name _____ David.

e My parents _____ at work.

f I _____ married.

g Champagne _____ a drink from Portugal.

h Egypt and Morocco _____ in Europe. They _____ in Africa.

14

PRESENTATION (2)

Possessive *'s*

T 10 Look at the photograph of Martin Peters with his family. Read and listen to the text. Write the names of the people in the correct places.

This is a photo of Martin, his wife, and his children. His wife's name is Jennifer. She's a dentist. His daughter's name is Alison. She's twenty-three and she's a hairdresser. His son's name is Andy. He's nineteen and he's a student. Alison's boyfriend is a travel agent. His name is Joe.

> **!**
>
> | His wife**'s** name | **'s** = possession. It is *not* the short form of *is*. |
> | | His wife**'s** name = her name |
> | She**'s** a dentist. | She**'s** = She is. *Is* is part of the verb *to be*. |

● Grammar question

Find other examples in the text of *'s* = possession, and *'s* = *is*.

Practice

1 Speaking

1 Ask and answer questions about Martin's family.

> Who's Jennifer?

> She's Martin's wife.

2 Ask your teacher questions about the names of his/her family.

> What's your mother's name?

> What's your sister's name?

2 Vocabulary

Use your dictionary and fill in the gaps.

husband	*wife*
son	
father	
	sister
uncle	
	niece
grandfather	

3 Speaking

Write down the names of some of the people in your family. Work in pairs. Ask your partner questions about his/her family.

> Who's Juan?

> He's my brother.

> Who's Sylvie?

> She's my aunt. She's my mother's sister.

4 Choosing the correct sentence

One sentence has a mistake. Choose the correct sentence. Put ✔ and ✗.

1 a He's a engineer.
  b He's an engineer. ·
2 a I'm a hairdresser. ·
  b I'm hairdresser.
3 a I have twenty-one years old. ·
  b I am twenty-one years old.
4 a My sister's name is Carmen. ·
  b My sisters name is Carmen.
5 a She isn't married. ·
  b She no married.
6 a I have two brothers. ·
  b I have two brother.
7 a Where Wolfgang from?
  b Where's Wolfgang from? ·
8 a That's Peter's book. ·
  b That's the book of Peter.

● VOCABULARY

Adjectives

1 Use your dictionary and match the opposites.

Example
old – young

difficult	horrible	lovely	easy
expensive	cold	small	right
old	cheap	old	young
hot	new	big	wrong

2 Write a sentence for each picture, using a word from Exercise 1.

a *It's big.*

b *It's small.*

c _Ste's_

d _____

e _____

f _____

g the frut its so.w

h _____

i _easy_

j _difficult_

k _____

l _____

m _it hot_

n _____

o _____

p _____

T11 Listen and check. Practise saying the sentences.

15

READING AND LISTENING

T 12a Paola is an Italian student of English at a school in London. Read and listen to her letter to David, her penfriend.

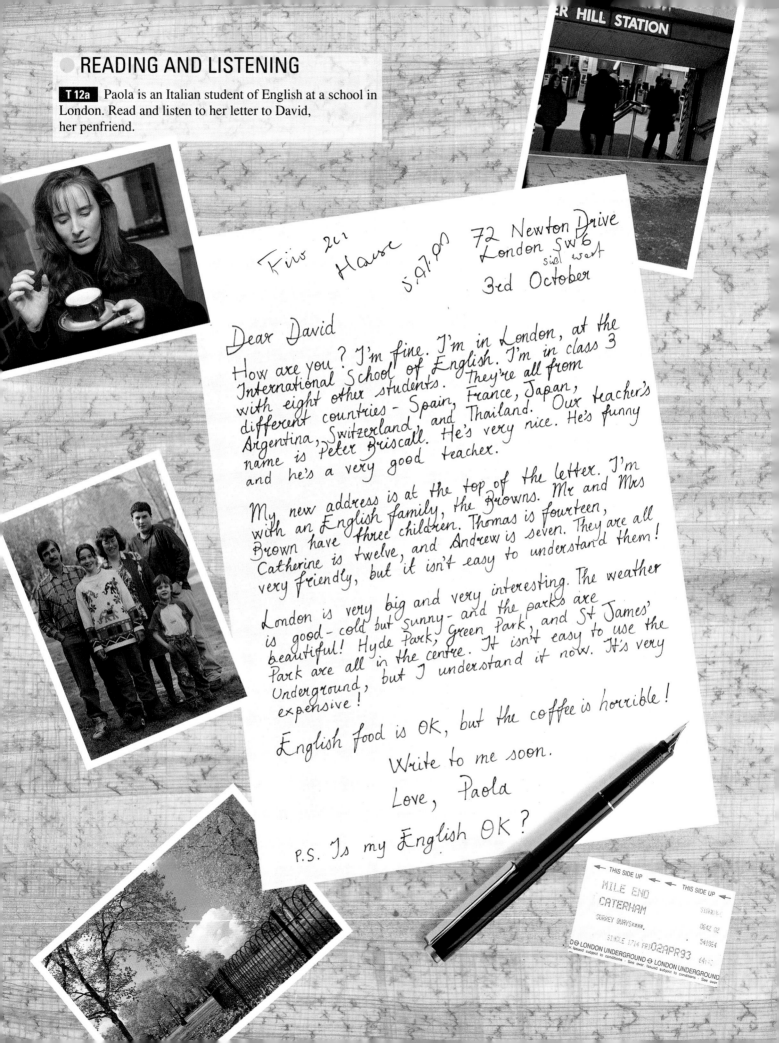

72 Newton Drive
London SW6
3rd October

Dear David

How are you? I'm fine. I'm in London, at the International School of English. I'm in class 3 with eight other students. They're all from different countries - Spain, France, Japan, Argentina, Switzerland, and Thailand. Our teacher's name is Peter Briscall. He's very nice. He's funny and he's a very good teacher.

My new address is at the top of the letter. I'm with an English family, the Browns. Mr and Mrs Brown have three children. Thomas is fourteen, Catherine is twelve, and Andrew is seven. They are all very friendly, but it isn't easy to understand them!

London is very big and very interesting. The weather is good - cold but sunny - and the parks are beautiful! Hyde Park, Green Park, and St James' Park are all in the centre. It isn't easy to use the Underground, but I understand it now. It's very expensive!

English food is OK, but the coffee is horrible!

Write to me soon.

Love, Paola

P.S. Is my English OK?

Comprehension check

1 Match a picture with a part of the letter.

In House
5.97.0

2 Are the sentences true (✔) or false (✘)?

Examples

Paola is Italian. ✔
She's in Rome. ✘ *No, she isn't. She's in London.*

a Paola's happy in London.
b She's on holiday.
c It's a very big class.
d The students in her class are all from Europe.
e Mr and Mrs Brown have two sons and a daughter.
f The Underground is cheap.
g The food in London is horrible.

3 Here are the answers to some questions about Paola's letter. Write the questions.

Example
Where's she from?
Italy.

a Pauela oie it's Ital_____?
  Spain, France, Japan, Argentina, Switzerland, and Thailand.

b _____?
  Peter Briscall.

c _____?
  Fourteen.

d _____?
  Yes, it is. Cold but sunny.

e _____?
  No, it isn't. It's horrible.

4 **T 12b** Listen to five conversations Paola has in London. Who is she with? Where is she?

Writing

Write a similar letter to a friend about your class.

● EVERYDAY ENGLISH

In a café

1 Look at the menu. Check the meaning of new words in your dictionary.

Kate's Corner Café

Sandwiches

Ham	£1.50
Cheese	£1.30
Tuna	£1.70
Chicken	£2.00
Piece of pizza	90p
Hamburger	£2.50
Ice cream	80p
Cup of tea	50p
Cup of coffee	70p
Coke	60p
Orange juice	60p
Mineral water	80p

2 **T 13a** Listen and repeat.

3 Ask and answer questions.

> How much is a tuna sandwich?

> One pound seventy.

> How much is a chicken sandwich and a mineral water?

> Two pounds eighty.

17

4 **T 13b** Listen to the conversations and complete them.

a A Hello.
   B Hello. Can I have a <u>sdus san</u>, please?
   A Here you are. Anything else?
   B No, thanks.
   A One pound _____, please.
   B Thanks.
   A Thank you.

b A Hi.
   B Hello. Can I have a cheese sandwich, please?
   A Anything to drink?
   B Yes. A <u>capity tee</u> _____, please.
   A OK. Here you are.
   B <u>Hanatschis</u> that?
   A One pound eighty, please.
   B Thanks.

c A Good morning.
   B Morning.
   A <u>Keu cW</u> _____ a hamburger and a cup of coffee, please?
   B OK. <u>nw you a</u>.
   A Thanks. How much is that?
   B <u>Tri Pan</u> twenty.
   A One, two, three pounds ... twenty p.
   B Thanks.
   A Thank you.

5 Work in pairs. Practise the conversations, then make more conversations. Use real British money if you can!

GRAMMAR SUMMARY

Verb *to be*

Questions with question words   **Answers**

What	is her surname?		Lucas.
	is his job?		He's a policeman.
	is her address?		34, Church Street.
Where	is she		
	are you	from?	Portugal.
	are they		
Who	is Jennifer?		
	is she?		She's John's daughter.
How old	is he?		
	are you?		Twenty-two.
How much	is a Coke?		Sixty pence.

Yes/No questions   **Short answers**

| Is | he she it | hot? | Yes, he is. No, she isn't. Yes, it is. |
| Are | you they | married? | No, I'm not./No, we aren't. Yes, they are. |

Negative

I	am			I'm not = I am not (I amn't)
He She It	is	not	from the States.	He isn't = He is not She isn't = She is not It isn't = It is not
We You They	are			We aren't = We are not You aren't = You are not They aren't = They are not

Possessive *'s*

My husband**'s** name is Martin.
That**'s** Andrea**'s** dictionary.

Prepositions

I'm **in** London. I'm **in** class 3 **with** eight other students.
Green Park is **in** the centre.

I'm **at** home. My parents are **at** work.
I'm **at** the International School **of** Languages.

She isn't **on** holiday.
This is a photo **of** my family.

Study the Word List for this unit on page 123.

UNIT 3

Present Simple (1) – *What time is it?*

Work

PRESENTATION (1)

Present Simple

1 **T14** Look at the photographs. Read and listen to the texts.

Sister Mary comes from Ireland. She is a nun and she lives and works in a girls' school in Cork. She teaches French and Spanish. She likes her job and she loves the green countryside of Ireland. She goes walking in her free time.

Hans Huser is a ski-instructor. He is Swiss and lives in Villars, a village in the mountains. In summer he works in a sports shop and in winter he teaches skiing. He speaks four languages, French, German, Italian, and English. He is married and has two sons. He plays football with them in his free time.

Grammar questions

– <u>Underline</u> the verbs in the texts.

Examples

<u>comes</u>   <u>is</u>

– What is the last letter of these verbs?

2 In pairs, practise saying the verbs. Read one of the texts aloud.

Practice

1 Grammar

Complete the sentences about Sister Mary and Hans.

a She comes from Ireland. He _____ _____ Switzerland.

b He lives in a village, but she _____ _____ a town.

c She works in a school. He _____ _____ a sports shop.

d He _____ skiing. She _____ _____ and Spanish.

e She _____ near the sea, but he _____ in the mountains.

f He likes his job and she _____ _____ _____ , too.

g He _____ _____ sons.

h She _____ walking in her free time. He _____ _____ with his sons.

i He _____ four languages. She _____ three.

19

2 Speaking

Look at the photograph of Georges and the information.
Make sentences about him.

> Georges is a taxi driver. He comes from
> France and he lives in Paris.

> He works ...

> He isn't ...

> He has ...

> ... in his free time.

In pairs, talk about Keiko and Mark.

Georges Teste	a taxi driver
Country	France
Town	Paris
Place of work	in the centre of Paris
Married?	No
Family	a dog (!)
Free time	walking with his dog and football

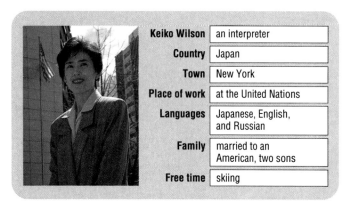

Keiko Wilson	an interpreter
Country	Japan
Town	New York
Place of work	at the United Nations
Languages	Japanese, English, and Russian
Family	married to an American, two sons
Free time	skiing

Mark King	a journalist for the BBC
Country	England
Town	Moscow
Place of work	in an office
Languages	English, Russian, and German
Family	married, three daughters
Free time	tennis

3 Writing

Write about a friend, or your mother or father.

Example

My friend Anna is a student. She lives in ...

20

PRESENTATION (2)

Questions and negatives

1 **T 15a** Read and listen to the questions and answers.
Practise saying them.

Where does Sister Mary come from?	Ireland.
What does she do?	She's a teacher.
Does she speak French?	Yes, she does.
Does she speak German?	No, she doesn't.

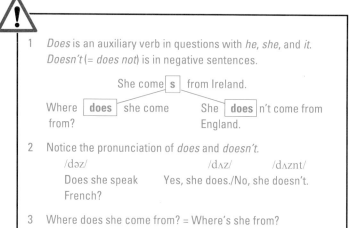

1 *Does* is an auxiliary verb in questions with *he*, *she*, and *it*.
Doesn't (= *does not*) is in negative sentences.

> She come **s** from Ireland.

> Where **does** she come
> from?

> She **does** n't come from
> England.

2 Notice the pronunciation of *does* and *doesn't*.

/dəz/	/dʌz/	/dʌznt/
Does she speak French?	Yes, she does./No, she doesn't.	

3 Where does she come from? = Where's she from?

4 What does he do? = What's his job?

2 Complete the questions and answers.

a Where _____ Hans _____ from? Switzerland.

b What _____ he _____ ? He's a ski-instructor.

c _____ he _____ French and German? Yes, he _____ .

d _____ he _____ Spanish? No, he _____ .

T 15b Listen and check.

Practice

1 Writing and speaking

1 Write questions about Georges, Keiko, and Mark.

Example

Where/come from? *Where does he come from?*

a Where/live?
b What/do?
c Where/work?
d Does he/she speak French/Spanish ...?
e What ... in his/her free time?
f ... play tennis?
g How many children ...?
h ... a dog?

2 Work in pairs. Ask and answer your questions, but don't look at the information.

3 Now ask your partner the same questions about a member of his or her family.

2 Listening and pronunciation

1 **T 16a** Listen to the sentences about Georges, Keiko, and Mark. Some are right and some are wrong. Correct the wrong sentences.

Example

Georges comes from Paris.   Yes, that's right.

Georges lives in London.   No, he doesn't.
He lives in Paris.

2 **T 16b** Tick (✔) the sentence you hear.

1 a He likes his job.
  b She likes her job.
2 a She loves walking.
  b She loves working.
3 a She's married.
  b She isn't married.
4 a Does she have three children?
  b Does he have three children?
5 a What does he do?
  b Where does he go?
6 a She watches the television.
  b She washes the television.

3 Choosing the correct sentence

One sentence has a mistake. Choose the correct sentence. Put ✔ and ✗.

1 a She comes from Spain.
  b She come from Spain.
2 a What he do in his free time?
  b What does he do in his free time?
3 a Where lives she?
  b Where does she live?
4 a He isn't married.
  b He doesn't married.
5 a Does she has two sons?
  b Does she have two sons?
6 a He doesn't play football.
  b He no plays football.
7 a She doesn't love Peter.
  b She doesn't loves Peter.
8 a What's he's address?
  b What's his address?

● VOCABULARY AND PRONUNCIATION

Jobs

1 Use your dictionary and match a picture with a job in column A.

2 Match a line in A with a line in B.

A	B
A pilot	makes bread.
An interpreter	looks after people in hospital.
A hairdresser	writes for a newspaper.
A singer	works in a hotel.
A nurse	translates things.
An actor	sells things.
A mechanic	flies a plane.
A journalist	works in a night club.
A receptionist	cuts hair.
A baker	mends cars.
A shop assistant	makes films.

3 Look at the phonetic spelling of some of the words. Practise saying them.

a /nɜːs/   b /ɪntɜːprɪtə/   c /rɪsepʃənɪst/
d /æktə/   e /sɪŋə/   f /məkænɪk/

4 Memorize the lines in A and B! Close your books. Ask and answer questions.

● READING AND LISTENING

Pre-reading task

1 Look at the map. Which two countries are they?
Write the names of the capital cities on the map.

2 Check the meaning of the <u>underlined</u> words in your
dictionary.
He <u>leaves</u> home.
She <u>drives</u> to work.
He <u>catches</u> a train at 9.00.
a <u>ferry</u>
She <u>arrives</u> at work at 8.30.
The <u>journey</u> <u>takes</u> twenty minutes.
It <u>costs</u> <u>only</u> ten pence.
<u>fortunately</u>

Reading

Read the text. Answer the three questions.

a Where does Mr Garret live?
b What's his job?
c Where does he work?

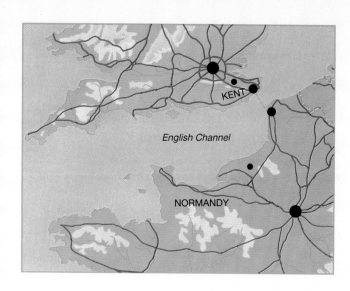

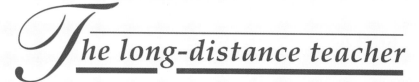

The long-distance teacher

Mr Frank Garret, 65, is a schoolteacher. He is English, but he lives in France, in the Normandy village of Yerville. Mr Garret lives in France, but he works in England.

Every Monday he leaves home at 2.30 in the morning and drives 101 miles from his village to Boulogne, where he leaves his car and catches the ferry to Folkestone. Then he catches the train to Maidstone in Kent and he arrives at Manor School at 8.25. He teaches French from 9.00 in the morning to 3.30 in the afternoon, and then leaves school. He arrives home at 9.30 in the evening. The journey there and back takes twelve hours and costs only £16!

Fortunately, Mr Garret works in England only one day a week.

And what does he do on the other days? He teaches English! He has a class of eighteen French students in Yerville.

'Yes, on Tuesdays I'm tired,' he says, 'but I love my job in England and I love my home in France. I'm a happy man!'

Comprehension check

1 Write Folkestone, Boulogne, Maidstone, and Yerville on the map. Mark Mr Garret's journey.

2 Answer the questions.

    a Is Mr Garret French?
    b How many jobs does he have?
    c Does he go to Boulogne by train?
    d Where does he leave his car?
    e Where does he catch the train?
    f Is the journey cheap or expensive? How much does it cost?
    g Does Mr Garret go to Manor School every day?
    h Why does Mr Garret live in France but work in England? (*Because …*)

3 Complete the text about Mr Garret's journey back home from his school.

Mr Garret _____ Manor School at 3.30 in the afternoon

and he _____ the train to Folkestone, where he _____

the ferry to Boulogne.

Then he _____ from Boulogne back to his village. The

journey _____ six hours. He _____ home at 9.30.

Language work

Complete the questions.

Example
What time *does he leave* home in the morning?
At 2.30.

    a What time _____ _____ _____ at Manor School?
       At 8.25.
    b What time _____ _____ _____ ?
       At 3.30.
    c When _____ _____ _____ home in the evening?
       At 9.30.
    d How much _____ the journey _____ ?
       Sixteen pounds.
    e How long _____ the journey home _____ ?
       Six hours.
    f How many students _____ he _____ in his English class?
       Eighteen.

Listening and speaking

1 **T 17** Listen to five conversations from Frank Garret's day and complete them.

    a A _____ _____ , sir. Can I see your _____ ?
       B Yes, of course. Here you _____ .
       A Thank you. Maidstone next _____ .
       B Thank you.

    b A _____ _____ , boys and girls.
       B _____ _____ , Mr Garret.
       A _____ _____ _____ your homework, please?
       B It's on your _____ , Mr Garret.
       A Thank you.

    c A _____ , Frank. Have a good _____ .
       B Thank you very _____ .
       A See you next _____ !
       B Yes, _____ course. Goodbye!

    d A _____ _____ . Is this seat _____ ?
       B Yes, it is.
       A Thank you. It's _____ this evening.
       B _____ certainly _____ . And the sea's very _____ !

    e A Hello, darling! Are you _____ ?
       B Yes, I am. And _____ .
       A Sit down and _____ a glass of wine.
       B Mmmm! Thank you. I'm _____ , too.

2 What time of day is it, morning, afternoon, or evening? Where are they? Who are the people? Choose from the boxes.

Places	People
at home	Frank's wife
on the ferry	a teacher
on the train	school children
at school	a ticket inspector
	a ferry passenger

3 Work in pairs and practise the conversations.

● EVERYDAY ENGLISH

What time is it?

1 Look at the clocks. Write the times. Practise saying them.

It's five
o'clock. _____

It's half
past five. _____

It's quarter
past five. _____

It's quarter
to six. _____

It's five
past five. _____

It's twenty-five
past five. _____

_____

It's twenty
to six.

It's ten to six.

_____

T 18a Listen and check.

2 Look at the times.

It's exactly half
past three.

It's nearly half
past three.

It's just after half
past three.

3 **T 18b** In pairs, draw clocks on a piece of paper.
Practise the conversations.

> Excuse me. Can
> you tell me the
> time, please?

> Yes, of course. It's
> six o'clock.

> Thanks.

> I'm sorry. I don't know.
> I don't have a watch.

24

GRAMMAR SUMMARY

Present Simple *he, she, it*

Positive

| He
She
It	lives	in the mountains.

Have is irregular.
She **has** a dog.   NOT ~~she haves~~

Negative

| He
She
It	does not	live	in France.	doesn't = does not

Question

| Where | does | he
she
it | live? |
|---|---|---|---|

Yes/No questions   **Short answers**

| Does | he
she
it | live | in France?

in the mountains? |
|---|---|---|---|

Yes, he does.
No, she doesn't.
Yes, it does.

Prepositions

She works **in** a girls' school.
He lives **in** a village **in** the mountains.
In winter he teaches skiing.

On Tuesdays I'm tired.

He plays football **with** his sons **in** his free time.
She is married **to** an American.
A nurse looks **after** people in a hospital.

He arrives **at** school **at** 8.45.
He catches a train **to** London.
He drives **from** his village **to** Boulogne.
He goes **to** Boulogne **by** train.

No preposition

He leaves ___ home at 8.00.
He arrives ___ home at 9.30.

Study the Word List for this unit on page 123.

UNIT 4

Present Simple (2) – Articles – Social English

Free time

PRESENTATION (1)

Present Simple

1 Practise saying the days of the week round the class.

2 Look at the photograph and read about Ann McGregor.

Ann McGregor lives in London. She is thirty-four and works for the BBC. She interviews people on an early morning news programme called The World Today. Every weekday she gets up at 3.00 in the morning because the programme starts at 6.30. She loves her work because it is exciting and she meets a lot of very interesting people, but she loves her weekends, too.

3 Look at the verbs in the box. Check the meaning of new verbs in your dictionary.

love	relax	stay	cook	have	like
chat	eat	go	live	arrive	come
visit	bring	listen	go out	get up	leave

4 **T 19a** Read and listen to what Ann says about her weekends.

On Fridays I _____ home from the BBC at about 2.00 in the afternoon and I just _____ .

On Friday evenings I don't _____ , but sometimes a friend _____ for dinner. He or she _____ the wine and I _____ the meal. I _____ cooking! We _____ to music or we just _____ .

On Saturday mornings I _____ at 9.00 and I _____ shopping. Then in the evenings I sometimes _____ to the theatre or the opera with a friend. I _____ opera! Then we _____ in my favourite Chinese restaurant.

On Sunday... Oh, on Sunday mornings I _____ in bed late, I don't _____ until 11.00! Sometimes in the afternoon I _____ my sister. She _____ in the country and _____ two children. I _____ playing with my niece and nephew, but I _____ early because I _____ to bed at 8.00 on Sunday evenings!

5 Fill in the gaps with the correct form of the verbs in the box. Listen again and check. Read the text aloud.

● Grammar questions

– Find four verbs which end in -*s*. Why do they end in -*s*?

– Find two negatives.

– Complete the rules.
   In the Present Simple positive we add _____ to the verb with *he*, *she*, and *it*, but not with *I*, *you*, *we*, and *they*.
   With *I*, *you*, *we*, and *they*, the negative is _____ + infinitive. With *he*, *she*, and *it*, the negative is _____ + infinitive.

PRESENTATION (2)

Questions

1 **T 19b** Read and listen to the questions and answers. Practise saying them.

Do you go out on Friday afternoons?	No, I don't.
What do you do?	I just relax.
Do you stay at home on Friday evenings?	Yes, I do.
What do you do?	I cook dinner for friends.

2 Work in pairs. One of you is Ann McGregor. Ask and answer questions about:

Saturday mornings/evenings

Sunday mornings/afternoons/evenings

● Grammar question

Complete the rule.

The auxiliary verb in questions with *I*, *you*, *we*, and *they* is

_____ . With *he*, *she*, and *it* the auxiliary verb is _____ .

Practice

1 Questions and answers

Match a line in A with a line in B to make a question. Then find an answer in C.

Questions		Answers
A	B	C
What time	do you like your job?	My grandmother.
Where	do you travel to work?	To a disco.
What	do you go on Saturday evenings?	After dinner.
When	do you visit on Sundays?	At 11 o'clock.
Who	do you go to bed?	I watch TV.
Why	do you do in the evenings?	Because it's interesting.
How	do you do your homework?	By train.

2 Speaking

1 Work in pairs. Ask and answer questions about your weekdays and weekends.

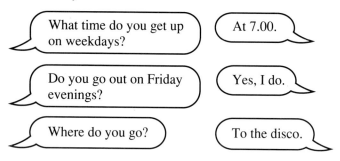

2 Tell the class about you and your partner.

Maria goes to the disco on Friday evenings and I usually watch TV.

3 Listening and pronunciation

T 20 Tick (✔) the sentence you hear.

1 a What does he do on Sundays?
  b What does she do on Sundays?
2 a I stay at home on Tuesday evenings.
  b I stay at home on Thursday evenings.
3 a He lives here.
  b He leaves here.
4 a I read a lot.
  b I eat a lot.
5 a Where do you go on Saturday evenings?
  b What do you do on Saturday evenings?
6 a She likes cars.
  b She likes cards.

4 Speaking and writing

1 Look at the questionnaire. Ask your teacher the questions, then ask two other students. Put ✔ or ✘ in the columns.

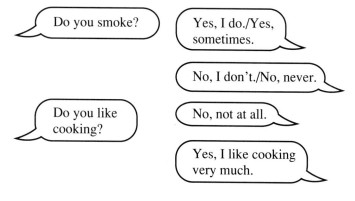

2 Now answer the questions about you.

Questions	T	S 1	S 2	Me
smoke?	☐	☐	☐	☐
drink wine?	☐	☐	☐	☐
like Chinese food?	☐	☐	☐	☐
like cooking?	☐	☐	☐	☐
play cards?	☐	☐	☐	☐
play tennis?	☐	☐	☐	☐
read a lot?	☐	☐	☐	☐
listen to music a lot?	☐	☐	☐	☐
watch TV a lot?	☐	☐	☐	☐

3 Use the information in the questionnaire. Write about you and your teacher, or you and another student.

Example

I don't smoke, but Marc smokes a lot. We both like Chinese food. ...

5 Grammar

Make the positive sentences negative and make the negative sentences positive.

Examples

She's French.   *She isn't French.*
I don't like cooking.   *I like cooking.*

  a She doesn't speak German.
  b They want to learn English.
  c We're tired and we want to go to bed.
  d John likes watching football on TV, but he doesn't like playing it.
  e I work at home because I have a word processor.
  f Sarah isn't happy because she doesn't have a nice flat.
  g I smoke, I drink, and I don't go to bed early.
  h He doesn't smoke, he doesn't drink, and he goes to bed early.

PRESENTATION (3)
Articles

1 Read the text about the Forrester family. Put *a*, *the*, or nothing into the gaps.

Mr and Mrs Forrester have (a) _____ son and (b) _____ daughter. (c) _____ son lives at (d) _____ home and (e) _____ daughter is (f) _____ student at (g) _____ university. Mr Forrester is (h) _____ journalist. He works for (i) _____ *Times*. He writes (j) _____ articles about (k) _____ restaurants. 'I love (l) _____ food!' he says.

T 21a Listen and check.

2 Read about articles in the Grammar Summary on page 31.

3 Mr Forrester talks about his holidays. Put *a*, *the*, or nothing into the gaps.

'Every spring (a) _____ children go skiing, so my wife and I go to Paris on (b) _____ holiday. We stay in (c) _____ hotel near (d) _____ River Seine. We have (e) _____ breakfast in (f) _____ hotel, but we have (g) _____ lunch in a restaurant. (h) _____ French food is delicious! We walk a lot, but sometimes we go by (i) _____ taxi. After four days we don't want to go (j) _____ home and go back to (k) _____ work.'

T 21b Listen and check.

Practice

1 Listening and speaking

Listen to your teacher say some incorrect sentences about the Forresters. Correct the sentences.

Example

The son lives with friends.

> No, he doesn't. He lives at home with his parents.

2 Grammar

Put *a*, *the*, or nothing into the gaps.

a Oxford is _____ town in _____ England, on _____ River Thames.

b _____ Queen lives in _____ very big house in London.

c I have _____ breakfast in _____ bed on _____ Sundays.

d Do you go to _____ work by _____ car?

e My sister is _____ student. She comes _____ home at weekends.

f Do you like _____ Chinese food?

3 Choosing the correct sentence

One sentence has a mistake. Choose the correct sentence. Put ✔ and ✘.

1 a Where do they live?
   b Where they live?
2 a She goes to home by taxi.
   b She goes home by taxi.
3 a Mr and Mrs Smith go walking in summer.
   b Mr and Mrs Smith goes walking in summer.
4 a I don't understand the question.
   b I no understand the question.
5 a She goes at weekends swimming.
   b She goes swimming at weekends.
6 a What you do on Sunday mornings?
   b What do you do on Sunday mornings?
7 a Do you play tennis sometimes?
   b You play tennis sometimes?
8 a I like very much football.
   b I like football very much.
9 a He doesn't know the answer.
   b He don't know the answer.

● VOCABULARY

Free time activities

1 Check the meaning of new words in your dictionary. Match a picture with an activity.

dancing
visiting museums
doing crosswords
walking
skiing
listening to music
watching TV
taking photographs
ice-skating
cooking
playing computer games
sailing
painting
swimming
reading
eating in restaurants
going to the cinema
playing volleyball
windsurfing
sunbathing
playing cards
fishing

2 Work in pairs.
Tell your partner what you like doing and what you don't like doing from the list.
Ask questions about the activities.

> I don't like watching TV, but I like reading very much.

> Oh, really? What do you read?

> When do you read?

Think of two things you like doing which are not on the list. Tell your partner.

READING AND LISTENING

1 What season is it now? What are the seasons?
What month is it now? What are the months?
When are the different seasons in your country?

2 **T 22a** Read and listen to three people from different countries talking about their free time.

AL WHEELER FROM CANADA

We have long, cold winters and short, hot summers. In summer I go sailing and I play baseball, but in winter I play ice hockey and go ice-skating. We have a holiday home near a lake, so I go fishing a lot, too. My favourite season is autumn, or fall, as we say in North America. I love the colours of the trees – red, gold, orange, yellow, and brown.

MANUELA DA SILVA FROM PORTUGAL

People think it's always warm and sunny in Portugal, but January and February are often cold, wet, and grey. I don't like winter. I meet friends in restaurants and bars and we chat. Sometimes we go to a Brazilian bar. I love Brazilian music. But then suddenly it's summer and at weekends we drive to the beach, sunbathe, and go windsurfing. I love summer.

TOSHI SUZUKI FROM JAPAN

I work for Pentax cameras, in the export department. I don't have a lot of free time, but I have one special hobby – taking photographs, of course! I like taking photographs of flowers, especially in spring. Sometimes, after work, I relax in a bar near my office with friends. My friend, Shigeru, likes singing pop songs in the bar. This has a special name, Karaoke. I don't sing – I'm too shy! I just watch him.

Comprehension check

1 Answer the questions.
   a Do they all play sports?
   b What do Al and Manuela do in winter?
   c Do Manuela and Toshi like going to bars?
   d Where is Al's holiday home?
   e When does Toshi like taking photographs of flowers?
   f What do Manuela and her friends do in summer?
   g Do you know all their jobs?
   h Why does Al like autumn?
   i Who does Toshi watch? Why doesn't Toshi sing?
   j Which colours are in the texts?

2 Find five mistakes in this summary and correct them.

> **Al comes from Canada. In winter he plays ice hockey and goes skiing. He has a holiday home near the sea.**
>
> **Manuela comes from Brazil. She likes sunbathing and windsurfing in summer.**
>
> **Toshi comes from Japan. He has a lot of free time. He likes taking photographs and singing pop songs in bars.**

3 **T 22b** Listen to the conversations. Is it Al, Manuela, or Toshi? Where are they? How do you know?

4 What is your favourite season? Why? What do you do in the different seasons?

Vocabulary

Write *play* or *go*.

_____ football	_____ walking	_____ sailing
_____ swimming	_____ volleyball	_____ tennis
_____ golf	_____ ice-skating	_____ dancing
_____ ice hockey	_____ windsurfing	_____ skiing
_____ fishing	_____ baseball	

● EVERYDAY ENGLISH

Social English

1 Complete the conversations with the sentences on the right.

a A _____ .

B Yes?

A Do you have a light?

B _____ . I don't smoke.

A _____ .

> I'm sorry.
>
> Excuse me!
>
> That's OK.

b A _____ . The traffic is bad today.

B _____ . Come and sit down. We're on page 25.

> Don't worry.
>
> I'm sorry I'm late.

c A _____ . It's very hot in here.

B _____ . I'm quite cold.

A OK. _____ .

> Really?
>
> Can I open the window?
>
> It doesn't matter.

d A _____ .

B Can I help you?

A Can I have a film for my camera?

B How many exposures?

A _____ .

B How many exposures?

A _____ .

B How many pictures? 24? 36?

A Ah! _____ . 36, please.

> Pardon?
>
> Now I understand!
>
> Excuse me!
>
> What does 'exposures' mean?

T 23 Listen and check.

2 In pairs, practise the conversations.

GRAMMAR SUMMARY

Present Simple

Positive

I You We They	start	
		at 6.30.
He She It	starts	

Negative

I You We They	don't		
		start	at 6.30.
He She It	doesn't		

Question

When	do	I you we they	start?
	does	he she it	

Yes/No questions

Do	you they	have	a camera?
Does	he she it	like	Chinese food?

Short answers

No, I don't./No, we don't.
Yes, they do.

Yes, he does.
No, she doesn't.
Yes, it does.

like/love + verb + *-ing*

When *like* and *love* are followed by a verb, it is usually verb + *-ing*.

I like swim**ming**.
She loves listen**ing** to music.
They like sail**ing** very much.

Articles

a = **indefinite article**

1   She has **a** flat in London.
    Can I have **a** ham sandwich?
2   She's **a** nurse. (jobs)

the = **definite article**

3   **The** flat (= her flat) is very nice.
    The ham sandwich is horrible!
4   **The** Times; **the** Thames (newspapers and rivers)

No article

5   **Things in general**
    I have ___ tea and toast for breakfast.
    ___ Books are expensive.
    I like taking ___ photographs.
    Do you like ___ Chinese food?

6   **Meals, places, transport**
    I have ___ breakfast/lunch/dinner.
    I go/come ___ home.
    I go/come to ___ school/university/work/bed.
    I'm at ___ work/on ___ holiday.
    I go/come by ___ train/car/bus/taxi.

Prepositions

I stay in bed **until** 11.00.
She works **for** the BBC.
We listen **to** music.

on | Friday mornings/evenings
       | Saturday
at weekends
in | the morning/evening
       | (the) spring
We stay **in** a hotel.

Study the Word List for this unit on page 123.

STOP AND CHECK

1 Correcting the mistakes

Each sentence has a mistake. Find it and correct it!

Example
Antonia is ~~Italiana~~.   *Antonia is Italian.*

a London is a city very big.
b My mother works in a hotel is a receptionist.
c My father watch TV in the evening.
d He's like watching football.
e On Sundays we go in a restaurant.
f Hans is businessman.
g You family is very nice.
h I like listen to music.
i Our school have a lot of students.
j The childrens go to school near here.
k We have the dinner at 7.00.
l Buses in London are reds.
m My brother no have a job.
n Do you want a ice-cream?
o Is near here, my flat.

15

2 Word order

Put the words in the correct order.

Example
Madrid Jorge from comes   *Jorge comes from Madrid.*

a policeman   from   is   John   a   New York

   _____ .

b married   sister   is   your?

   _____ ?

c mountains   sister   skiing   goes   the   in   my

   _____ .

d isn't   coffee   nice   English   very

   _____ .

e your   what   name   teacher's   is?

   _____ ?

f surname   how   spell   do   your   you?

   _____ ?

g often   weekends   go   I   at   swimming

   _____ .

7

3 Choosing the correct sentence

One sentence is correct. Which one?

Example
Where she from?   ✗
Where does she from?   ✗
Where is she from?   ✔

1 a Sally is a nice girl, and I like.
   b Sally is a nice girl, and I like her.
   c Sally is a nice girl, and I like him.
2 a Coffee English is horrible.
   b The English coffee is horrible.
   c English coffee is horrible.
3 a Peter works with his father.
   b Peter works with he's father.
   c Peter works with him father.
4 a Sally and Tim live in Madrid. They're flat is lovely.
   b Sally and Tim live in Madrid. Their flat is lovely.
   c Sally and Tim live in Madrid. There flat is lovely.
5 a She lives in a house or a flat?
   b Does she lives in a house or a flat?
   c Does she live in a house or a flat?
6 a I don't like going to discos.
   b I don't like go to discos.
   c I no like going to discos.
7 a How many languages you speak?
   b How many languages do you speak?
   c How many languages does you speak?
8 a My brother work in a bank.
   b My brother he works in a bank.
   c My brother works in a bank.

8

4 Questions

1 Match a line in A with a line in B to make a question.

A	B
What	do you go to bed?
Where	languages do you speak?
What time	is a cup of coffee and a sandwich?
Who	do you usually sit next to?
How much	do you do at weekends?
How many	do you go on holiday?

5

2 Here are the answers to some questions. Write the questions. Use the words in brackets.

Example
What do you do? (you / do)   I'm a hairdresser.

a _____ ?
(Peter / start work)   At 8.00.

b _____ ?
(Sylvie and Jacques / come)   From France.

c _____ ?
(your wife's)   Jackie.

d _____ ?
(you / have)   Three. Two girls and a boy.

e _____ ?
(you / like / gardening)   Yes, I do. I grow a lot of vegetables.

`5`

5 Prepositions

Put a preposition from the box into each gap.

| at | in | about | after | for | with | by | to | on | after |

James lives __*in*__ a small flat (a) _____ Cambridge. He lives (b) _____ two other boys who are students (c) _____ Cambridge University. They work hard during the week, but (d) _____ weekends they invite a lot of friends to their house. They cook a meal (e) _____ their friends, and then they go out (f) _____ the pub (g) _____ a drink, or they stay (h) _____ home and listen (i) _____ music.

James has two jobs. (j) _____ Mondays, Tuesdays, and Wednesdays he works (k) _____ a hospital, where he helps to look (l) _____ children who are ill. He goes to the hospital (m) _____ bus. He starts (n) _____ ten o'clock and works until quarter (o) _____ five. On Thursdays and Fridays he works (p) _____ home. He has a word processor (q) _____ his bedroom and he writes stories. (r) _____ the evening, one of the boys cooks a meal. (s) _____ dinner they look in the newspaper to see what's on TV or they talk (t) _____ their day. They usually go to bed at about midnight.

`20`

6 Vocabulary

Put the words into the correct columns. There are five words for each column.

cheese	map	actor	favourite	toast	dentist	arrive
palace	ham	village	want	bring	notebook	easy
expensive	chicken	journalist	dictionary	leave	friendly
interpreter	magazine	orange	night club	beach	engineer
office	newspaper	funny	listen

Things to read	Professions	Things to eat	Places	Verbs	Adjectives
		cheese			

`30`

7 am/is/do/does (not)

Put a verb from the box into each gap.

| am/'m not   is/isn't   are/aren't   does/doesn't   do/don't |

Example
I *'m not* English, I'm French.

a Vienna _____ in Austria.

b Where _____ you from?

c I _____ on holiday. I'm at work.

d My teacher _____ very funny.

e What time _____ the bank open?

f My sister _____ eat meat because she _____ like it.

g I _____ hungry. How much _____ a cheese sandwich?

h Where _____ you usually go on holiday?

i Daddy, we _____ want to go to bed. We _____ tired.

j Learning English _____ boring! It's interesting!

`10`

Total `100`

TRANSLATE

Translate the sentences into your language. Translate the *ideas*, not word by word.

1 I am a student.

_____

2 My sister isn't at home. She's at work.

_____

3 I live in a flat.

_____

4 My mother works in a bank.

_____

5 I don't smoke.

_____

6 My father doesn't like rock music.

_____

7 What do you do at weekends?

_____

8 John's flat is in the centre of town.

_____

9 Can I have a cup of coffee, please?

UNIT 5

Places

PRESENTATION (1)

There is/are – any – Prepositions

1 What are the names of the rooms in a house? Think of one or two things that we do in the rooms.

> We watch TV in the living room.

2 Look at the photograph of a living room.
  Find these objects.

a chair	an armchair	a table	a sofa	a window
a picture	a telephone	a television	a lamp	
a mirror	a stereo	a fireplace	a plant	

3 Describe the room.

> There's a sofa.   There's a television.

> There are two lamps and an armchair.

4 **T 24** Listen to the questions and answers, and practise saying them.

Is there a stereo?	Yes, there is.
Is there a clock?	No, there isn't.
Are there any books?	Yes, there are.
Are there any magazines?	No, there aren't.

In pairs, ask and answer questions about these objects.

a table	a dog	a desk	lamps	pictures
a fire	a stereo	a camera	flowers	plants
a mirror	an armchair	a newspaper	photos	books

5 Look at the photograph of the living room. Put a preposition from the box into each gap.

near	on	next to	in front of	behind

a The telephone is _____ the table.

b The table is _____ the sofa.

c The chair is _____ the stereo.

d The lamp is _____ the chair.

e The dog is _____ the fire.

Practice

1 Grammar

Complete the sentences about the living room in the photograph.

a There _____ two books _____ the sofa.

b The sofa is _____ _____ _____ the window.

c There _____ a lamp _____ _____ the television.

d The telephone is _____ one of the lamps.

e '_____ there _____ pictures on the wall?'
'Yes, _____ _____.'

f There _____ _____ desk.

g There's a plant _____ the sofa in front of the window.

h Is _____ _____ fire?

i '_____ there _____ people in the living room?'
'No, _____ _____.'

2 Speaking and listening

1 Work in pairs.
Your teacher will give you each a picture of a living room. There are ten differences! Don't show your picture!
Talk about the pictures to find the ten differences.

> Is there a table?

> Yes, there is.

> How many people are there?

> Two, and there's a cat on the sofa.

2 **T 25** Look at the pictures together. Listen to someone describing them. There are five mistakes in each description. Say 'Stop!' when you hear a mistake.

> Stop! There aren't three people! There are four people!

PRESENTATION (2)

some and *any*

1 Look at the photograph of the kitchen. What can you see?

2 **T 26** Listen to the description of the kitchen and fill in the gaps.

It's a modern kitchen, nice and clean with a lot of cupboards. _____'s a washing machine, a fridge, and a cooker, but there isn't a dishwasher. There are some lovely _____ on the walls, but there aren't any photographs. There's a radio _____ the cooker. There are some flowers, but there aren't _____ plants. On the table there are some apples and oranges. Ah! And there are _____ cups and plates next to the sink.

● Grammar questions

– Look at the sentences. When do we say *There isn't a ...* and when do we say *There aren't any ...*?

> There isn't a dishwasher.
> There aren't any photographs.

– Look at the sentences. What is the difference?

> There are two books.
> There are some flowers.

1 When we use *some*, we are not interested in the exact number.
   I have ten fingers. (NOT I have ~~some~~ fingers.)
   I have some friends in Berlin.

2 We use *any* in questions and negatives.
   Are there any photographs?
   There aren't any people.

3 Notice the pronunciation of *some* and *any*.
   /səm/   /enɪ/
   There are some flowers. There aren't any plants.

Practice

1 Speaking

1 Look again at the photograph of the kitchen. Make sentences with *There's a ...* and *There are some ...* about the kitchen.

> There's a fridge.   There are some flowers.

2 Have a class discussion.
   What is there in *your* kitchen? How is your kitchen different from the one in the picture?
   Why do you think kitchens are different in different parts of the world?

2 Grammar

1 Put *some* or *any* into the gaps.

   a In our classroom there are _____ books on the floor.
   b There aren't _____ flowers.
   c Are there _____ German students in your class?
   d There aren't _____ Chinese students.
   e We have _____ dictionaries in the cupboard.
   f There are _____ pens on the table.

2 What is there in your classroom?

3 Listening and speaking

1 **T 27** Listen to a man describing what is in his briefcase. Tick (✔) the things you hear.

   ___ a newspaper ___ some pens   ___ a bus ticket
   ___ a dictionary ___ a notebook   ___ an address book
   ___ a sandwich   ___ a letter   ___ some stamps
   ___ some keys   ___ some photos

2 What is there in *your* bag?

4 Choosing the correct sentence

One sentence has a mistake. Choose the correct sentence. Put ✔ and ✘.

1 a There's a dog in front of the fire.
   b There's in front of the fire a dog.
2 a There isn't a desk in the room.
   b There isn't an desk in the room.
3 a Near of my house there's a park.
   b Near my house there's a park.
4 a We eat in the kitchen.
   b We eat in kitchen.
5 a We have a fridge, a table, and a cooker.
   b We have a fridge, a table, and any cooker.
6 a My room isn't big, but I like it very much.
   b My room isn't big, but I like very much.
7 a There isn't television in the living room.
   b There isn't a television in the living room.
8 a In the evening my mother go for a walk.
   b In the evening my mother goes for a walk.
9 a He gets up at 7.00 every day.
   b He's get up at 7.00 every day.

● READING

Pre-reading task

1 Look at the photographs. Can you answer these questions?

Where are these buildings?
What are they?
Who lives in them?

2 Check the meaning of new words in your dictionary or with your teacher.

inside (*prep*)   to prepare (*v*)   do the washing-up (*v*)
the whole world   own (*adj*)   everybody (*pron*)
famous (*adj*)   piper (*n*)   during (*prep*)
grow up (*v*)   outside (*prep*)   course (food) (*n*)
like (*prep*)

Reading

Read the text.

INSIDE

Buckingham Palace

THE PALACE

There are two addresses in London that the whole world knows. One is 10 Downing Street, where the Prime Minister lives. The other is Buckingham Palace. This famous palace, first built in 1703, is in the very centre of London.

It is two places, not one. It is a family house, where children play and grow up. It is also the place where presidents, kings, and politicians go to meet the Queen.

Buckingham Palace is like a small town, with a police station, two post offices, a hospital, a bar, two sports clubs, a disco, a cinema, and a swimming pool. There are 600 rooms and three miles of red carpet. Two men work full-time to look after the 300 clocks. About 700 people work in the Palace.

Comprehension check

1 Are the sentences true (✔) or false (✘)? Correct the false sentences.

a The Palace is more than two hundred years old.
b It is famous because it is in the centre of London.
c The same person starts the Queen's bath, prepares her clothes, and feeds the dogs.
d The dogs sleep in the Queen's bedroom.
e The Queen and the Prime Minister go out for a drink on Tuesday nights.

2 Answer the questions.

a 'Buckingham Palace is two places, not one.' How?
b Why is it like a small town?
c Are there a lot of clocks?
d How many dogs does the Queen have?
e What newspaper does she read?
f What sort of music does the piper play?
g Why do people have five glasses on the table?
h Who does the Queen speak to during a meal?
i What happens when the Queen finishes her food?

THE QUEEN'S DAY

When the Queen gets up in the morning, seven people look after her. One starts her bath, one prepares her clothes, and one feeds the Royal dogs. She has eight or nine dogs, and they sleep in their own bedroom near the Queen's bedroom. Two people bring her breakfast. She has coffee from Harrods, toast, and eggs. Every day for fifteen minutes, a piper plays Scottish music outside her room and the Queen reads *The Times*.

Every Tuesday evening, she meets the Prime Minister. They talk about world news and have a drink, perhaps a gin and tonic or a whisky.

AN INVITATION TO THE PALACE

When the Queen invites a lot of people for dinner, it takes three days to prepare the table and three days to do the washing-up. Everybody has five glasses: one for red wine, one for white

wine, one for water, one for port, and one for liqueur. During the first and second courses, the Queen speaks to the person on her left and then she speaks to the person on her right for the rest of the meal. When the Queen finishes her food, everybody finishes, and it is time for the next course!

Language work

1 Work in pairs. Ask and answer questions about Buckingham Palace.

> Is there a police station? Yes, there is.

> Is there a post office? Yes, there are two.

Ask about:
a swimming pool	a school	a sports club	a disco
a supermarket	a bar	a cinema	a hospital

2 Here are the answers to some questions about the text. Write the questions.

a 10 Downing Street.
b 600.
c 300.
d Coffee, toast, and eggs.
e In their own bedroom.
f On Tuesday evenings.

● VOCABULARY AND PRONUNCIATION

Places, people, food and drink

1 Put words from the text *Inside Buckingham Palace* into the correct columns. Mark the stress on words with two syllables or more.

Places	People	Food and drink
• palace house	• Prime Minister • family	• breakfast • coffee

2 Can you add more words to the columns?

● LISTENING AND SPEAKING

1 **T 28** Listen to five people talking about where they live. Fill in the chart.

	Anne-Marie	Harry	Dave and Maggie	Thanos
House or flat?				
Old or new?				
Where?				
Number of bedrooms?				
Garden?				
Live(s) with?				

2 Talk about where you live.
Do you live in a house or a flat?
How many rooms are there?
Do you have a garden? A terrace?
What's in your bedroom?

Writing

3 Write a paragraph about where you live.

● EVERYDAY ENGLISH

Directions (1)

1 Look at the street map. Where can you buy these things?

bread   a CD   cigarettes   a book   a plane ticket

Where can you borrow a book?

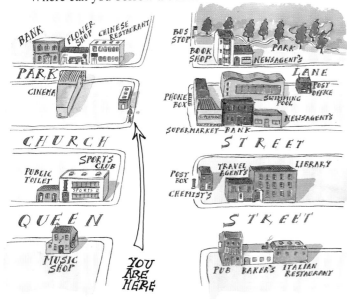

2 **T 29** Listen to the conversations and complete them.

a A Excuse me! Is _____ a chemist's _____ here?
  B Yes. It's over _____ .
  A Thanks.

b A _____ me! Is there a _____ club near here?
  B Yes. _____ _____ Queen Street. Take the
    second _____ _____ _____ right.
  A Thanks.

c A Excuse me! Is there a _____ near here?
  B There's _____ in Church Street _____ _____
    the bank, and there's one in Park Lane opposite
    the _____ _____ .
  A Is that one _____ ?
  B No. Just two minutes, that's all.

d A Is there a cinema near here?
  B _____ the first left, and it's _____ _____ left,
    _____ the flower shop.
  A Thanks a lot.

3 Work in pairs. Practise the conversations. Then make
  more conversations about other places on the map.

4 Talk about where *you* are.
  Is there a chemist's near here? Is it far?
  What about a bank/a post office/a sports club?

GRAMMAR SUMMARY

There is/are

Positive

| There | is | a sofa. | (singular) |
| | are | two books. | (plural) |

Negative

| There | isn't | an | armchair. | (singular) |
| | aren't | any | flowers. | (plural) |

Yes/No questions

| Is | there | a table? |
| Are | | any photos? |

Short answers

Yes, there is.
No, there isn't.
Yes, there are.
No, there aren't.

some/any

Positive
There are some flowers.   *some* + plural noun

Negative
There aren't any cups.   *any* + plural noun

Question
Are there any books?   *any* + plural noun

Prepositions

There is a photo **on** the television.

The bank is **next to** the supermarket.

The bus stop is **near** the park.

There is a post box **in front of** the chemist's.

The cinema is **on** the left, **opposite** the
flower shop.

There are two pictures **on** the wall.

The lamp is **behind** the sofa.

Your dictionary is **like** my dictionary.
She speaks **to** people **during** the meal.
Why don't we go out **for** a drink?
They talk **about** the news.
She has coffee **from** Harrods.

Study the Word List for this unit on page 124.

39

UNIT 6

can/could – was/were – At the airport

What can you do?

PRESENTATION (1)

can/can't

1 **T 30a** Look at the pictures. Match a sentence with a picture. Then, listen and check.

1 Cats can see in the dark.
2 She can type fifty words a minute.
3 'Can you use a word processor?' 'Yes, I can.'
4 'Can you speak Japanese?' ' No, I can't.'
5 I can't spell your name.
6 I can't hear you. The line's bad.

2 Listen again carefully.

What is the pronunciation of *can*
– in the positive and in questions?
– in short answers?
What is the pronunciation of *can't*?

1	I can speak French. Can you speak French?	=	/kən/ or /kn/
	Yes, I can.	=	/kæn/
	I can't speak German.	=	/kɑ:nt/

2 Look at the sentence stress.

• • ●
I can swim.

● • ●
I can't cook.

3 I can't speak Japanese. NOT I ~~don't can~~ speak Japanese.

3 **T 30b** Listen and complete the sentences with *can* or *can't* + verb.

a I _____ _____ , but I _____ _____ .
b He _____ _____ and he _____ _____ .
c '_____ you _____ ?' 'Yes, I _____ .'
d They _____ _____ , but they _____ _____ .
e We _____ _____ and we _____ _____ .
f '_____ she _____ ?' 'No, she _____ .'

Practice

1 Listening and speaking

1 **T 31** Listen to Sarah. What can she do? What can't she do? Put ✔ or ✘.

drive a car · speak Italian · play the piano · use a word processor · speak German · draw · cook · type · speak Spanish · ski · play tennis · swim · speak French

2 Work in pairs.
Use the words in Exercise 1. Ask and answer questions.

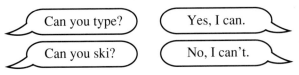

Can you type? — Yes, I can.

Can you ski? — No, I can't.

Tell the class about your partner.

2 Speaking

1 Work in pairs.
Look at the list. Talk about computers.
What can they do? What can't they do?

They can count, but they can't translate. — Yes, they can!

> # Computers
> ## Can they...?
>
> count · smell
> translate · forecast the weather
> speak English · check spellings
> play chess · make music
> do crosswords · have conversations
> hear · write books
> see · think

2 What can people do that computers can't do?

PRESENTATION (2)

was/were – could

1 Read the questions. Check the meaning of new words. Complete the answers.

Present	Past
a What day is it today? It's _____ .	What day was it yesterday? It was _____ .
b What month is it now? It's _____ .	What month was it last month? It was _____ .
c Where are you now? I'm in/at _____ .	Where were you yesterday morning? I was in/at _____ .
d Are you in England? _____ , I am./ _____ , I'm not.	Were you in England in 1990? _____ , I was./ _____ , I wasn't.
e Can you swim? _____ , I can./ _____ , I can't.	Could you swim when you were five? _____ , I could./ _____ , I couldn't.
f Can your teacher cook? Yes, _____ can./No, _____ can't.	Could he/she cook when he/she was sixteen? Yes, _____ could./No, _____ couldn't.

● Grammar questions

– What are the past tense forms of the verb *to be*?

	Positive	Negative
I	*was*	*wasn't*
you	*were*	*weren't*
he/she/it	_____	_____
we	_____	_____
they	_____	_____

– What is the past tense form of *can* in all persons?

Positive _____ Negative _____

Notice the pronunciation of *was* and *were*.

/wəz/   /wə/

It was Monday yesterday. We were at school.

In short answers the pronunciation is different.

                              /wɒz/

'Was it hot?'   'Yes, it was.'

                              /wɜː/

'Were you tired?'   'Yes, we were.'

2 **T 32** Listen and repeat.

3 Ask and answer questions.

Where were you ...
at eight o'clock this morning? at half past six yesterday
                                evening?
at two o'clock this morning?   at this time yesterday?
at ten o'clock last night?   last Sunday lunchtime?

Practice

1 Listening and pronunciation

1 Read the conversation between two friends, Sue and Bill.
   Put *was*, *were*, *wasn't*, or *couldn't* into the gaps.

Sue _____ you at Eve's
party last Saturday?

Bill Yes, I _____ .

Sue _____ it good?

Bill Well, it _____ OK.

Sue _____ there many
people?

Bill Yes, there _____ .

Sue _____ Tom there?

Bill No, he _____ . And
where _____ you?

Sue Oh ... I _____ go
because I _____ at
Adam's party! It
_____ brilliant!

T 33 Listen and check. Listen again for the
pronunciation of *was* and *were*.

2 Work in pairs. Practise the conversation. Then make
   similar conversations about:
       John's barbecue last Sunday
       the disco last Friday evening
       the football match last week

2 Speaking

1 Look at the sentences.
       My sister *could* read *when she was* four.
       I *couldn't* read *until I was* seven.
   Make similar sentences, using these words.

   a Mozart/play the piano/three. I/play the piano/ten.
   b Picasso/draw/one. I/draw/six.
   c Nureyev/dance/three. I/dance/seven.
   d I/speak/two. Einstein/speak/eight. (True!)

Memorize some of the sentences! Practise saying them.

2 Match a line in A with a line in B.

A	B
Mozart was born in	Siberia.
Picasso was born in	Ulm.
Nureyev was born in	Salzburg.
Einstein was born in	Malaga.

Where were you born? When?

I was born in Madrid in 1975.

3 Choosing the correct sentence

One sentence has a mistake. Which is the correct sentence?
Put ✔ and ✘.

1 a I don't can use a word processor.
   b I can't use a word processor.
2 a Was they at the party?
   b Were they at the party?
3 a I'm sorry. I can't go to the party.
   b I'm sorry. I no can go to the party.
4 a She no was at home.
   b She wasn't at home.
5 a He could play chess when he was five.
   b He can play chess when he was five.
6 a I was in New York the last week.
   b I was in New York last week.

● READING AND SPEAKING

Pre-reading task

What do teenagers like doing in your country?
Think of three things and tell the others in the class.

Reading

Divide into two groups.

Group A   Read about Ivan Mirsky.
Group B   Read about Jaya Rajah.

Answer the questions.

Comprehension check

a How old is he?
b Does he go to school?
c Where was he born?
d Where does he live now?
e Who does he live with?
f What does his father do?
g How was he different when he was very young?
h What does he do in the evening?
i Can his father speak English?
j Does he have any friends?
k What does he do in his free time?

Check your answers with your group.

Ivan Mirsky is thirteen and he is the number 13 chess player in the world.

He was born in Russia but now lives in America with his father, Vadim. They live in a one-room flat in Brooklyn. Ivan doesn't go to school and his father doesn't have a job. They practise chess problems all day, every day, morning, afternoon, and evening.

Ivan was different from a very young age: he could ride a bike when he was eighteen months old and read before he was two. He could play cards at three and the piano at four. When he was twelve, he was the under-20 chess champion of Russia.

His father can't speak English and can't play chess, either! Ivan translates for him. Vadim says, 'I know that I can't play chess, but I can still help Ivan. He and I don't have any friends – we don't want any friends. Other teenagers are boring! We don't like playing sports or watching TV. We live for chess!'

TWO TEENAGE GENIUSES

Jaya Rajah is fourteen, but he doesn't go to school. He studies medicine at New York University in a class of twenty-year-olds. Jaya was born in Madras in India but now lives in a house in New York with his mother, father, and brother. They can all speak English fluently. His father is a doctor.

Jaya was different from a very young age. He could count before he could say 'Mummy' or 'Daddy'. He could answer questions on calculus when he was five and do algebra when he was eight. Now he studies from 8.15 to 4.00 every day at the university. Then he studies at home with his father from 6.30 to 10.00 every evening. Jaya doesn't have any friends. He never goes out in the evenings, but he sometimes watches TV. He says, 'I live for one thing – I want to be a doctor before I am seventeen. Other children of my age are boring. They can't understand me.'

Speaking

1   Find a partner from the other group.
    Discuss the answers again and tell your partner about the teenager in your text.

2   Now read the other text.
    How many similarities and differences can you find?

> They both live in New York.

> Ivan lives with just his father, but Jaya lives with his parents and his brother.

3   What do you think?
    a   Are Ivan and Jaya happy?
    b   Are friends important? Why?

Roleplay

Work in pairs.
Student A is a journalist, Student B is Ivan or Jaya.
Ask and answer questions. Use the questions in the Comprehension Check to help you prepare the interview.

> Hello, Ivan! Can I ask you one or two questions?

> Yes, of course.

> First of all, how old are you?

> I'm thirteen.

●VOCABULARY AND PRONUNCIATION

Words that sound the same

1   Look at the sentences. What do you notice about the underlined words?
    I have a black eye.
    No, he doesn't know the answer.

2   Find the words in B that have the same pronunciation as the words in A.
    Check the meaning of new words in your dictionary.

A
hear   see   write
eye   there   for
know   by   knows
wear   son   hour
meat   cheque   too

B
right   no   check
where   buy   I
nose   two   sea
four   meet   their
our   here   sun

3   Each sentence has two words with the wrong spelling. Correct the spelling mistakes.

a   I can here you, but I can't sea you.
b   Their are three bedrooms in hour house.
c   John nose wear Jill lives.
d   My sun lives near the see.
e   Don't where that hat when you meat the Queen!
f   They no Anna two.
g   You were write. Sally and Peter don't eat meet.
h   There daughter could right when she was three.
i   I want to by too new pens.
j   Cheque that your answers are write.

4   Here are some spellings in phonetics. Write the two words which sound the same.

a   /nəʊz/   _____   _____
b   /sʌn/   _____   _____
c   /miːt/   _____   _____
d   /tʃek/   _____   _____
e   /tuː/   _____   _____
f   /raɪt/   _____   _____
g   /hɪə/   _____   _____
h   /weə/   _____   _____

● EVERYDAY ENGLISH

At the airport

1 **T 34a** Listen to the airport announcements and complete the chart.

FLIGHT NUMBER	• DESTINATION	GATE NUMBER	● ●	REMARK
B A 5 1 6	• G E N E V A	1 4	● ●	LAST CALL
S K	•		● ●	LAST CALL
A F	•		● ●	DELAYED 30 mins
L H	•		● ●	NOW BOARDING
V S	•		● ●	NOW BOARDING

2 Where do you go first when you travel by plane? Put these places in the correct order. Write 1-5 on the left.

___	passport control	___
___	baggage reclaim	___
1	the check-in desk	___
___	the plane	___
___	the arrival hall	___
___	the departure lounge	**a**

3 **T 34b** Read and listen to the conversations. Where are they? Write the letter next to the correct place on the right in Exercise 2.

a A Ah! … BA 476 to Madrid. That's our flight.
   B Was it gate 4 or 14?
   A I couldn't hear. I think it was 4.
   B Ssssh! There it is again. It *is* gate 4.
   A OK. Come on!

b A Can I see your passport, please?
   B Yes, of course. Here you are.
   A Thank you very much. That's fine.

c A Can I have your ticket, please?
   B Yes, of course. Here you are.
   A Do you have just one suitcase?
   B Yes. This bag is hand luggage.
   A That's fine. Smoking or non-smoking?
   B Non-smoking, please. Oh ... and can I have a seat next to the window?
   A Yes, that's OK. Here's your boarding pass. Have a nice flight!

d A Can I have your tray please, madam?
   B Yes. Here you are.
   A Thank you. And can you fasten your seat belt? We land in ten minutes.
   B Yes, of course.

e A Excuse me. I think that's my suitcase.
   B I'm sorry. My suitcase is red, too.
   A Is this yours?
   B Yes, it is. Thank you very much.

f A Hello. Are you Marie-Thérèse Scherer from Switzerland?
   B Yes, I am. Are you Mr and Mrs Barnes?
   A Yes, we are. Welcome to England, Marie-Thérèse. Was your flight good?
   B Yes, it was, but I don't like flying.
   C Never mind. You're here safely now. Come on, the car's outside.

4 Read the conversations again carefully. Who are the people?

5 **T 34c** Close your books.
Listen to some of the lines from the conversations. There is a pause after each one for you to respond. You can use the ideas from the conversations in the book or your own ideas.

6 Work in groups of two or three.
Think of some roleplays in an airport or on a plane.
Choose a place and some characters.
You can be travellers from different countries, pilots, customs officers ...!

GRAMMAR SUMMARY

can/can't

Can and *can't* have the same form in all persons. There is no *do* or *does*.
Can is followed by the infinitive (without *to*).

could/couldn't

Could is the past of *can*. *Could* and *couldn't* have the same form in all persons.
Could is followed by the infinitive (without *to*).

Positive

I You He/She/It We They	can could	swim.

Negative

I You He/She/It We They	can't couldn't	dance.

NOT He ~~doesn't can~~ dance.

Question

What	can could	I you he/she/it we they	do?

Yes/No questions

Can Could	you she they etc.	drive? cook?

Short answers

No, I can't./No, we couldn't.
Yes, she can/could.
Yes, they can/could.

NOT ~~Do you can~~ drive?

was/were

Was/were is the past of *am/is/are*.

Positive

I She/He/It	was	in Paris yesterday.
We You They	were	in England last year.

Negative

I He/She/It	wasn't	at school yesterday.
We You They	weren't	at the party last night.

Question

Where	was	I? he/she/it?
	were	we? you? they?

Yes/No questions

Was	he she	at work?
Were	you they etc.	at home?

Short answers

No, he wasn't.
Yes, she was.

Yes, I was./Yes, we were.
No, they weren't.

was born

Where	was	she he	born?
	were	you they etc.	

I was born in Manchester in 1970. NOT I ~~am born~~ in 1970.

Prepositions

They were **in** England **in** 1980.
I was **at** a party.
We land **in** ten minutes.
He studies **from** 8.15 **to** 4.00.

Study the Word List for this unit on page 124.

Past Simple (1) – Special occasions

Then and now

PRESENTATION (1)

Regular verbs

1 Check the meaning of these verbs.

earn	move (house)	retire	die

2 Look at the photograph and read text A about Ellen Peel.

A

Ellen Peel is over ninety years old. She lives in a village in the country with her five cats. She is not married, but she loves children. She is very happy, but she can remember times when her life was difficult. She often thinks about her past.

3 **T 35a** Read and listen to text B.

B

Ellen's father died in the war in 1915 and her mother died a year later. Ellen was twelve years old. Immediately she started work as a housemaid with a rich family in London.

Now answer the Grammar questions.

● Grammar questions

– Which text is about the present?
Which is about the past?

– Find an example of the past of *is*.
What are the last two letters of the other verbs in text B?

– Complete the rule.
To form the Past Simple of regular verbs, add _____ to the infinitive.

4 **T 35b** Read and listen to text C.
Fill in the gaps. Use the Past Simple form of the verbs in the box.

love stay retire look work move earn clean like

C

She _____ from 5.30 in the morning until 9.00 at night.
She _____ all the rooms in the house before breakfast. She _____ £25 a year.
In 1921 she _____ to another family. She _____ her new job because she _____ after the children. There were five children, four sons and one daughter.
She _____ them, especially the baby, Robert. She _____ with that family for twenty years. Ellen never married. She just looked after other people's children until she _____ when she was seventy years old.

Practice

1 Grammar

Match a line in A with a line in B. Put the verb in B into the Past Simple.

A	B
a I was only twelve years old	because I _____ (work) very long hours.
b I was always tired in my first job	but in 1920 I _____ (live) in London.
c I started work at 5.30 in the morning	when my mother _____ (die) and I _____ (start) work.
d Now I live in a village,	but I _____ (love) Robert especially.
e Now I look after my five cats.	and I _____ (finish) at 9.00 in the evening.
f I loved all the children,	In the 1920s I _____ (look) after five children.
g Robert's over seventy now and I still see him.	He _____ (visit) me just last month.

2 Listening and pronunciation

1 **T 36a** Listen to Ellen and check your answers.

2 **T 36b** The past tense ending -ed has three different pronunciations. Listen and put the verbs in the correct columns.

/t/	/d/	/ɪd/
_____	_____	_____
_____	_____	_____
_____	_____	
	_____	
	_____	

Practise saying the verbs.

PRESENTATION (2)

Questions and negatives

1 Read about Queen Victoria. Ask your teacher the questions below the text to find the missing information.

Queen Victoria was born in _____ (?) in 1819 and she died in _____(?). She was Queen of the United Kingdom for nearly sixty-four years.
Her father died when she was _____(?) and she was Queen from 1837 to 1901. She didn't have any brothers or sisters. She married Prince Albert in _____(?) and they lived in _____(?) with their _____(?) children.

When did she die?
When did she marry Prince Albert?
How many children did they have?
Where was she born?
Where did they live?
When did her father die?

2 **T 37** Listen and practise saying the questions.

> ⚠
>
> 1 *Did* is the past of *do* and *does*. We use *did* to form a question about the past.
>
> Where **do** you work (now)?   Where **does** she live (now)?
> Where **did** you work in 1980? Where **did** she live in 1950?
>
> 2 We use *didn't* to form a negative.
>
> She **didn't** have any brothers or sisters.

● Grammar question

Complete the rule.
To form questions in the Past Simple, we use the auxiliary

verb _____ and the _____ (without *to*).

Practice

1 Speaking

Work in pairs. Your teacher will give you some more information about Queen Victoria and Prince Albert, but you don't have the same information as your partner. Ask and answer questions to complete the information.

Example

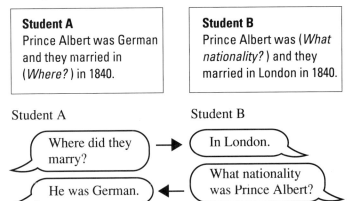

Student A	Student B
Prince Albert was German and they married in (*Where?*) in 1840.	Prince Albert was (*What nationality?*) and they married in London in 1840.

Student A

Student B

Where did they marry? → In London.

What nationality was Prince Albert?

He was German. ←

2 Grammar and speaking

1 Put *did*, *was*, or *were* into the gaps.

a Where _____ you born? Where _____ your mother born?

b When _____ you start school?

c How many schools _____ you go to?

d What _____ your favourite subject?

e Where _____ you live when you _____ a child?

f _____ you live in a house or a flat?

2 Stand up!
Ask two or three students the questions in Exercise 1.

3 Tell the class some of the information you learned.

Enrico was born in ...

He started school ...

His mother ...

PRESENTATION (3)

Irregular verbs

1 Three of the verbs in the box are regular. Which are they? The others are irregular. Check the meanings in your dictionary and write in the Past Simple forms of all the verbs. There is a list of irregular verbs on page 127.

have	_____	come	_____	work	_____	go	_____
leave	_____	hate	_____	get	_____	give	_____
become	_____	write	_____	change	_____	win	_____
lose	_____	find	_____	buy	_____	sell	_____

2 **T 38** Listen and repeat the Past Simple verb forms.

3 How old were you in 1980? What can you remember about the 1980s?
Think about your life, sport, and politics.

4 **T 39** Listen to Kevin talking about the 1980s.

ABOUT HIM

a He _____ school in 1982. He was unemployed, but then he _____ a job in an office. He _____ computer software.

b His parents _____ a video recorder in 1985 and his brother _____ a video computer game for his birthday in 1986.

c Kevin _____ his job in 1990.

SPORT

d The USSR _____ _____ to the Olympics in 1984, but both the United States and the USSR _____ to Seoul in 1988.

e Argentina _____ the World Cup in 1986.

POLITICS

f Reagan _____ the US president in 1981, Gorbachev _____ the world *glasnost* and *perestroika*, and the Berlin Wall _____ down in 1989.

Complete the sentences. Listen again and check.

5 Here are the answers to some questions about the listening text. Write the questions.

Example
In 1982.
When did Kevin leave school?

a Computer software.
b In 1985.
c A video computer game.
d In 1990.
e In 1986.
f In 1989.

Practice

1 Speaking

1 Look at the past time expressions.

last	night Monday week month year	yesterday	morning afternoon evening

We cannot say ~~last evening~~ or ~~last afternoon~~.

2 Work in pairs. Ask and answer questions with *When did you last ...?* Ask one more question each time.

Example
have a holiday

When did you last have a holiday?

Last August.

Where did you go?

To Spain.

a see a video
b go shopping
c give someone a kiss
d take a photograph
e go to a party
f lose something
g write a letter
h get a present
i have dinner in a restaurant

Tell the class some things you learned about your partner.

Keiko had a holiday last August and she went to Spain.

2 Choosing the correct sentence

One sentence has a mistake. Choose the correct sentence. Put ✔ and ✘.

1 a He bought some new shoes.
   b He buyed some new shoes.
2 a Where did you go yesterday?
   b Where you went yesterday?
3 a You see Jane last week?
   b Did you see Jane last week?
4 a Did she found a job?
   b Did she find a job?
5 a We didn't enjoyed the film.
   b We didn't enjoy the film.
6 a I didn't go out yesterday evening.
   b I didn't go out last evening.
7 a I was to school for the first time when I was six.
   b I went to school for the first time when I was six.
8 a Last night I have dinner with friends.
   b Last night I had dinner with friends.

● READING

Pre-reading task

1 Do you know any British or American writers? What do you know about them?

2 Do you know any books by Charles Dickens? When did he live? Do you know anything about Victorian England?

3 Check the meaning of these words in your dictionary. Put one of the words into each gap.

novelist (*n*)	clerk (*n*)	debt (*n*)	prison (*n*)
factory (*n*)	popular (*adj*)	experience (*n*)	
lawcourt (*n*)	abroad (*adv*)	successful (*adj*)	

a All the students like Anna. She's a very _____ girl.
b My mother writes books, but she isn't a famous _____ .
c Alan started work in a bank last week. He's a _____ .
d He has ten clothes shops. He's a rich, _____ businessman.
e I don't like borrowing money. I hate being in _____ .
f I live near a very big _____ that makes cars.
g I went round the world for a year. It was a wonderful _____ .
h She often goes _____ in her job, sometimes to Hong Kong, sometimes to Canada.

Reading

Read the text about the life of Charles Dickens.

Comprehension check

1 Are the sentences true (✔) or false (✘)? Correct the false sentences.

a Charles Dickens wrote novels.
b He wrote only about the lives of rich and famous people.
c His father had a good job.
d Charles never went to school.
e He went to prison when he was eleven.
f His first job was in a factory.
g He became a journalist when he was fifteen.
h He never married.

Charles Dickens (1812–1870)

Charles Dickens is one of the greatest novelists in the English language. He wrote about the real world of Victorian England and many of his characters were not rich, middle-class ladies and gentlemen, but poor and hungry people.

DICKENS THE CHILD

His family lived in London. His father was a clerk in an office. It was a good job, but he always spent more money than he earned and he was often in debt. There were eight children in the family, so life was hard.

Charles went to school and his teachers thought he was very clever. But suddenly, when he was only eleven, his father went to prison for his debts and the family went, too. Only Charles didn't go to prison. He went to work in a factory, where he washed bottles. He

worked ten hours a day and earned six shillings (30p) a week. Every night, after work, he walked four miles back to his room. Charles hated it and never forgot the experience. He used it in many novels, especially *David Copperfield* and *Oliver Twist*.

DICKENS THE WRITER

When he was sixteen, he started work for a newspaper. He visited law courts and the Houses of Parliament. Soon he was one of the *Morning Chronicle*'s best journalists. He also wrote short stories for magazines. These were funny descriptions of people that he met. Dickens' characters were full of colour and life – good people were very, very good and bad people were horrible. His books became popular in many countries and he spent a lot of time abroad, in America, Italy, and Switzerland.

DICKENS THE MAN

Dickens had ten children, but he didn't have a happy family life. He was successful in his work but not at home, and his wife left him. He never stopped writing and travelling, and he died very suddenly in 1870.

2 Answer the questions.

a How old was Dickens when he died?
b How many brothers and sisters did he have?
c Was he good at school?
d Why did he leave school when he was eleven?
e Who was in prison?
f What did Charles do in his first job?
g What was his next job?
h Was he happy at home?
i When did he stop writing?

Writing

Write about your past. Use these ideas to help you.

Born	Parents	School	Free time	First job
when?	work?	like?	sports?	what?
where?	live?	not like?	hobbies?	when?
				earn?

● VOCABULARY AND PRONUNCIATON

Silent letters

1 English spelling is not phonetic, so there are many silent letters in English words.

Here are some words from the text about Charles Dickens. Practise saying them.

de**b**t	/det/	ei**gh**t	/eɪt/
har**d**	/hɑːd/	thou**gh**t	/θɔːt/

Cross out the silent letters in these words.

Example
ni~~gh~~t

a walk	d writer	g work	j half
b listen	e autumn	h short	k foreign
c know	f farm	i high	l daughter

T 40a Listen and check. Practise saying the words.

2 Here are some of the words from Exercise 1 in phonetics. Write the words.

Example
/wɔːk/ = *walk*

a /wɜːk/ _____   d /ɔːtəm/ _____

b /fɑːm/ _____   e /raɪtə/ _____

c /lɪsən/ _____   f /dɔːtə/ _____

3 Here are some other words in phonetics. Write the words. Be careful! They all have silent letters.

a /tɔːk/ _____   f /waɪt/ _____

b /bɔːn/ _____   g /naɪf/ _____

c /bɔːt/ _____   h /rɒŋ/ _____

d /wɜːld/ _____   i /kʌbəd/ _____

e /ɑːnsə/ _____   j /krɪsməs/ _____

T 40b Listen and practise saying the words.

● EVERYDAY ENGLISH

Special occasions

1 Look at the list of days. Which are special? Check the meaning of new words in your dictionary. Match the special days with the photographs and objects.

```
Thursday
birthday
Monday
wedding day
Christmas Day
yesterday
New Year's Eve
Easter Day
tomorrow
Mother's Day
today
Valentine's Day
Friday
```

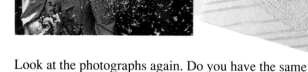

A Valentine Especially for You

Look at the photographs again. Do you have the same customs in your country?

2 Complete the conversations.

a A Ugh! Work again! I hate _____ !
   B Me, too. Did you have a nice weekend?
   A Yes. It was wonderful.

b Happy _____ to you.
   Happy _____ to you.
   Happy _____ , dear Katie.
   Happy _____ to you.

c A How many _____ eggs did you get?
   B Six. What about you?
   A Five. I had them all on _____ morning before lunch.
   B Did you?
   A And then I was sick!
   B Ugh!

d A Congratulations!
   B Oh … thank you very much.
   A When's the happy day?
   B Pardon?
   A Your _____ day. When is it?
   B Oh! We're not sure yet. Some time in June, probably.

e A Hello! Merry _____ , everyone!
   B Merry _____ ! Come in, come in. It's so cold outside.

f A Wonderful! It's _____ !
   B Yes. Have a nice weekend!
   A Same to you.

T 41a Listen and check. In pairs, practise the conversations.

3 **T 41b** Listen and answer.

GRAMMAR SUMMARY

Past Simple

The form of the Past Simple is the same in all persons.

Positive

I You He/She/It We They	went	to London in 1985.
	moved	

Negative

We use *didn't* + infinitive (without *to*) in all persons.

I You He/She/It We They	didn't	go	to London.
		move	

Question

We use *did* + infinitive (without *to*) in all persons.

When Where	did	I you he/she/it we they	go?

Yes/No questions

Did	you she they etc.	like	the film?
			the family?

Short answers

No, I didn't./No, we didn't.
Yes, she did.
No, they didn't.

Remember the list of irregular verbs on page 127.

Time expressions

last	night Saturday week month year	yesterday	morning afternoon evening

Prepositions

I often think **about** you.
I have a shower **before** breakfast.
I am always **in** debt.
Write **about** when you were young.
The box is full **of** books.

Study the Word List for this unit on page 124.

53

UNIT 8

Past Simple (2) – Time expressions – Ordinals and dates

How things began

PRESENTATION (1)

Negatives and *ago*

1 What century is it now? What was the last century? What year is it now? What year was it one hundred years ago?

2 Look at the photographs. Complete the questions with the correct verb from the box.

drive	eat	listen to	make	write	ride
take	travel (× 2)	use	watch	wear	

3 Ask and answer questions.

Did people drive cars one hundred years ago?

Yes, I think they did.

I'm not sure.

No, they didn't.

4 Say the things people did and the things people didn't do.

People rode bikes.

They didn't watch TV.

5 Listen! Your teacher knows the answers and the correct dates.

● Grammar question

Complete the rule.
To form the negative in the Past Simple, we use the auxiliary

verb _____ + _____ and the _____ (without *to*).

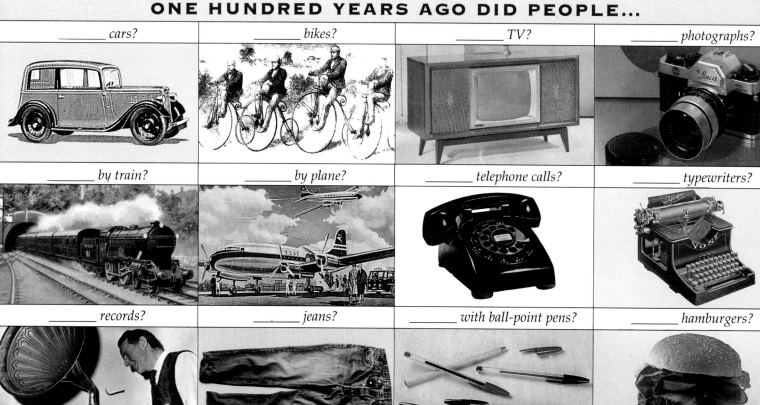

ONE HUNDRED YEARS AGO DID PEOPLE...

_____ cars? _____ bikes? _____ TV? _____ photographs?

_____ by train? _____ by plane? _____ telephone calls? _____ typewriters?

_____ records? _____ jeans? _____ with ball-point pens? _____ hamburgers?

Practice

1 Reading and listening

1 Read the three texts. Check the meaning of new words in your dictionary.
There are three mistakes in each text. Can you find any of them?

2 **T 42** Listen and correct the mistakes.

> He didn't make the first hamburgers in 1985. He made them in 1895.

THE HAMBURGER	TELEVISION	THE BALL-POINT PEN
An American chef from Connecticut, Louis Lassen, made and sold the first hamburgers in 1985. He called them hamburgers because sailors from Hamburg in Germany gave him the recipe. Teachers from Yale University and businessmen loved them and bought them. Kenneth Lassen, Louis' son, still sells hamburgers in Connecticut.	A Scotsman, John Logie Baird, transmitted the first television picture on 25 October, 1825. The first thing on television was a cat from the office next to Baird's workroom in London. In 1927 Baird sent pictures from London to Glasgow. In 1928 he sent pictures to Paris and also produced the first colour TV pictures.	A Hungarian, Laszlo Biro, made the first ball-point pen in 1838. In 1944 the American Army bought thirty thousand because soldiers could write with them outside in the rain. At the end of the war 'Biros' quickly became very popular all over the world. In 1948 a shop in New York sold ten on one day.

2 Listening and pronunciation

1 **T 43** Read and listen to the conversations. Listen carefully to the intonation.

> Did you know that Marco Polo brought spaghetti back from China?

> Really? He didn't! That's incredible!

> Well, it's true!

> Did you know that Napoleon was afraid of cats?

> He wasn't! I don't believe it!

> Well, it's true!

2 Work in pairs.
Your teacher will give you two different lists of more incredible information!

Student A   Give the information, beginning *Did you know that ...?*

Student B   Make a reply.

Then change!

PRESENTATION (2)

Time expressions

How many correct time expressions can you make?

	the twentieth century
	1924
	winter
	September
in	10 October
on	weekends
at	Christmas day
	Saturday
	Sunday evening
	the evening
	seven o'clock

Practice

1 Grammar and speaking

Ask and answer questions with *when*. Use a time expression and *ago* in the answer.

> When did you get up?

> At seven o'clock.
> Three hours ago.

> When did this term start?

> In September. Two months ago.

a ... have breakfast?
b ... arrive at school?
c ... start learning English?
d ... start this school?
e ... first travel by plane?
f ... last have a holiday?
g ... last eat a hamburger?
h ... learn to ride a bicycle?
i ... your parents marry?
j ... Shakespeare die?

2 Listening and speaking

1 What is the Past Simple of these verbs?

| break into   steal   eat   drink   feel   fall   wake up |

2 **T 44** Look at the pictures about a burglar and listen. It's a true story!

Complete the sentences with verbs from the box and your own ideas.
Don't write! Practise saying the story until you can remember it.

Picture 1
On 1 June 1992, a French burglar ... a house ... He ... living room and ...

Picture 2
Then ... kitchen. He opened ... cheese.

Picture 3
... hungry, so ... Next ... champagne.

Picture 4
... thirsty, so ... Then ... felt ...

Picture 5
... upstairs for ..., but ... tired ... fell ...

Picture 6
When ... the next ..., there were ... bed!

4

5

6

3 Complete the questions about the story.

Example
When *did he break into* the house?
On 1 June, 1992.

a How many pictures _____ ?
Two.

b What _____ see _____ ?
Some cheese.

c How _____ bottles _____ ?
Two.

d Why _____ upstairs?
Because he wanted a rest.

e When _____ up?
Next morning.

f How many _____ ?
Four.

4 Write the story for homework!

● VOCABULARY AND PRONUNCIATON

Odd one out

1 Which word is the odd one out? Why?

Example
orange   apple   ~~chicken~~   banana

> Chicken is the odd one out because it's an animal.
> The others are kinds of fruit.

Check the meaning of new words in your dictionary.

a	camera	stereo	photograph	computer
b	recipe	cake	bread	biscuit
c	met	laughed	wrote	spoke
d	fall in love	get married	get engaged	be retired
e	pink	yellow	warm	blue
f	war	sailor	soldier	pilot
g	hair	voice	eyes	hand
h	century	clock	season	month
i	shy	nervous	angry	hungry
j	fridge	dishwasher	television	washing machine

2 Where is the stress on these words? Put them in the correct column.

photograph   machine   recipe   camera   engaged
dishwasher   century   computer   married

● ● ●	● ●	● ● ●	● ●

3 Here are some words in phonetics. Practise saying the words.

a /bred/   c /lɑːft/   e /heə/   g /æŋgrɪ/
b /bɪskɪt/   d /wɔː/   f /mærɪd/   h /hʌŋgrɪ/

4 Put one of the words from Exercise 1 into each gap.

a My American cousin was a _____ in the Vietnam war.

b My daughter doesn't like parties because she's very _____ .

c He took a lovely _____ of the baby.

d They _____ when I told them the joke.

e Can I have that _____ for chocolate cake? It was wonderful.

f I _____ to our neighbour, Mrs Jones, today. She said she was fine.

g She's a very good singer. She has a beautiful _____ .

h 'How did you feel before the exam?' 'Very _____ .'

i I broke my father's camera yesterday. He was very _____ .

OLIVER AND WENDY MINT ▲

HOW ♥ we ♥ MET

▼ TREVOR AND ASTRID RICHARDS

● LISTENING AND SPEAKING

Pre-listening task

1 Put the sentences in order. There is more than one answer!

____ They got married.

____ They fell in love.

____ Jane and Roger met at a party.

____ He liked her before she liked him.

____ They have two children.

____ They went out together for a long time.

____ They wrote love letters.

2 Are you married? How did you meet your husband/wife? When did your parents meet? Where?

3 Look at the photographs of two couples. How old are they? What jobs do they do?

4 Check the meaning of new verbs in your dictionary. What is the past tense form of each verb?

| hear think wait smile ring tell forget speak laugh |

Listening

T 45 Divide into two groups.

Group A   Listen to Wendy Mint.
Group B   Listen to Trevor Richards.

Answer the questions about your couple.

Comprehension check

a When did they meet?
b How did they meet?
c What is his job?
d Was he at work when they met?
e What did he/she like about him/her?
f Are they both English?
g Who is shy?
h Wendy talks about a restaurant.
   Trevor talks about a cake. Why?
i When did they get married?
j Do they work together?
k Do they have any children?

Speaking

1 Find a partner from the other group. Discuss the answers and compare information.
2 Imagine that you are Oliver or Astrid. Tell the story of how you met your wife/husband.

● EVERYDAY ENGLISH

1 Ordinals

1 Write the correct word next to the numbers.

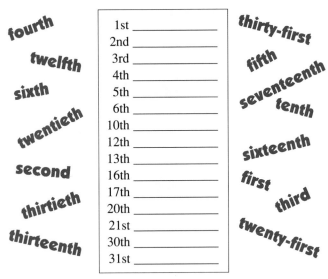

fourth *twelfth* *sixth* *twentieth* *second* *thirtieth* *thirteenth*

1st	_____
2nd	_____
3rd	_____
4th	_____
5th	_____
6th	_____
10th	_____
12th	_____
13th	_____
16th	_____
17th	_____
20th	_____
21st	_____
30th	_____
31st	_____

thirty-first *fifth* *seventeenth* *tenth* *sixteenth* *first* *third* *twenty-first*

T 46a Listen and practise saying the ordinals.

2 Ask and answer questions about the months of the year.

Which is the first month? — January.

Which is the ninth month? — September.

2 Dates

⚠

We write:	We say:
3/4/1992	the third of April, nineteen ninety-two
or	or
3 April 1992	April the third, nineteen ninety-two

Practise saying these dates:

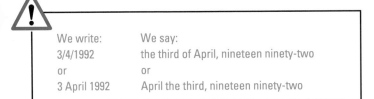

1 April	2 March	17 September	19 November	23 June
15/7/67	29/2/76	19/12/83	3/10/70	31/5/93

T 46b Listen and check.

2 **T 46c** Listen and write the dates you hear.

3 Work in pairs. Ask and answer these questions.

a What's the date today?
b When did this school term start? When does it end?
c When's Christmas Day?
d When's Valentine's Day?
e When's Mothers' Day this year?
f When's American Independence Day?
g What century is it now?
h What are the dates of public holidays in your country?
i When were you born?
j When's your birthday?

GRAMMAR SUMMARY

Past Simple

Negative
Negatives in the Past Simple are the same in all persons.

I You She We They etc.	didn't	go out	last night.

ago

I went to the States	ten years two weeks a month	ago.

Time expressions

in	the twentieth century 1924 winter/summer the evening/the morning September
on	10 October Christmas Day Saturday Sunday evening
at	seven o'clock weekends

Prepositions

I phoned him **at** the end **of** the programme.
My birthday is **on** the tenth **of** October.
Can I ask a question **about** your country?
She fell **in** love **with** his voice.

Study the Word List for this unit on page 125.

STOP AND CHECK

Units 5–8

1 Correcting the mistakes

Each sentence has a mistake. Find it and correct it!

Example
Where ~~you live~~?   *Where do you live?*

a   My brother go to university.
b   English is a language international.
c   I don't like swim.
d   I arrive at Heathrow airport at ten o'clock last night.
e   She could to speak three languages when she was ten.
f   Where did you went last night?
g   I saw the wife of Jeremy at the shops.
h   I don't can go out because I have a lot of homework.
i   In the kitchen is a table.
j   I was to the cinema last weekend.
k   My children like they're school very much.
l   I buyed a new video.
m   Did you watch the football on TV last evening?
n   Italian people is very artistic.
o   I like cities because I can to go to the theatre.

15

2 can/could/was/were (not)

Put a verb from the box into each gap.

> can/can't could/couldn't was/wasn't were/weren't

Example
I _can't_ drive. I'm only 14 years old.

a   Our teacher _____ at school last week because she
    _____ ill.

b   Leonardo _____ a student in Florence. He _____
    draw, write music, and design buildings.

c   We _____ see the Mona Lisa in the Louvre in Paris.

d   'Where _____ you last night? You _____ at home.
    I phoned you, but there _____ no answer.'
    'I _____ get into my flat because I lost my keys. I
    _____ at a friend's house.'

10

3 Irregular verbs

Write the Past Simple form of these irregular verbs.

a   give   _____   f   make   _____
b   leave _____   g   break _____
c   sell   _____   h   meet   _____
d   speak _____   i   win   _____
e   lose   _____   j   take   _____

10

4 Past Simple

Fill in the gaps with the Past Simple form of the verbs in brackets. There are regular and irregular verbs.

Example
Leonardo da Vinci _lived_ (live) in Italy in the fifteenth and sixteenth centuries.

> He was a student in Florence, where he (a) _____ (study) painting, sculpture, and design. He (b) _____ (begin) a lot of paintings, but he (c) _____ (not finish) many of them. His picture of the Mona Lisa is the most famous portrait in the world.
>
> Leonardo (d) _____ (be) interested in many things. He (e) _____ (want) to know about everything he saw. He examined the human body. He (f) _____ (think) that the sun (g) _____ (not go) round the earth. He (h) _____ (write) music. He designed a flying machine 400 years before the first one flew. Many people
>
>
>
> (i) _____ (not understand) his ideas. It is difficult to think that one man (j) _____ (can) do so much.

20

60

5 *a/an* or nothing?

Some of the sentences need *a* or *an*. Some of the sentences are correct. Put *a/an* or ✔.

Examples

He has good~~job~~. *He has a good job.*

I don't like cheese. ✔

a   I have toast for breakfast. _____

b   My sister works in office. _____

c   Do you like Indian food? _____

d   Is there Indian restaurant
near here? _____

e   Have nice weekend! _____

f   There's good library near
my house. _____

g   Meat is expensive. _____

h   My grandfather is
engineer. _____ **16**

6 *some/any/a/an*

Put *some*, *any*, *a*, or *an* into each gap.

Example

Heathrow is ___*an*___ international airport.

a   Did Charles Dickens have _____ children?

b   I bought _____ newspaper and _____ magazines.

c   Jane lives in _____ old house in France.

d   There are _____ trees in my garden, but there aren't
_____ flowers.

e   Do you have _____ books by Gabriel García
Márquez?

f   There are _____ letters for you on the table. **8**

7 Vocabulary – connections

Match a line in A with a line in B.

Example

Easter Day – egg

A	B
Easter Day	sun
cupboard	war
wallet	borrow
library	kitchen
check-in desk	egg
smell	wedding
Welcome to Britain!	luggage
son	chef
Congratulations!	arrival hall
recipe	nose
soldier	money

11

8 Vocabulary – opposites

Match a word in A with its opposite in B.

Example

wonderful – horrible

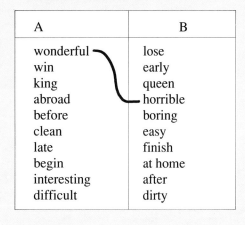

A	B
wonderful	lose
win	early
king	queen
abroad	horrible
before	boring
clean	easy
late	finish
begin	at home
interesting	after
difficult	dirty

10

Total **100**

TRANSLATE

Translate the sentences into your language. Translate the *ideas*, not word by word.

1   Is there a chemist's near here?
_____

2   There are two books on the table.
_____

3   There are some flowers in the living room.
_____

4   Are there any glasses?
_____

5   I can type, but I can't spell.
_____

6   I couldn't go to the party last night.
_____

7   I was ill.
_____

8   Where were you born?
_____

9   I was born in Mexico.
_____

10   She started work when she was twelve.
_____

11   He didn't like his first job.
_____

12   Where did you go on holiday last year?
_____

UNIT 9

like and *would like* – *some/any* – Requests

Food and drink

PRESENTATION (1)

like and *would like* – *some*

1 Look at the lists of food and drink. What do you like?
What don't you like?

> I like tea, but I
> don't like coffee.

> I really like apples.

> I don't like milk
> very much.

> I don't like tomatoes
> at all!

2 **T 47** Listen to two children talking about what they
like. Tick (✔) the things they *both* like.
Practise saying some of the sentences.

● Grammar questions

– Look at the sentences. Why is there no *-s* on *rice*?
Why is there an *-s* on *apples*?
> I like rice.
> I like apples.
Can we count apples? Can we count rice?

– Look at the two lists of words in Exercise 1. What is
the grammatical difference between them?

```
Do you like ... ?

A              B
tea            apples
coffee         oranges
wine           bananas
apple juice    grapes
beer           strawberries
milk           eggs
water          biscuits
bread          sandwiches
cheese         tomatoes
ice-cream      hamburgers
chocolate
rice
fruit
```

3 **T 48** Look at the pictures and listen to the conversations.

a A I'm thirsty.
   B Would you like some tea?
   A No, thanks.
   B Would you like some apple juice?
   A Oh, yes, please!

b A I'm hungry. Is there anything to eat?
   B Would you like a biscuit?
   A No, thanks. I'd like a sandwich.
   B Cheese? Ham?
   A Cheese *and* ham, please!

● Grammar question

What is the difference between the sentences in each pair?

I like hamburgers.
I'd like a hamburger, please.

Do you like apple juice?
Would you like some apple juice?

Which sentences are about all time?
Which sentences are about now?

---

1 I'd = I would

2 We use *some* with plural and uncountable nouns:
   some bananas
   some rice

3 When we ask for things and offer things, we use *some*, not *any*, in the question.
   Would you like some grapes?
   Can I have some milk, please?

   But:
   Would you like a hamburger? (Just one.)

---

4 Practise the dialogues in Exercise 3. Make more dialogues with other food and drink.

Practice

1 Grammar

Choose the correct sentence. Put ✔ and ✘.

Example
A Would you like | a cigarette? ✔
   Do you like | ✘
B No, thanks. I don't smoke.

a A Do you like | your teacher?
      Would you like |
   B Yes. She's very nice.

b A Do you like | a drink?
      Would you like |
   B Yes, please. Some Coke, please.

c A Can I help you?
   B Yes. I like | a packet of cigarettes, please.
      Yes. I'd like |

d A What sports do you do?
   B Well, I'd like | swimming very much.
      Well, I like |

e A Are you ready to order your meal, sir?
   B Yes. I like | a steak, please.
      Yes. I'd like |

2 Listening

T 49a Listen to what A says. Choose the correct answer for B. Put ✔ and ✘.

1 a I like all sorts of fruit.
   b Yes. I'd like some fruit, please.
2 a I'd like a book by John le Carré.
   b I like books by John le Carré.
3 a I'd like a new bike.
   b I like riding my bike.
4 a I'd like a cat but not a dog.
   b I like cats, but I don't like dogs.
5 a I like French wine, especially red wine.
   b We'd like a bottle of French red wine.
6 a No, thanks. I don't like cream.
   b I wouldn't like it.

T 49b Listen and check.

3 Vocabulary

1 Write *a* or *some*.

a _____ book

b _____ air

c _____ rice

d _____ mushroom

e _____ music

f _____ rain

g _____ ice

h _____ kiss

i _____ bacon

j _____ money

k _____ five-pound note

l _____ fruit

2 Write *a*, *an*, or *some*.

a _____ flower

b _____ flowers

c _____ grape

d _____ grapes

e _____ cake

f _____ cake

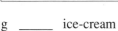

g _____ ice-cream

h _____ ice-cream

64

PRESENTATION (2)

some/any

1 Look at the picture. What is there in the shop?

> There's some bacon.

> There are some newspapers.

> She doesn't have any milk.

> I can't see any eggs.

2 Work in pairs. Ask and answer questions about what there is in the shop.

> Is there any orange juice?

> Yes, there is.

> Does she have any sandwiches?

> No, she doesn't.

3 **T 50** Listen to the conversation in the shop and look at the shopping list. Tick (✔) what the man buys. Why doesn't he buy the other things?

THINGS TO BUY

Orange juice   Coffee
Potatoes   Apples
Milk   Bread
Pizza   Cheese

Practice

1 Speaking

Look at the price lists. Check the meaning of new words in your dictionary.

Chemist's

toothpaste	75p
a bottle of aspirin	£1.80
soap	60p
shampoo	£1.40
conditioner	£1.50
a film	£4.50

Art Shop

a pen	45p
writing paper	£1.15
a birthday card	95p
glue	75p
paints	£3.60
a file	£2.50

NEWSAGENT'S

a packet of cigarettes	£2.50
a box of matches	10p
a book of stamps	£2.20
a phone card	£5.00
chewing gum	20p
paper hankies	40p

Roleplay

Work in pairs. Student A is a shop assistant, Student B is a customer.

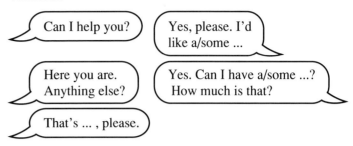

Can I help you?

Yes, please. I'd like a/some ...

Here you are. Anything else?

Yes. Can I have a/some ...? How much is that?

That's ... , please.

2 Questions and answers

1 Complete the questions using *much* or *many*.

a How _____ people are there in the room?

b How _____ money do you have in your pocket?

c How _____ cigarettes do you smoke a day?

d How _____ petrol is there in the car?

e How _____ potatoes do you want?

f How _____ eggs do you want?

g How _____ beer is there in the fridge?

2 Choose an answer for each question in Exercise 1.

h A kilo.
i There are six cans.
j A packet of twenty.
k Three pounds fifty p.
l Half a dozen.
m Twenty. Nine men and eleven women.
n It's full.

3 Correcting the mistakes

Each sentence has a mistake. Find it and correct it!

Example
How ~~much~~ apples do you want?
How many apples do you want?

a I don't like an ice-cream.
b Can I have a bread, please?
c I'm hungry. I like a sandwich.
d Would like you a cup of coffee?
e I have thirsty. Can I have a drink?
f I'd like some fruits, please.
g How many money do you have?

READING AND LISTENING

Pre-reading task

1 What's your favourite food?
What do you eat with it?
When do you have it?

2 You are going to read a text about what British people eat and when.
What do you want to know? Write some questions.

Examples
What do they have for breakfast?
Do they have hot things or cold things?
Do they eat a lot of fish?

Reading

Read the text and match a photograph with each paragraph.

Comprehension check

1 Can you answer your questions from the Pre-reading task?

2 Are the sentences true (✔) or false (✘)? Correct the false sentences.

   a   Many British people have a big breakfast.
   b   People often have cereal or toast for breakfast.
   c   Marmalade is different from jam.
   d   People drink tea with hot milk.
   e   Many foreign visitors love instant coffee.
   f   All British people have a hot lunch.
   g   Pubs are good places to go for lunch.
   h   British people eat dinner late in the evening.
   i   Sunday lunch is a special meal.
   j   When you get a take-away meal, you eat it at home.

MEALS IN BRITAIN

A traditional English breakfast is a very big meal – sausages, bacon, eggs, tomatoes, mushrooms …. But nowadays many people just have cereal with milk and sugar, or toast with marmalade, jam, or honey. Marmalade and jam are not the same! Marmalade is made from oranges and jam is made from other fruit. The traditional breakfast drink is tea, which people have with cold milk. Some people have coffee, often instant coffee, which is made with just hot water. Many visitors to Britain find this coffee disgusting!

For many people lunch is a quick meal. In cities there are a lot of sandwich bars, where office workers can choose the kind of bread they want – brown, white, or a roll – and then all sorts of salad and meat or fish to go in the sandwich. Pubs often serve good, cheap food, both hot and cold. School-children can have a hot meal at school, but many just take a snack from home – a sandwich, a drink, some fruit, and perhaps some crisps.

'Tea' means two things. It is a drink and a meal! Some people have afternoon tea, with sandwiches, cakes, and, of course, a cup of tea. Cream teas are popular. You have scones (a kind of cake) with cream and jam.

The evening meal is the main meal of the day for many people. They usually have it quite early, between 6.00 and 8.00, and often the whole family eats together.

On Sundays many families have a traditional lunch. They have roast meat, either beef, lamb, chicken, or pork, with potatoes, vegetables, and gravy. Gravy is a sauce made from the meat juices.

The British like food from other countries, too, especially Italian, French, Chinese, and Indian. People often get take-away meals – you buy the food at the restaurant and then bring it home to eat. Eating in Britain is quite international!

Listening

T 51 You are going to hear six short conversations. Match each conversation with a photograph on page 66. What is the relationship between the people?

Examples
Mother and daughter./Two friends.

Speaking and writing

1 What do you know about meals in other countries?

> People in Japan eat a lot of fish and rice.

> Spanish people eat late in the evening.

2 Talk about what people in your country eat and when they eat it.

3 Write a similar paragraph about meals in your country.

● VOCABULARY

Food

Look at the word search below. There are seventeen words connected with food.
They go across ➡ and down ⬇.
Find them and write them here. The words begin with these letters.

M _____	B _____	C _____
C _____	R _____	F _____
B _____	V _____	Y _____
P _____	E _____	G _____
S teak	B _____	H _____
J _____	L _____	

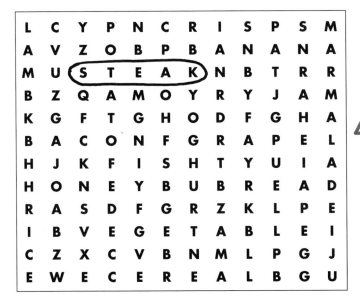

L	C	Y	P	N	C	R	I	S	P	S	M
A	V	Z	O	B	P	B	A	N	A	N	A
M	U	S	T	E	A	K	N	B	T	R	R
B	Z	Q	A	M	O	Y	R	Y	J	A	M
K	G	F	T	G	H	O	D	F	G	H	A
B	A	C	O	N	F	G	R	A	P	E	L
H	J	K	F	I	S	H	T	Y	U	I	A
H	O	N	E	Y	B	U	B	R	E	A	D
R	A	S	D	F	G	R	Z	K	L	P	E
I	B	V	E	G	E	T	A	B	L	E	I
C	Z	X	C	V	B	N	M	L	P	G	J
E	W	E	C	E	R	E	A	L	B	G	U

Make your own word search. Use words connected with drinks. Give it to a partner.

● EVERYDAY ENGLISH

In a hotel

1 Read this conversation in a hotel and put the lines in the correct order.

___ Certainly. A single room or a double?

___ Just this one bag.

___ Yes, sure. Do you want my address, too?

___ Here's your key. Your room number is 311. I hope you enjoy your stay.

___ Single, please.

_1_ Good evening. Can I help you?

___ A shower. How much is the room?

___ Yes, please. Could I have a room for the night?

___ No, thanks. Just breakfast. Can I pay by credit card?

___ Yes, of course. We take Visa and Access. Could you sign the register, please?

___ No. Just a signature. Do you have any luggage?

___ Would you like a room with a shower or a bath?

___ £72 for the room and breakfast. Would you like an evening meal?

_14_ Thanks.

> ⚠️
>
> We use *Could I ...?* to ask for things.
>
> Could I have a room for the night?
>
> We use *Could you ...?* to ask other people to do things for us.
>
> Could you sign the register, please?

T 52 Listen and check.

2 Look at the tapescript on page 119 and practise the conversation.

3 Look at the requests of a hotel guest. Complete them, using *Could I …?* or *Could you …?*

In the restaurant

____ ____ have the menu, please?

____ ____ give me the bill?

____ ____ have some coffee, please?

In the bedroom

____ ____ have breakfast in my room, please?

____ ____ clean my shirts, please?

____ ____ wake me up at 7.00 tomorrow morning?

At the reception desk

____ ____ change some traveller's cheques?

____ ____ recommend a good restaurant?

4 Work in pairs. Practise some conversations in a hotel, using the ideas above. One of you is the guest, the other the waiter or receptionist.

GRAMMAR SUMMARY

would like

Would is the same in all persons. We use *would like* in offers and requests.

Positive

I You He/She/It We They	'd like	a drink.	'd = would

Yes/No questions

Would	you · he/she/it they	like a biscuit?

Short answers

Yes, please.
No, thank you.

Countable and uncountable nouns

Some nouns are countable.

> a book – two books
> an egg – six eggs

Some nouns are uncountable.

> bread
> rice

Some nouns are both!

> Do you like ice-cream?
> We'd like three ice-creams, please.

How much …? and *How many …?*

We use *How much …?* with uncountable nouns.

> How much rice would you like?

We use *How many …?* with countable nouns.

> How many cigarettes do you smoke a day?

some

We use *some* in positive sentences with uncountable nouns and plural nouns.

There is	some	bread	on the table.
There are		oranges	

We use *some* in questions when we ask for things and offer things.

Can I have	some	coffee, please?	(I *know* there is some coffee.)
Would you like		grapes?	(I *know* there are some grapes.)

any

We use *any* in questions and negative sentences with uncountable nouns and plural nouns.

Is there	any	water?	(I *don't know* if there is any water.)
Does she have		children?	(I *don't know* if she has any children.)
I can't see		rice.	
There aren't		people.	

Prepositions

a bottle **of** aspirin
a packet **of** cigarettes

They have cereal **for** breakfast.
Marmalade is made **from** oranges.

Study the Word List for this unit on page 125.

UNIT 10

Comparatives and superlatives – *have got* – Directions (2)

Describing places

PRESENTATION (1)

Comparative adjectives

1 Match an adjective in A with its opposite in B. Check the meaning of new words in your dictionary.

A	B
fast	cheap
small	slow
clean	bad
safe	unhealthy
quiet	unfriendly
old	dirty
healthy	noisy
friendly	modern
interesting	dangerous
expensive	boring
good	big

2 Which adjectives describe life in a city? Which describe life in the country?

3 Make sentences comparing life in the city and country.

| The city is / The country is | cheaper
safer
noisier
healthier
more expensive
more interesting
better | than the country.
than the city. |

4 **T 53** Listen and compare your sentences with the ones on the tape. Are they the same or different?
Practise saying some of the sentences. Be careful with the sound /ə/.

　/ə/　　　　　　/ə/ /ə/ /ə/
The country is cheaper than the city.
　/ə/　　　　　　/ə/ /ə/ /ə/
The city is noisier than the country.

● Grammar question

We use -(e)r and *more* to make comparative adjectives.
Can you make any rules?

Practice

1 Using dictionaries

1 Dictionaries usually show irregular comparative and superlative forms of adjectives. Does your dictionary do this?

> **big** /bɪg/ *adj.* (bigger, biggest)

> **good** /gʊd/ *adj.* (better, best)

2 What is the comparative form of the other adjectives in A and B on page 69?

3 Make more sentences comparing life in the city and life in the country.

2 Grammar and listening

Complete the conversations as shown in the example.

Example
A Life in the country is *slower* *than* city life. (slow)
B Yes, the city's much *faster*.

a A The country is _____ _____ the city. (quiet)

  B Yes, that's true. The city is much _____ .

b A New York is _____ _____ London. (safe)

  B No, it isn't. New York is much _____ _____ .

c A The streets of New York are _____ _____ the streets of Paris. (clean)

  B No, they aren't. They're much _____ .

d A Paris is _____ _____ Madrid. (big)

  B No, it isn't. It's much _____ .

e A Madrid is _____ _____ _____ Rome. (expensive)

  B No, it isn't. Madrid is much _____ .

f A The buildings in Rome are _____ _____ _____ the buildings in New York. (modern)

  B No, they aren't. They're much _____ .

g A The Underground in London is _____ _____ the Metro in Paris. (good)

  B No, it isn't! The Underground is much _____ .

T 54 Listen and check. Practise saying some of the sentences.

PRESENTATION (2)

have got

Amy moved from London to Seaton, a small country town on the south coast of England. Her friend Fran can't understand why she left London.

1 **T 55** Listen to their telephone conversation.

Fran	Why did you leave? You had a _____ job in London.
Amy	Yes, but I've got a _____ job here.
Fran	And you had a _____ flat in London.

Amy Well, I've got a house here.
Fran Really? How many bedrooms has it got?

Amy Three. And it's got a garden. It's _____ than my flat and it's _____ . Everything is much _____ here.

Fran But you haven't got any friends!
Amy I've got a lot of friends here. Everybody is very _____ . People are much _____ than in London.

Fran But the country's so _____ !

Amy No, it isn't. It's much _____ _____ than London. Seaton has got shops, cinemas, theatres, and parks. And the air is _____ and the streets are _____ .

Fran OK. OK. Everything is _____ ! So when can I visit you?

Complete the conversation with the correct adjectives. Some are comparatives and some are not.

> ⚠️
>
> 1   When we talk about possession, *have got* means the same as *have*. We often use *have got* in spoken English.
>
>   I've (I have) got a house. = I have a house.
>   He's (He has) got a car. = He has a car.
>
> 2   The past of both *have* and *have got* is *had*.

2 Find other examples of *have got* in the text. Change them to *have* and use the correct form of *do* when necessary.

  Example
  I've got a better job.   *I have a better job.*

3 Work in pairs. Practise the conversation using *have got*. Try to change some of the adjectives.

Practice

1 Grammar

Read about *have got* in the Grammar Summary on page 76. Rewrite the sentences using the correct form of *have got*.

Example

London has a lot of parks.   *London's got a lot of parks.*
I don't have much money.   *I haven't got much money.*

a I have a lot of homework tonight.
b Do you have any children?
c Our school has a library, but it doesn't have any computers.
d My friends have a CD player.
e I don't have a Walkman.
f Does your house have a garden?

2 Speaking

Roleplay

Work in pairs. Student A is a king, Student B is a queen of a different country. Your teacher will give you each some information. Ask and answer questions to find out who is richer!

PRESENTATION (3)

Superlative adjectives

FOR SALE

ROSE COTTAGE

* £115,000
* Built in 1750
* 2 bedrooms, bathroom, living room, kitchen
* Beautiful garden, 20 metres long
* 50 metres from the sea
* 2 kilometres from the shops and town centre

SEAVIEW

* £135,000
* Built in 1927
* 3 bedrooms, 2 bathrooms, living room, dining room, kitchen, study
* Garage
* Garden, 30 metres long
* 500 metres from the sea
* 1 kilometre from the shops and town centre.

PARK HOUSE

* £ 95,000
* Built in 1975
* Three bedrooms, bathroom, living room, kitchen/ breakfast room
* Big garage
* Small garden, 8 metres long
* 1.5 kilometres from the sea.
* 50 metres from the town centre, next to the park.

1 Look at the photographs and read about the three houses.

Here are some sentences about the houses. Are they true (✔) or false (✗)?
Correct the false sentences.

Examples
Seaview is cheaper than Rose Cottage. ✗
No, it isn't. It's more expensive.
Park House is the cheapest. ✔

a Seaview is the most expensive house.
b Seaview is more modern than Park House.
c Park House is the most modern house.
d Seaview is the biggest house.
e Park House is smaller than Rose Cottage.
f Seaview hasn't got a garage.
g Park House has got a bigger garden than Rose Cottage.
h Seaview has got the biggest garden.
i Park House is the nearest to the town centre.
j Park House is the farthest from the sea.

● Grammar questions

Look at the correct (✔) answers. They all have superlatives. Answer the questions.

– How do we make the superlative of one-syllable adjectives?
– How do we make the superlative of longer adjectives?
– Which adjectives are irregular?

2 **T 56** Listen and repeat.

Practice

1 Writing and speaking

1 Complete the questions about Park House.

a How much _____ _____ _____ ?
b How old _____ _____ ?
c How many bedrooms _____ _____ _____ ?
d _____ it _____ _____ garden?
e How big _____ _____ ?
f How far _____ _____ from the sea/town centre?

2 Work in pairs. Ask and answer questions comparing all the houses.

> How much does Park House cost?

> £95,000.

> Is it the cheapest?

> Yes, it is.

> Has it got the biggest garden?

> No, it hasn't.

2 Grammar and listening

1 Complete the sentences using the superlative form of the adjective.

Example

That house is very old.
Yes, *it's the oldest house* in the village.

a The Ritz is a very expensive hotel.

Yes, _____ in London.
b Hambledon is a very pretty village.

Yes, _____ in England.
c Everest is a very high mountain.

Yes, _____ in the world.
d Meryl Streep is a very popular actress.

Yes, _____ in America.

e Mr Clark is a very funny teacher.

Yes, _____ in our school.
f Maria is a very intelligent student.

Yes, _____ in our class.
g This is a very easy exercise.

Yes, _____ in the book.

T 57a Listen and check.

2 **T 57b** Close your books. Listen to the first line and give the answer.

3 Speaking

How well do you know the other students in your class? Describe them using comparative and superlative adjectives.

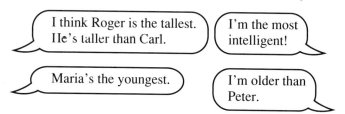

> I think Roger is the tallest. He's taller than Carl.

> I'm the most intelligent!

> Maria's the youngest.

> I'm older than Peter.

4 Choosing the correct sentence

One sentence has a mistake. Choose the correct sentence. Put ✔ and ✘.

1 a Yesterday was more hot than today.
  b Yesterday was hotter than today.
2 a She's taller than her brother.
  b She's taller that her brother.
3 a I'm the most young in the class.
  b I'm the youngest in the class.
4 a Last week was busier than this week.
  b Last week was busyer than this week.
5 a He hasn't got any sisters.
  b He doesn't got any sisters.
6 a Do you have any bread?
  b Do you got any bread?
7 a My homework is the baddest in the class.
  b My homework is the worst in the class.
8 a Exercise 2 is the most difficult in the book.
  b Exercise 2 is most difficult in the book.

● VOCABULARY AND PRONUNCIATION

Town and country words

1 Look at the words in the box. Match a picture with a word. Which things do you usually find in towns? Which in the country? Which in both? Put them into the correct columns.

Town	Country	Both

hills	woods
traffic lights	bridge
farm	car park
factory	swimming pool
field	theatre
lake	village
mountains	cottage
tall buildings	underground
statue	tram
pollution	concert hall
fresh air	river bank

2 Put a word or phrase from Exercise 1 into each gap.

a There's a _____ of Prince Albert near the Royal Albert Hall.

b _____ are bigger than hills.

c It's cheaper to travel by _____ than by underground.

d Stop! The _____ are red.

e She lives in the prettiest _____ in the village.

f New York has got a lot of _____ .

g There was a famous musician at the _____ last week.

h _____ is a problem in many big towns. The air is much dirtier than in the country.

3 Is the letter *r* pronounced in these words?

Example
farm ✗   factory ✔

traffic	bridge	car park	theatre
underground	tram	concert	river

T 58a Listen and repeat.

4 Look at the phonetic spelling of some of the other words.

/leɪk/   /maʊntɪnz/   /bɪldɪŋz/   /stætʃuː/
/vɪlɪdʒ/   /kɒtɪdʒ/

T 58b Listen and repeat.

● READING AND SPEAKING

Two capital cities

Pre-reading task

1 Match a country in Eastern Europe with its capital city.

Budapest	Romania
Sofia	Poland
Prague	Bulgaria
Warsaw	The Czech Republic
Bucharest	Albania
Tirana	Hungary

2 There were a lot of changes in the countries of Eastern Europe in the 1980s and 1990s. What were they?

Reading

Divide into two groups.
Group A   Read about Budapest.
Group B   Read about Prague.
Answer the questions in the
Comprehension Check. Check the
meaning of new words in your
dictionary.

▲ *Chain Bridge over the Danube*

BUDAPEST

Budapest has a population of over two million people. One in every five Hungarians lives there. The River Danube divides the city into two parts. On the west bank there are the woods and hills of Buda and the old town. On the east bank there is the bigger and more modern Pest, the business and shopping centre. From Buda there are wonderful views of Pest and the river. Six bridges join Buda and Pest.

Important dates in the history of Budapest

For nearly a thousand years Buda and Pest were two towns. Then in 1873 they joined and became one city, Budapest. Until 1939 Budapest was one of the most important cultural capitals of Europe. Then World War II started. In 1945 the city was in ruins and the Communists took control. In 1956 the people tried to free themselves. They pulled down a statue of Stalin and fought the soldiers, but they were not successful. Communist rule did not end until 1989.

The city today

Budapest is very unusual because it has two completely different parts. You can choose the peace and quiet of Buda's woods or the excitement of Pest, where there are good

▲ *Relaxing in one of the city's spa baths*

theatres, restaurants, bars, and shops.
The public transport system in Budapest is one of the best and cheapest in the world. You can travel easily by underground, bus, tram, and taxi, but driving a car in Budapest is not a good idea! There are not many car parks. Most cars are old, so pollution is very bad.
The healthiest thing to do in the city is to visit one of the thirty spa baths and swimming pools. The mineral waters of Budapest are famous, and a very popular way to relax.

▲ *Bridges over the River Vltava*
▼ *Prague Castle and Charles Bridge*

PRAGUE

Prague has a population of over one million people. It is not the biggest city in Europe, but it is certainly one of the most beautiful. It is built on seven hills on the banks of the River Vltava. Fifteen bridges cross the river. The most famous is Charles Bridge, which joins Prague Castle and the old town. The view of the castle from the river is very famous.

Important dates in the history of Prague

Prague did not become the capital until October 1918, after World War I, when Czechoslovakia became an independent country. Twenty years later, in 1938, it lost its independence again before World War II. After the war, in 1948, the Communists took control. In 1968 the people tried to free themselves. They fought the soldiers in Wenceslas Square, but they were not successful. Communist rule did not end until 1989.

The city today

Some people say Prague is the most beautiful city in the world! They call it 'The Golden City' and 'The Mother of Cities' because it still has many beautiful medieval buildings and statues. Perhaps the most popular building is the Old Town Hall with its amazing 15th

▲ *Old Town Hall with its famous clock*

century astronomical clock.
People also call Prague 'Europe's School of Music'. There are many concert halls, and every May there is a famous music festival: 'Prague Spring'. There are also twenty theatres and many old pubs, wine bars, and restaurants.
There is now a modern underground, but traffic is still a problem. It is often better to walk and feel the atmosphere of the pretty little streets.

Comprehension check

1 What can you see in the photos of your city?
2 How many people live there?
3 What is the name of its river?
4 How many bridges are there?
5 When did it become the capital?
6 When did the Communists take control? When did they lose control?
7 When and how did the people try to free themselves?
8 What is the best way to get round the city?

9 Which of these things can you do if you visit the city? Put ✔ or ✗.

a go to the theatre
b walk in the woods
c walk round the old town
d travel by tram
e travel by underground
f go to a famous music festival
g relax in the spa waters
h see a famous astronomical clock

Check your answers with your group.

Speaking

1 Find a partner from the other group. Compare the two cities.
2 Now read the other text. Ask your partner about new words.

● EVERYDAY ENGLISH

Directions (2)

1 **T 59a** Look at the pictures and listen to Robert talking about his driving lesson. Put a preposition from the box into each gap.

along	down	into	out of	over
past	through	under	up	

Robert's driving lesson

Robert drove

_____ the garage,

_____ the road, and

_____ the bridge.

Then he drove

_____ the pub,

_____ the hill, and

_____ the hill.

Next he drove

_____ the river,

_____ the hedge, and

_____ the lake!

Look at the pictures again and tell the story of Robert's driving lesson.

2 **T 59b** Listen to Louisa giving directions from her school to her house. Mark the route on the map. Then fill in the gaps.

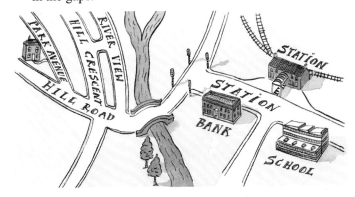

Go _____ the school and turn _____ . Walk

_____ Station Road _____ the railway station

and the _____ . Turn _____ at the _____

and walk _____ the _____ and _____ the

_____ . Turn right _____ Park Avenue. My

house is the _____ on the left. It's number

_____ . It takes ten minutes.

3 Work in pairs.
Student A Think of a place near your school. Give your partner directions, but don't say what the place is!
Student B Listen to the directions. Where are you?

GRAMMAR SUMMARY

Comparative and superlative adjectives

	Adjective	Comparative	Superlative
One-syllable adjectives	old	older	the oldest
	safe	safer	the safest
	big	bigger	the biggest*
	hot	hotter	the hottest*
Adjectives ending in -y	noisy	noisier	the noisiest
	dirty	dirtier	the dirtiest
Adjectives with two or more syllables	boring	**more** boring	the **most** boring
	beautiful	**more** beautiful	the **most** beautiful
Irregular adjectives	good	**better**	the **best**
	bad	**worse**	the **worst**
	far	**farther**	the **farthest**

* Adjectives which end in one vowel and one consonant double the consonant.

Examples
You're **older than** me.
New York is **dirtier than** Paris.
Prague is one of **the most beautiful** cities in Europe.

have got and *have*

Have got means the same as *have* to talk about possession, but the form is very different. We often use *have got* in spoken English.

have got

Positive

I You We They	have		a cat.
		got	
He She It	has		a garden.

Negative

I You We They	haven't		a dog.
		got	
He She It	hasn't		a garage.

Questions

Have	I you we they		any money?
		got	
Has	he she it		a sister?
How many children have they got?			

Short answers

Yes, I have./No, I haven't.
Yes, she has./No, she hasn't.

have

Positive

I You We They	have	a cat.
He She It	has	a garden.

Negative

I You We They	don't		a dog.
		have	
He She It	doesn't		a garage.

Questions

Do	I you we they		any money?
		have	
Does	he she it		a sister?
How many children do they have?			

Short answers

Yes, I do./No, I don't.
Yes, she does./No, she doesn't.

Prepositions

The country is quieter **than** the city.
The house is 50 metres **from** the sea.
Everest is the highest mountain **in** the world.

Study the Word List for this unit on page 125.

UNIT 11

Present Continuous – *Whose ...? It's mine.* – In a clothes shop

Describing people

PRESENTATION (1)

Present Continuous

1 Look around the classroom. Find things that are these colours.

red blue brown black green yellow grey pink

Can you see these clothes?

| a jumper   a shirt   a T-shirt   a dress   a skirt |
| a jacket   a suit   a tie |
trousers   jeans   trainers   shoes   boots

2 Look at the photographs. Who's got ...?

long		blue	
short		brown	eyes
blond	hair		
fair			
brown		a moustache	
black		a beard	

> Len's got short black hair and a beard.

Who ...?

is pretty	is quite tall
is handsome	isn't very tall
is good-looking	is slim

Who ...?

is smiling	is cooking
is wearing glasses	is holding a dog
is writing	is wearing earrings
is standing up	is sitting down

> Emma's smiling.

> Peter's sitting down.

⚠

1 *Am/is/are* + adjective describes people and things.
   He is old/tall/hungry/tired.

2 *Am/is/are* + verb+ -*ing* describes activities happening now.
   I'm learning English.
   He's wearing a suit.
   They're cooking.
   She isn't smiling.
   This is the Present Continuous tense.

3 Work in pairs.

Student A   Choose someone in the classroom, but don't say who.

Student B   Ask Yes/No questions to find out who it is!

- Is it a girl?
- Yes, it is.
- Is she sitting near the window?
- No, she isn't.
- Has she got blond hair?
- No, she hasn't.

Practice

1 Listening and writing

1 **T 60** Peter is at a party, but he doesn't know anyone. Listen to Mary, who's giving the party, telling him about the other guests. Write the names next to the people.

2 Mary uses the Present Simple tense and the Present Continuous tense. Can you remember what she says and complete the sentences below?

	Present Continuous	Present Simple
Paul	*He's sitting at the table.*	
	_____ to Kathy.	_____ in LA.
Kathy	_____ T-shirt.	_____ house.
Suzie	_____ wine.	_____ books.
Alex	_____ a cigar.	_____ world.
Laura and Ellie	_____ crisps.	_____ School.

Listen again and check.

2 Grammar

1 Put the verb in brackets into the Present Continuous tense.

a   Oh, no! It _____ . What a pity! (rain)

b   I _____ a very good book at the moment. (read)

c   We _____ champagne because it's our wedding anniversary. (drink)

d   I _____ hard because we have exams next week. (work)

e   'What _____ Peter _____ on the floor?' (do)

   'He _____ for his glasses.' (look)

f   'Why _____ you _____ ?' (run)

   'Because I _____ to a party and I'm late.' (go)

g   The photocopier _____ . Phone the engineer. (not work)

h   I _____ any more work. I'm tired. (not do)

78

2 Look at the picture and answer the questions.

a What does Captain Biggles do?
b Is he flying a plane now?
c What does Fiona do?
d Is she acting now?
e What's she doing?
f What does Wendy do?
g What's she doing now?
h What does Frank do?
i Is he playing football now?
j What's he doing?

3 Speaking

Work in pairs.
Your teacher is going to give you each a picture of a holiday scene. There are ten differences! Don't show your picture! Talk about the pictures to find the ten differences.

> Three people are having a drink.

> How many people are swimming?

PRESENTATION (2)

Whose ...? It's mine.

1 Look at the pictures. Put a word from the box into each gap.

ours	mine	his	hers	theirs	yours

a Excuse me! Is this your ball?

No, it isn't mine. It's __his__ .

b Is this _____ ?

No, it isn't _____ . It's _____ .

c Excuse me! Is this your ball?

No, it isn't _____ . I think it's _____ .

d Hello. Is this yours?

No, it isn't _____ . It's the dog's!

T 61 Listen and check.

2 Ask and answer questions with *Whose ...?* about these things.

> Whose is this hat?

> It's his.

---

1 *Whose ...?* asks about possession.
   Whose hat is this?
   Whose is this hat?
   Whose is it?

2 Careful!
   Who's your teacher? = Who is your teacher?

3 It's hers. = It's her hat.

79

Practice

1 Grammar

1 Choose the correct word.

Example

✔   ✗

I like your/~~yours~~ house.

a Ours/Our house is smaller than their/theirs.
b And their/theirs garden is bigger than our/ours, too.
c My/Mine children are older than her/hers.
d Her/Hers children go to the same school as my/mine.
e This book isn't my/mine. Is it your/yours?
f 'Whose/Who's winning the match?' 'Peter is.'
g 'Jamie's crying, but it wasn't my/mine fault.'
   'Well, whose/who's fault was it, then?'
h Whose/Who's going to the party tonight?

2 **T 62** Listen to the sentences.
If the word is *Whose ...?*, shout '1'!
If the word is *Who's...?*, shout '2'!

2 Speaking

1 The house is in a mess! Read the conversation.

A Whose is this tennis racket?
B It's mine.
A What's it doing here?
B I'm playing tennis this afternoon.

> The Present Continuous can also describe activities happening in the near future.
>
> I'm playing tennis this afternoon.
> We're having fish for dinner tonight.

2 Work in pairs. Make more dialogues.

a football boots? / John's / playing football later
b ballet shoes? / Mary's / going dancing tonight
c suitcase? / mine / going on holiday tomorrow
d coat? / Jane's / going for a walk soon
e plane ticket? / Jo's / flying to Rome this afternoon
f all these glasses? / ours / having a party tonight

3 Correcting the mistakes

Each sentence has a mistake. Find it and correct it!

a Alice is tall and she's got long, black hairs.
b James is quiet old, about sixty-five.
c I'm wearing a jeans.
d Look at Roger. He stands next to Jeremy.
e He's work in a bank. He's the manager.
f What is drinking Suzie?
g I no working any more. I'm tired.
h Where you going tonight?
i What you do after school today?

80

● VOCABULARY AND PRONUNCIATION

Words that rhyme

1 Match the words that rhyme.

A
bread
steak
lamb
lose
sign
half

B
laugh
wake
head
ham
shoes
wine

C
soap
when
near
suit
wait
heart

D
again
boot
late
part
hope
beer

E
meat
dead
hair
war
ball
list

F
said
kissed
door
Paul
feet
wear

T 63 Listen and check. Practise saying the words.

2 Write one of the words on each line according to the vowel sound.

a /e/ **bread**   g /uː/ _____
b /ɪ/ _____   h /aɪ/ _____
c /æ/ _____   i /ɪə/ _____
d /ɑː/ _____   j /eɪ/ _____
e /iː/ _____   k /eə/ _____
f /ɔː/ _____   l /əʊ/ _____

LISTENING

Pre-listening task

1 What do you do before you go to a big party? Does it take you a long time to get ready? What are your favourite clothes? Do you dance?

2 You are going to hear a song written by Eric Clapton called *Wonderful tonight*. Read the words of the song and put one of the words or phrases in the list into each gap. There are more words than gaps!

Listening

1 **T 64** Listen to the song and check the words.

2 Find the mistakes in this summary and correct them.

> A husband and wife got ready and went to a party. The party started in the early evening. He thought she looked very pretty, but he didn't say anything. There were only two or three other people at the party. He was angry with his wife, and she was worried about him. He loves her very much, but she doesn't love him.
> At the end of the party he didn't feel very well. He drove the car home. He had another drink before he went to bed.

wonderful **TONIGHT**

It's late in the _____
She's wondering what _____ to wear.
She _____ on her make-up,
Then _____ her long _____ hair.
And then she asks me,
'Do I look _____?'
And I say, 'Yes,
You _____ wonderful tonight.'
We go to a party
And _____ turns to see
This _____ lady
That's _____ around with me.
And then she asks me,
'Do you feel all right?'
And I say, 'Yes,
I _____ wonderful tonight.'
I feel wonderful
_____ I see
The love light in your _____.
And the wonder of it all
Is that you just don't realize
How much I _____ you.
It's time to go _____ now
And I've got an aching _____.
So I give her the _____,
She helps me to bed.
And then I tell her
As I turn out the _____,
I say, 'My, _____,
You _____ wonderful tonight.'

feel

head

heart

eyes

all right

because

were

blond

light

darling

everyone

morning

evening

home

bed

walking

beautiful

clothes

puts

love

car keys

brushes

look

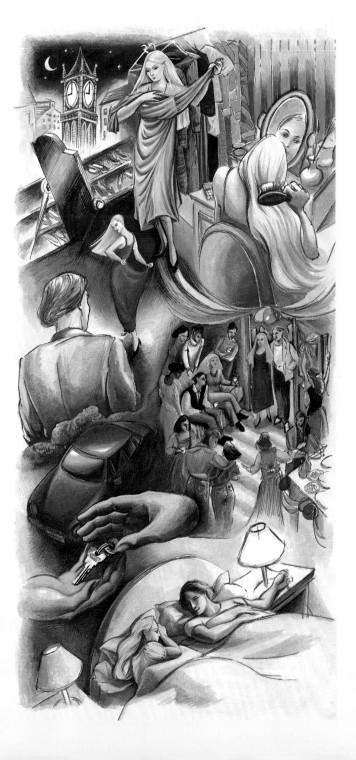

● EVERYDAY ENGLISH

In a clothes shop

1 Look at the lines of some conversations in a clothes shop. Who says them, the customer or the shop assistant? Put C or A.

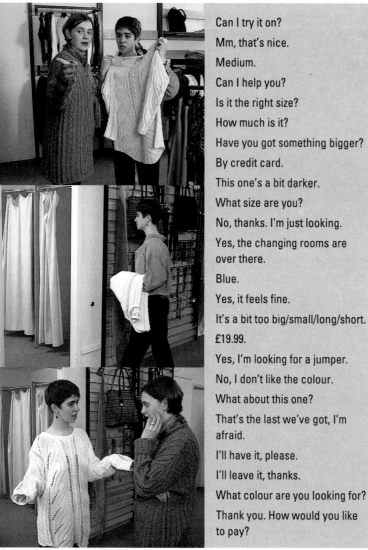

Can I try it on?

Mm, that's nice.

Medium.

Can I help you?

Is it the right size?

How much is it?

Have you got something bigger?

By credit card.

This one's a bit darker.

What size are you?

No, thanks. I'm just looking.

Yes, the changing rooms are over there.

Blue.

Yes, it feels fine.

It's a bit too big/small/long/short.

£19.99.

Yes, I'm looking for a jumper.

No, I don't like the colour.

What about this one?

That's the last we've got, I'm afraid.

I'll have it, please.

I'll leave it, thanks.

What colour are you looking for?

Thank you. How would you like to pay?

'll = will. Will is an auxiliary verb.
I'll have it.
I'll leave it.
In these sentences, will expresses a decision.

2 Can you match any lines?

Example
'Can I help you?'   'No, thanks. I'm just looking.'

T 65 Listen and check. In pairs, practise the dialogues.

3 Work in pairs. Make more conversations in a clothes shop. Use real clothes if you can.

82

GRAMMAR SUMMARY

Present Continuous

The Present Continuous describes an activity happening now.
　　She's wearing jeans.
　　I'm studying English.
It also describes an activity in the near future.
　　I'm playing tennis this afternoon.
　　Jane's seeing her boyfriend tonight.

Positive and negative

I	am			
He She It	is	(not)	go**ing**	outside.
We You They	are			

Question

	am	I		
Where	is	he/she/it	go**ing**?	
	are	we you they		

Yes/No questions	**Short answers**
Are you hav**ing** a good time?	Yes, we are.
Is my English gett**ing** better?	Yes, it is.
Are they hav**ing** a party?	No, they aren't.

Present Simple and Present Continuous

The Present Simple describes things that are always true, or true for a long time.
　　I come from Switzerland.
　　He works in a bank.

The Present Continuous describes activities happening *now*, and temporary activities.
　　Why are you wearing a suit? You usually wear jeans.

Whose + possessive pronouns

Whose is this book?	It's	mine.
Whose book is this?		yours.
		hers.
		his.
		ours.
		theirs.

Prepositions

I'm looking **for** a jacket.

Study the Word List for this unit on page 125.

UNIT 12

going to – Infinitive of purpose – Suggestions

Planning the future

PRESENTATION (1)

going to

1   Look at the photographs of Gemma, 11, and her teacher Miss Black, 62. They both have plans for the future.

When I grow up ...

When I retire ...

Read the future plans. Which do you think are Gemma's? Which are Miss Black's? Write G or B next to each sentence.

G I'm going to be a ballet dancer.

___ I'm going to travel all over the world.

___ I'm going to learn to drive.

___ I'm going to learn Russian.

___ I'm going to write a book.

___ I'm going to open a school.

___ I'm not going to marry until I'm thirty-five.

___ I'm not going to wear skirts and blouses.

___ I'm going to wear jeans and tracksuits all the time.

___ I'm going to become a TV star.

T 66   Listen and check. Were you correct?

2   Talk first about Gemma, then about Miss Black. Use the ideas in Exercise 1.

> Gemma's going to be a ballet dancer.

> She's going to ...

> She isn't going to ...

Which two plans are the same for both of them?

> They're both going to ...

● Grammar questions

–   What are the present tense forms of the verb *to be*? What are the negatives?
–   Complete the rule.
    We make the *going to* future with the auxiliary verbs

    am, _____ , _____ + *going to* + _____ .

3   **T 67a**   Listen and repeat the questions and answers about Gemma.

What's she going to be?	A ballet dancer.
What's she going to do?	Travel all over the world.

4   Make more questions about Gemma's plans and match them with an answer.

Why/she/learn French and Russian?	Until she's seventy-five.
When/marry?	Two.
How many children/have?	Dancing.
How long/work?	Not until she's thirty-five.
What/teach?	Because she wants to dance in Paris and Moscow.

T 67b   Listen and check. In pairs, practise saying the questions and answers.

Practice

1 Writing and speaking

1 Are you going to do any of these things after the lesson? Write your answers.

Example
watch TV
I'm going to watch TV./I'm not going to watch TV.

a have a coffee   e cook a meal
b catch a bus   f go shopping
c eat in a restaurant g wash my hair
d meet some friends   h do my homework

2 In pairs, ask and answer the questions in Exercise 1. Give short answers.

> Are you going to watch TV?

> Yes, I am./ No, I'm not.

Tell the class some of the things your partner is or is not going to do.

2 Writing and listening

1 We also use *going to* when we can see *now* that something is sure to happen in the future.
Look at the pictures and say what is going to happen. Use the verbs in the box.

| have sneeze pass fail miss kiss rain drop |

1 It …
2 I …
3 We …
4 They …
5 I …
6 He …
7 You …
8 They …

2 Put a sentence from Exercise 1 into each gap.

a Take an umbrella. _____.

b Hurry up! _____.

c I'm very worried about this exam. I know
_____.

d Jack is studying very hard. I know
_____.

e Careful! _____.

f Look at all that wine and food!
_____.

g There's my sister and her boyfriend! Yuk!
_____.

h 'Oh dear, _____.
Aaattishooo!' 'Bless you!'

T 68 Listen and check.

PRESENTATION (2)

Infinitive of purpose

1 Match a country or a city with an activity. Check the meaning of new words with your teacher.

Holland	visit the pyramids
Norway	drive through the Grand Canyon
Moscow	see the midnight sun
Spain	see the tulips
Egypt	walk along the Great Wall
Kenya	watch Flamenco dancing
India	take photographs of the lions
China	sunbathe on Copacabana beach
USA	walk in Red Square
Rio	visit the Taj Mahal

2 Miss Black is going to travel round the world. She is going to visit all these countries. She is telling her friend, Arthur, about her plans. Read their conversation and complete the last sentence.

Miss Black	First I'm going to Holland.
Arthur	Why?
Miss Black	To see the tulips, of course!
Arthur	Oh yes! How wonderful! Where are you going after that?
Miss Black	Well, then I'm going to Norway to _____ .

T 69 Listen and check.

⚠️ With the verbs *to go* and *to come*, we usually use the Present Continuous for future plans.

> I'm going to Holland tomorrow.

NOT   I'm ~~going to go~~ to Holland tomorrow.

> She's coming this evening.

NOT   She's ~~going to come~~ this evening.

● Grammar question

– Do these sentences mean the same?

> I'm going to Holland to see the tulips.
> I'm going to Holland because I want to see the tulips.

Practice

1 Speaking

1 Work in pairs. Student A is Miss Black, Student B is Arthur. Ask and answer questions about the places.

> Why are you going to Holland?

> To see the tulips, of course!

> How wonderful!

2 Take turns to talk about Miss Black's journey. Use *first*, *then*, *next*, *after that*.

> First she's going to Holland to see the tulips.

> Then she's …

3 Write down the names of some places you went to last year.
In pairs, ask and answer questions about the places.

> Why did you go to England?

> To learn English.

> Why did you go to Melbourne?

> To visit my cousins.

Tell the class about your partner.

2 Grammar

Rewrite the sentences using the infinitive of purpose.

Examples
I'm going upstairs because I want to have a shower.
I'm going upstairs to have a shower.

I went to the supermarket and I bought some biscuits.
I went to the supermarket to buy some biscuits.

a He went to the station and he caught the train.
b She turned on the TV because she wanted to watch the film.
c Are you going to the pub because you want to have a beer?
d Did you open the door because you wanted to get some fresh air?
e I phoned Bill and I told him the news.
f Are you learning English because you want to get a better job?
g They're studying hard because they want to pass their exams.
h I'm going home early because I want to finish my homework.

3 Choosing the correct sentence

One sentence has a mistake. Which is the correct sentence? Put ✔ and ✗.

1 a Is going to rain.
  b It's going to rain.
2 a Do you wash your hair this evening?
  b Are you going to wash your hair this evening?
3 a She's going to have a baby.
  b She's going to has a baby.
4 a Are they many students in your class?
  b Are there many students in your class?
5 a I'm going to the Post Office to buy some stamps.
  b I'm going to the Post Office for buy some stamps.
6 a Every evening I go home and I listen to music.
  b Every evening I'm go home and I listen to music.
7 a They waited for me in the garden.
  b They waited for my in the garden.
8 a He can't answer the phone because he's having a bath.
  b He can't answer the phone because he has a bath.

READING AND SPEAKING

Pre-reading task

1 Which of these sports do you think is the most dangerous? Put them in order 1–8. 1 is the most dangerous.

___ cycling ___ motor racing ___ football
___ sailing ___ windsurfing ___ skiing
___ golf ___ mountain climbing

Compare your ideas with a partner and then the class.

2 Look at the photographs and find:
a mountain a rock a rope a climber a bivouac

Reading

Quickly read the text about a famous mountain climber, Catherine Destivelle, and answer the questions.

1 The title *Rock Star* has two meanings. What are they?
2 Put the four paragraph headings into the correct places in the text.

a WHY DOES SHE CLIMB?
b HER FUTURE
c HOW DID SHE BEGIN?
d HER BEST CLIMB

THE ROCK STAR!

Catherine Destivelle is a rock star. She loves rock, but she can't sing or play the guitar! She is a rock climber and a big star in France and Italy. She is probably the most famous woman climber in the world because she often climbs without ropes. She climbs in many countries but most often in the French Alps near Chamonix, where she lives.

1

She started climbing near her home in Paris when she was five. Then, at fourteen, she joined the French Alpine Club to learn more, but immediately she climbed better and more quickly than the older members of the club. She won her first competition in Italy in 1985.

2

Three years ago she found a new route up the Dru Mountain near Chamonix. The climb took eleven days and for four days the snow was so heavy that she could not move. She slept and ate in a bivouac on the side of the mountain. Last year other climbers tried to follow the new Destivelle Route, but they failed. They are going to try again this year.

3

People always ask her this question. She says 'I climb because I'm in love with mountains. I like touching the rock and reading the face of the rock. I like it a lot. I feel comfortable and at home on the side of a mountain. I prepare well before I go, so I'm never worried.'

4

Catherine chooses new mountains from books – like buying from a shopping catalogue! 'I see a nice mountain and I go to climb it!' Her next mountain is in Pakistan. She is going there next month. 'It's much bigger than the Dru, so it's going to take longer to climb. An American climber, Jeff Lowe, is coming with me to help.'

Comprehension check

Read the article again. Correct these false statements about Catherine.

Example
She lives in Italy.
No, she doesn't. She lives near Chamonix in France.

a   She's good at singing and playing the guitar.
b   She's famous because she climbs in France and Italy.
c   She didn't start climbing until she was fourteen.
d   She learned a lot from the older members of the Alpine Club.
e   The climb up the Dru took four days.
f   She slept and ate in a tent.
g   Climbers followed Catherine's new route last year.
h   She likes reading books when she's on the mountains.
i   She's going to buy a mountain in Pakistan.
j   It's going to take three days to climb this mountain.

Language work

Find examples of the following in the text:

three sentences with a verb in the Present Simple
one sentence with the past of *can*
four sentences with a verb in the Past Simple
four sentences about future plans
two comparative or superlative sentences

Speaking

Roleplay
Work in pairs. Student A is a journalist, Student B is Catherine Destivelle.
Ask and answer questions. Use the paragraph headings to help you.

Good morning, Catherine! Can I ask you one or two questions?

Yes, of course.

First of all, where do you live?

● VOCABULARY

The weather

1 Write the correct word under each symbol. Check the meaning of new words in your dictionary.

sunny	raining	windy	snowing	cloudy	foggy

☁	25 ➚	☀	FOG	☁☂	☁❄
___	___	___	___	___	___

Which symbols can the following adjectives go with?

hot	warm	cold	wet	dry

2 **T 70** Listen to the questions and answers and fill in the gaps.

What's the weather like today?   It's _____

and _____ .

What was it like yesterday?   Oh, it was _____

and _____ .

⚠

In the question *What … like?*, *like* is a preposition.
It is not a verb as in *I like ice-cream; Do you like playing tennis?*

Practise saying the questions and answers.
Ask and answer about the weather today and yesterday.

> What's the weather like today?

> It's cold and wet.

3 Work in pairs. Find out about the weather round the world yesterday.

Student A Look at the information on this page.
Student B Look at the information from your teacher.

Ask and answer questions to complete the information.

> What was the weather like in Athens?

> It was sunny and warm. 18 degrees Celsius.

WORLD WEATHER: NOON YESTERDAY

		°C
Athens	S	18
Berlin	R	7
Bombay	—	—
Edinburgh...................................	C	5
Geneva	—	—
Hong Kong	S	29
Lisbon	—	—
London	R	10
Los Angeles	—	—
Luxor	S	40
Milan	—	—
Moscow	Sn	-1
Oslo	—	—

S = sunny C = cloudy Fg = foggy
R = raining Sn = snowing

Which city was the hottest? Which was the coldest? Which month do you think it is?

● EVERYDAY ENGLISH

Making suggestions

1 What do you like doing when the weather is good? What do you like doing when the weather is bad? In pairs, write two lists.

2 **T 71** Read and listen to the beginning of two conversations. In pairs, practise saying them.

A It's a lovely day! What shall we do?	A It's raining again! What shall we do?
B Let's play tennis!	B Let's stay at home and watch a video.

1   *Shall* is an auxiliary verb. We use it to ask for suggestions.

What shall we do tonight? = What do we want to do tonight?

Shall we go swimming?

2   *Let's go!* makes a suggestion for everyone. It is like an imperative in the first person plural.

Let's go! = I suggest that we go. (Let's = Let us)
Let's have a pizza!
Let's go home now. It's late.

3   Here are the next lines of the two conversations, but they are mixed up. Continue the conversations with the correct lines.

Well, let's go to the beach.
OK. What's on at the Odeon cinema?
Oh no! It's too hot to play tennis.
Oh no! We watched a video last night.
OK. I'll get my swimming costume.
Well, let's go to the cinema.

T 72   Listen and check. In pairs, practise saying the conversations.

4   Make more dialogues suggesting what to do when the weather is good or bad. Use the lists of activities you wrote in Exercise 1 to help you.

5   Your teacher will give you a list of TV programmes for tonight on channels 1 to 4. Imagine that you and your partner live in the same flat and you only have one TV. Decide together which programmes you are going to watch tonight.

What's on TV tonight?

Shall we watch The Big Match at 8.30?

No, I don't like football.

Well, let's watch the film.

What channel is it on?

GRAMMAR SUMMARY

going to

Going to expresses a person's plans and intentions.

She's going to be a ballet dancer when she grows up.
We're going to stay in a villa in France this summer.

We also use *going to* when we can see *now* that something is sure to happen in the future.

Careful! That glass is going to fall!

Positive and negative

I	am			have a break.
He/She/It	is	(not)	going to	
We You They	are			stay at home.

Question

	am	I		have a break?
	is	he/she/it	going to	
When	are	we you they		stay at home?

With the verbs *to go* and *to come*, we usually use the Present Continuous for future plans.

We're going to Paris next week.
Joe and Tim are coming for lunch tomorrow.

Infinitive of purpose

The infinitive can express *why* a person does something.

I'm saving my money **to buy** a CD player.
We're going to Paris **to have** a holiday.
NOT
I'm going shopping ~~for to buy~~ some new clothes.
I'm going shopping ~~for buy~~ some new clothes.

Prepositions

I'm worried **about** the exam.
She's good **at** singing.
She climbs **without** ropes.
What's the weather **like**?
What's **on** at the cinema?
What's **on** TV tonight?
There's a film **on** Channel 4.

Study the Word List for this unit on page 126.

STOP AND CHECK

UNITS 9–12

1 Correcting the mistakes

Each sentence has a mistake. Find it and correct it!

Example

Where ~~you live~~? *Where do you live?*

a   It's very hot today – do you like something to drink?
b   Peter's got a lot of books because he'd like reading.
c   How many children do you got?
d   How many money has he got?
e   Who's is that new car?
f   I'm go home now because it's late.
g   Last night I went to a cafe for to meet my friends.
h   We're going have a test next week.
i   I'm wear old clothes because I'm going to clean the car.
j   Pierre is French, he's coming from Paris.
k   What you doing tonight?
l   My sister is more old than me.
m   I think is going to rain.
n   Your house is bigger than my.
o   Who is the most rich person in the world?

15

2 Questions and answers

Match a question in A with an answer in B.

A	B
Whose is this coat?	Yes, of course. What can I do for you?
How many cats have you got?	Yes. I think he's very nice.
How much did your bike cost?	To buy some toothpaste.
Could you help me, please?	To Turkey.
Would you like some more to eat?	I stayed at home.
Do you like Henry?	Three.
Where are you going on holiday?	It's Jane's.
Why are you going to the chemist's?	£100.
What did you do last night?	Her name's Mrs Taylor.
Who's the new teacher?	No, thanks. I'm full.

10

3 Comparatives and superlatives

Complete the chart.

Adjective	Comparative	Superlative
big	_____	_____
_____	more beautiful	_____
_____	_____	worst
exciting	_____	_____
noisy	_____	_____

10

4 Comparing hotels

1   Look at the information about the two hotels. Write five sentences about the hotels using the comparative forms of the adjectives in the box.

Example

good – *The Ritz is a better hotel than The Strand.*

big   expensive   near   far   modern

	The Strand	The Ritz
Number of stars	★★★	★★★★
Number of rooms	102	55
Price	£56–£80	£90–£110
How many minutes to the sea?	10 minutes	15 minutes
How many minutes to the town centre?	20 minutes	8 minutes
Old or new?	New–1990	Old–1870

a   _____
b   _____
c   _____
d   _____
e   _____

10

2 Look at the information about The Star Hotel. Write five more sentences, comparing the three hotels. Use the superlative form of the adjectives.

Example
good – *The Star is the best hotel.*

	The Star
Number of stars	★★★★★
Number of rooms	45
Price	£120–£150
How many minutes to the sea?	1 minute
How many minutes to the town centre?	15 minutes
Old or new?	Old–1920

a _____

b _____

c _____

d _____

e _____

10

5 some and any

Put *some*, *any*, or *a* into each gap.

a Would you like _____ cup of tea?

b You have _____ lovely pictures on the walls!

c Is there _____ water in the fridge?

d Can I have _____ grapes, please?

e I'd like _____ hamburger and _____ chips, please.

f Do you want _____ sandwich?

g The shop doesn't have _____ eggs, peas, or bread.

h There are _____ eggs in the cupboard, but there isn't _____ sugar. **10**

6 Present Simple or Present Continuous

Put the verbs in brackets in the Present Simple or the Present Continuous.

a Pierre _____ (smoke) twenty cigarettes a day, but he _____ (not smoke) now because he's in class.

b Alice and Peter _____ (look) for a new house. They _____ (not like) living in London.

c I always _____ (wear) nice clothes for work. Today I _____ (wear) a blue jacket and skirt.

d 'Why _____ you _____ (go) to bed? It's only 10.00' 'I always _____ (go) to bed early.'

e Jane _____ (work) in a bank, but today she's at home. She _____ (write) letters. **10**

7 going to

Complete the sentences with *going to*. Use a verb and a place or person from the boxes.

Example
We're going to buy a book at the bookshop.

buy	write	see	borrow	have

the bookshop	my friend	Florida	the library
the theatre	the baker's		

a Peter _____ some bread at _____.

b I _____ some books from _____.

c We _____ a play at _____.

d They _____ a holiday in _____.

e I _____ a letter to _____.

10

8 Vocabulary

Put the words in the box in the right columns.

a film fruit a dress a suit mushrooms toothpaste a shirt
cheese aspirin rice jumper soap shampoo shorts cereal

Clothes shop	Food	Chemist's
a dress		

15

Total 100

TRANSLATE

Translate the sentences into your language. Translate the *ideas*, not word by word.

1 I like Coke. I'd like a Coke.

_____

2 There is some bread on the table. There isn't any coffee.

_____

3 You're older than me, but Tim is the oldest in the class.

_____

4 My sister has got three children.

_____

5 I usually wear jeans, but today I'm wearing a suit.

_____

6 'Whose is this book?' 'It's mine.'

_____

7 We're going to have a party.

_____

8 I went into London to buy some books.

_____

UNIT 13

Question forms – Adverbs – At the railway station

Did you know that?

PRESENTATION (1)

Question forms

1 Work in groups. Answer the quiz!

General Knowledge Quiz

(1) When did the Berlin Wall come down?
  a 1988   b 1989   c 1990

(2) When did the first American walk on the moon?
  a 1961   b 1965   c 1969

(3) Where are the Andes mountains?

(4) Who did the actress Elizabeth Taylor marry twice?

(5) Who won the 100 metres in the Seoul Olympics?
  a Ben Johnson   b Carl Lewis
  c Ed Moses

(6) How many countries are there in the European Community?

(7) How much does an African elephant weigh?
  a 3-5 tonnes   b 5-7 tonnes
  c 7-9 tonnes

(8) How fast does Concorde fly?
  a 2,000 kilometres an hour
  b 2,500 kilometres an hour
  c 3,000 kilometres an hour

(9) How far is it from London to New York?
  a 6,000 kilometres
  b 9,000 kilometres
  c 12,000 kilometres

(10) How old was Charlie Chaplin when he died?
  a 75   b 83   c 88

(11) What languages do Swiss people speak?

(12) What did Columbus discover in 1492?

(13) What sort of music did Elvis Presley play?
  a Jazz   b Blues   c Rock'n'roll

(14) What happens at the end of the story *Cinderella*?

(15) What happened in Chernobyl in 1986?

(16) Why do birds migrate?

(17) Which newspaper does Queen Elizabeth read?

(18) Which language has the most words?
  a French
  b Chinese
  c English

2 **T 73** Listen and check. Listen carefully to the intonation of the questions. Practise some of the questions.

● Grammar question

Underline the question words.
Which questions are in the Past Simple, and which are in the Present Simple?

3 In groups, write some general knowledge questions. Ask the class!

Practice

1 Question words

Match a question word in A with an answer in B.

A	B
When?	Five.
Where?	A book.
Who?	60p.
How?	The new one in the High Street.
How many?	Because I need it for my job.
How much?	Jenny.
What?	To the cinema.
Why?	By bus.
Which one?	Last Saturday.

2 Grammar

1 Put the words in the correct order to make questions. Then choose the correct answers from list B above.

a cigarettes you many do a day how smoke?

_____

b go you night where did last?

_____

c does petrol much a cost litre of how?

_____

d last go you shopping did when?

_____

e restaurant did go to which you?

_____

f come today school how you to did?

_____

g shops did buy the at you what?

_____

h party to speak who did the at you?

_____

i English want learn to you do why?

_____

2 In pairs, ask and answer the questions about yourselves.

3 Listening and pronunciation

T 74 Tick (✔) the sentence you hear.

1 a Where do you want to go?
   b Why do you want to go?
2 a Where does she work?
   b Where does he work?
3 a She walks to the bank.
   b She works in a bank.
4 a He won the match.
   b Who won the match?
5 a Did she marry him?
   b Is she married, Jim?
6 a How old was she?
   b How old is she?
7 a Johnny Page played the guitar.
   b Johnny Page plays the guitar.
8 a Where did you go last night?
   b Where do you go at night?

4 Speaking

Read the introduction about Laurel and Hardy.

LAUREL AND HARDY, THE COMEDY DUO

They are called El Gordo y el Flaco in Spain, Helan och Halvan in Sweden, and Stanlio e Olio in Italy, but in English they are called Laurel and Hardy, the most famous comedy duo in cinema history.

Work in pairs. Your teacher will give you some more information about Laurel and Hardy, but you do not have the same information.
Ask and answer questions to complete the information.

Example

Student A
Laurel and Hardy met in … (*Where?*) in 1926.

Student B
Laurel and Hardy met in Hollywood in … (*When?*).

Student A   Student B

(Where did they meet?) → (They met in Hollywood.)

(They met in 1926.) ← (When did they meet?)

93

PRESENTATION (2)

Adverbs

1 Look at the sentences.

> Lunch is a *quick* meal for many people.
> I ate my food *quickly* and left the restaurant.

> *Quick* is an adjective. It describes a noun.
> *Quickly* is an adverb. It describes a verb.

2 Are the words in italics adjectives or adverbs?

a Smoking is a *bad* habit.
b The team played *badly* and lost the match.
c Please listen *carefully*.
d Jane's a *careful* driver.
e The homework was *easy*.
f Peter's very good at tennis. He won the game *easily*.
g I know the Prime Minister *well*.
h My husband's a *good* cook.
i It's a *hard* life.
j Teachers work *hard* and don't earn much money.

● Grammar questions

– How do we make regular adverbs? What happens when the adjective ends in *-y*?
– Which adverbs are irregular?

Practice

1 Listening and speaking

1 Check the meaning of these adverbs in your dictionary.

___ quickly   ___ slowly
___ carefully   ___ suddenly
___ quietly   ___ immediately

2 **T 75** Listen to a man describing what happened to him in the middle of the night and put the adverbs in the correct order.

3 In pairs, tell the story again.

2 Grammar

1 Match a verb or phrase in A with an adverb in B. Sometimes, more than one answer is possible.

A	B
run	hard
work	early
get up	fluently
speak two languages	carefully
do your homework	fast

2 Put the word in brackets in the correct place in the sentence. If necessary, change the adjective to an adverb.

a We had a holiday in Spain, but unfortunately we had weather. (terrible)
b Maria dances. (good)
c When I saw the accident, I phoned the police. (immediate)
d Don't worry. Justin is a driver. (careful)
e Jean-Pierre is a Frenchman. He loves food, wine and rugby. (typical)
f Please speak. I can't understand you. (slow)
g We had a test today. (easy)
h We all passed. (easy)
i You speak English. (good)

3 Correcting the mistakes

Each sentence has a mistake. Find it and correct it.

a Where does live Anna's sister?
b What sort of music you like?
c What means *scream*?
d Did they went out last night?
e Do you can help me, please?
f When is going Peter on holiday?
g I last night to the cinema went.
h Do your homework very careful.
i You drive too fastly! Slow down!
j You're a beautifully dancer!

● VOCABULARY

Talking about a book

1 It is a good idea to read stories in English. You can read at home, in bed, on the train, anywhere!
Maria read a story called *The Monkey's Paw*. Match a question about the book with Maria's answers.

Questions about the book

1 What's the title of the book?
2 What sort of story is it?
3 Who are the main characters?
4 What's it about?
5 What happens in the end?
6 Did you enjoy it?
7 Do you recommend it?

Maria's answers

a The son dies in an accident at work.
b Yes, I do.
c Old Mr and Mrs White and their son, Herbert.
d It's called *The Monkey's Paw*.
e It's a horror story.
f Yes, I did. It was very interesting.
g A monkey's paw which is magic. It can give people three wishes, but the wishes don't bring happiness.

T 76 Listen to Maria and check your answers.

2 Here are four texts from four books. Match A, B, and C.

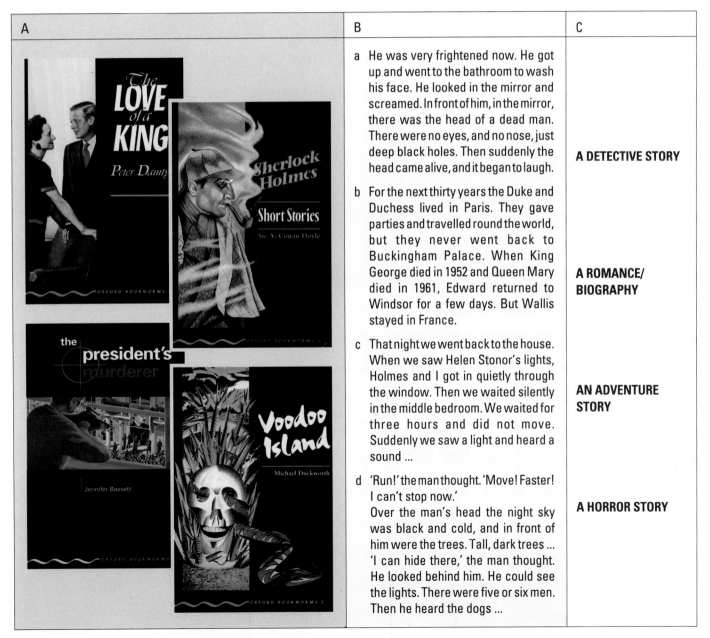

A	B	C
	a He was very frightened now. He got up and went to the bathroom to wash his face. He looked in the mirror and screamed. In front of him, in the mirror, there was the head of a dead man. There were no eyes, and no nose, just deep black holes. Then suddenly the head came alive, and it began to laugh.	A DETECTIVE STORY
	b For the next thirty years the Duke and Duchess lived in Paris. They gave parties and travelled round the world, but they never went back to Buckingham Palace. When King George died in 1952 and Queen Mary died in 1961, Edward returned to Windsor for a few days. But Wallis stayed in France.	A ROMANCE/ BIOGRAPHY
	c That night we went back to the house. When we saw Helen Stonor's lights, Holmes and I got in quietly through the window. Then we waited silently in the middle bedroom. We waited for three hours and did not move. Suddenly we saw a light and heard a sound ...	AN ADVENTURE STORY
	d 'Run!' the man thought. 'Move! Faster! I can't stop now.' Over the man's head the night sky was black and cold, and in front of him were the trees. Tall, dark trees ... 'I can hide there,' the man thought. He looked behind him. He could see the lights. There were five or six men. Then he heard the dogs ...	A HORROR STORY

(These books are part of the *Oxford Bookworm Series*).

● READING AND LISTENING

A short story

You will read a story called *The Girl with Green Eyes* from a book of short stories from the *Oxford Bookworm Series* called *One-Way Ticket*.

Pre-reading

1 Do you like train journeys? What can you do on a train journey that you can't do on a car journey?

2 Do you like looking at people on trains?

Look at picture 1.
Who are friends?
Who are strangers?
Who are husband and wife?

3 What do you think happens in the story?

Reading and listening

1 **T 77** Read and listen to part 1 of the story. Answer the questions.

   a Who is related to who?
   b Who is who in the pictures?
   c What does Julie think of her husband?
   d What do you think happens in the story?

2 Read and listen to part 2. Answer the questions.

   e What does Bill do? What does the tall dark man do?
   f Why does Julie read the back of the newspaper?
   g Does she look into the tall dark man's eyes the first time? And the second time?
   h What does she think of the tall dark man?

3 Read and listen to part 3. Answer the questions.

   i What happens when the train arrives at the station?
   j Who sees Julie get off the train?
   k 'People don't always need words, young man.' What does the mother mean?
   l Why does Julie leave her husband?

Vocabulary

Which parts of the body are in the story? Which parts especially? Why, do you think?

Speaking

1 Work in groups of three. Student A is Bill, Student B is the little girl, and Student C is the girl's mother. Practise the dialogue from '*Where's Julie?*' to the end.

2 Look back at the questions on page 95. Use them to ask and answer about *The Girl with Green Eyes*. Retell the story in the Past Simple.

1

There were seven people in the carriage.

2

Julie opened her eyes and looked at the back page of the tall dark man's newspaper.

3

Green eyes looked into dark brown eyes for a long, slow minute.

4

'She got off the train at Plymouth. With the tall dark man.'

The Girl with Green Eyes

Part 1

'Of course,' the man in the brown hat said, 'there are good policemen, and there are bad policemen, you know.'

'You're right,' the young man said. 'Yes. That's very true. Isn't it, Julie?'

Julie didn't answer and looked bored. She closed her eyes.

There were seven people in the carriage. There was the man in the brown hat; the young man and his wife, Julie; a mother and two children; and a tall dark man in an expensive suit.

The young man's name was Bill. He had short brown hair and a happy smile. His wife, Julie, had long red hair and very green eyes – the colour of sea water. They were very beautiful eyes.

Part 2

Bill and the man in the brown hat talked and talked. The tall dark man took out his newspaper and began to read. Julie opened her eyes and looked at the back page of his newspaper. She read about the weather in Budapest and about the football in Liverpool. She wasn't interested in the weather and she didn't like football, but she didn't want to listen to Bill and the man in the brown hat. 'Talk, talk, talk,' she thought. 'Bill never stops talking.'

Then suddenly she saw the tall man's eyes over the top of his newspaper. She could not see his mouth, but there was a smile in his eyes. Quickly, she looked down at the newspaper again. She read about the weather in Budapest for the third time. Then she looked at the tall man's hands. They were long, brown hands, very clean. 'Nice hands,' she thought. He wore a very expensive Japanese watch. 'Japan,' she thought. 'I'd like to go to Japan.' She looked up and saw the man's eyes again over the top of his newspaper. This time she did not look away. Green eyes looked into dark brown eyes for a long, slow minute.

Part 3

Bill and his new friend went to buy something to eat and drink. The train was nearly at Plymouth. The tall dark man stood up, put the newspaper in his bag, and left the carriage. The train stopped at the station. A lot of people got on the train, and two women and an old man came into the carriage.

The train moved slowly away from Plymouth station, and Bill came back to the carriage. 'Where's Julie?' he said. 'She's not here.'

The little girl looked at Bill. 'She got off the train at Plymouth,' she said. 'With the tall dark man. I saw them.'

'Of course she didn't!' Bill said. 'She's on this train. She didn't get off.'

'Yes, she did,' the children's mother said suddenly. 'I saw her too. The tall man waited for her on the platform.'

'He waited for her?' Bill's mouth was wide open. 'But ... But he read his newspaper all the time. He didn't talk to Julie. And she never talked to him. They didn't say a word.'

'People don't always need words, young man,' the children's mother said.

'But I don't understand,' said Bill. 'She's my wife. Why did she go? Why did she leave me? What am I going to do?'

(Adapted from a story by Jennifer Bassett)

● EVERYDAY ENGLISH

Catching a train

1 Ann lives in London. She wants to go to Newcastle for the day and decides to go by train. She phones the British Rail Talking Timetable Service.

T 78a Listen and complete the timetable. Notice we often use the twenty-four hour clock for timetables.

7.00 in the morning = 0700 (oh seven hundred hours)

DEPARTURE TIME from KING'S CROSS	ARRIVAL TIME in NEWCASTLE
0 7 0 0	
	1 1 3 0
0 9 5 0	
	1 4 3 7
1 2 0 0	

2 **T 78b** Ann goes to the Information Office at King's Cross station. She wants to know about train times back from Newcastle. Listen and complete the conversation.

A Good morning. (a) _____ the times of

trains (b) _____ Newcastle, please?

B Afternoon, evening? When (c) _____ ?

A About five o'clock this afternoon.

B About (d) _____ . Right. Let's have a

look. There's a train that (e) _____

4.45, and there's (f) _____ at 5.25.

A And (g) _____ get in?

B Back at King's Cross at 7.15 and (h) _____

A Thanks a lot.

3 Ann goes to the ticket office. Put the lines of the conversation in the correct order.

1 A Hello. I'd like a ticket to Newcastle, please.
___ A I want to come back this evening, so a day return.
___ C How do you want to pay?
___ A Return, please.
___ C Here's your change and your ticket.
___ C Single or return?
___ A Twenty, forty, sixty pounds.
___ C Day return or period return?
___ A Cash, please.
___ C Forty-eight pounds fifty, please.
11 A Thank you.

T 78c Listen and check. Close your books. Try to remember the conversations! In pairs, practise saying them.

4 **T 78d** Look at the noticeboards at the railway station and listen to the announcement. Correct the mistakes.

ARRIVALS				
FROM	• PLATFORM	TIME	• •	REMARK
Edinburgh	• 18	0830	• •	On time
Hertford	• 6	0835	• •	On time
Newcastle	• 15	0845	• •	Delay 30 mins
Darlington	• 9	0845	• •	On time
DEPARTURES				
DESTINATION	• PLATFORM	TIME	• •	REMARK
Peterborough	• 12	0825	• •	Ready
Newcastle	• 7	0840	• •	Ready
York	• 5	0850	• •	

GRAMMAR SUMMARY

Question forms

When	did Columbus discover America?
Where	are the Andes?
Who	did she marry?
How	do you get to school?
What	do you have for breakfast?
What	happens at the end of the story?
Why	do you want to learn English?

How many	people are there in the class?
How much	does she earn?
How far	is it to the centre?
What sort of	car do you have?
Which newspaper	do you read?

Adjectives and adverbs

Adjectives describe nouns.

a **big** dog
a **careful** driver

Adverbs describe verbs.

She ran **quickly**.
He drives too **fast**.

To form regular adverbs, add *-ly* to the adjective. Words ending in *-y* change to *-ily*.

Adjective	Adverb
quick	quickly
bad	badly
careful	carefully
easy	easily
immediate	immediately

Some adverbs are irregular.

good	well
hard	hard
early	early
fast	fast

Prepositions

What's the story **about**?
What happens **in** the end?
What do you think **of** Peter?
I want to go **round** the world.
A girl **with** green eyes.
Are you interested **in** ballet?
The train is **on** time.
The train leaves **from** platform 9.

Study the Word List for this unit on page 126.

UNIT 14

Present Perfect – Telephoning

In my life

PRESENTATION (1)

Present Perfect + *ever* and *never*

1 Look at the countries and tick (✔) those you have visited at some time in your life.

2 **T 79a** Read and listen to the sentences. Practise saying them.

> I've been to England. I haven't been to Scotland.
>
> I've been to the United States. I've never been to Mexico.
>
> I haven't been to *any* of the countries!

Work in groups. Tell each other which countries in Exercise 1 you have or have not been to.

3 **T 79b** Read and listen to the conversation. Practise saying it.

A Have you ever been to Ireland?
B No, I haven't.
A Have you ever been to Scotland?
B Yes, I have.
A When did you go?
B Two years ago.

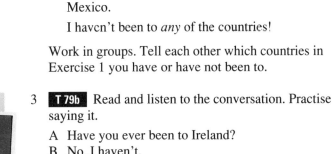

1 We use the Past Simple to talk about definite past time.

When did you go there?

I went there	last year.
	two years ago.
	in 1992.

We use the Present Perfect to talk about indefinite past time.

Have you ever (at some time in your life) been to Paris?

2 We make the Present Perfect tense with *has/have* + the past participle of the verb.

I've (= I have) been to France.
She's (= She has) been to Algeria.

4 Write down the names of four capital cities. In pairs, make more dialogues like the one in Exercise 3.

5 Tell the class about your partner.

> Maria's been to London. She went there two years ago. But she hasn't been to Paris.

Practice

1 Grammar

Here are the past participles of some verbs. Write the infinitive.

visited	**visit**	seen	_____	taken	_____
eaten	**eat**	met	_____	driven	_____
drunk	_____	cooked	_____	lived	_____
stayed	_____	flown	_____	bought	_____
won	_____	written	_____	had	_____
made	_____	sent	_____	done	_____

Which are the four regular verbs?
What is the Past Simple form of the irregular verbs? There is a list of irregular verbs on page 127.

2 Listening and speaking

1 **T 80** Listen to Roger talking about his life and tick (✔) the things he says he has done.

	Roger	Teacher	Student
lived in a foreign country	☐	☐	☐
worked for a big company	☐	☐	☐
stayed in an expensive hotel	☐	☐	☐
flown in a jumbo jet	☐	☐	☐
cooked a meal for ten (or more) people	☐	☐	☐
met a famous person	☐	☐	☐
seen a play by Shakespeare	☐	☐	☐
driven a tractor	☐	☐	☐
been to hospital	☐	☐	☐
won a competition	☐	☐	☐

2 Tell your teacher about Roger and answer your teacher's questions.

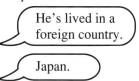

He's lived in a foreign country.

Which country did he live in?

Japan.

How long did he live there?

One year.

3 Ask your teacher the questions and fill in the chart.

Have you ever lived in a foreign country?

Which country did you live in?

4 Ask another student the questions. Tell the class about your partner.

3 Choosing the correct sentence

One sentence has a mistake. Choose the correct sentence. Put ✔ and ✗.

1 a I saw John yesterday.
   b I've seen John yesterday.
2 a Did you ever eat Indian food?
   b Have you ever eaten Indian food?
3 a Diana won £5,000 last month.
   b Diana has won £5,000 last month.
4 a I've never drank champagne.
   b I've never drunk champagne.
5 a Tom has ever been to America.
   b Tom has never been to America.
6 a Did they live in London five years ago?
   b Have they lived in London five years ago?
7 a Mary has wrote a lot of books.
   b Mary has written a lot of books.
8 a Did she write a book last year?
   b Has she written a book last year?

PRESENTATION (2)

Present Perfect + *yet* and *just*

1 Jack and Lilian are in New York on holiday. Before they went, they made a list of things they wanted to do there. Look at the list.

NOTES

The Big Apple !!

See a show on Broadway
Climb the Empire State Building
See the Statue of Liberty
Go to Greenwich Village
Walk in Central Park
Go to Chinatown
Take a helicopter tour

2 **T 81** Lilian is talking to her father on the telephone. Listen to their conversation. Put ✔ next to the things she has done and ✘ next to things she has not done yet.

3 Complete the sentences.

a We _____ been to Greenwich Village yet.

b Have you _____ the Statue of Liberty yet?

c We've just _____ a helicopter tour.

Listen and check. Find two more examples of *yet*.

● Grammar questions

– Where do we put *yet* in a sentence?
– Where do we put *just* in a sentence?
– Complete the rule.
  We do not use *yet* in positive sentences, only in

  _____ and _____ .

Practice

1 Speaking

1 Talk about Jack and Lilian. Say what they have done and what they haven't done yet.

> They've climbed the Empire State Building.

> They haven't seen a show on Broadway yet.

2 Work in pairs. Use the ideas to make questions with *yet* and answers with *just*.

Example
do the washing-up

> Have you done the washing-up yet?

> Yes, I've just done it.

a finish your homework
b wash your hair
c clean the car
d meet the new student
e make the dinner
f do the shopping
g talk to the teacher
h buy your plane ticket

2 Reading

Complete the story. Put the verb in brackets into the Present Perfect or Past Simple tense.

A SAD STORY OF A SAD MAN

One Sunday evening two men (a) _____ (**meet**) in a London pub. One of them was very unhappy.

'Life is terrible, everything in the world is really boring,' he said.

'Don't say that,' said the other man. 'Life is marvellous! The world is so exciting! Think about Italy. It's a wonderful country. (b) _____ you ever _____ (**be**) there?'

'Oh, yes. I (c) _____ (**go**) there last year and I (d) _____ (**not like**) it.'

'Well, (e) _____ you _____ (**be**) to Norway? (f) _____ you ever _____ (**see**) the midnight sun?'

'Oh, yes. I (g) _____ (**go**) in 1984 and I (h) _____ (**see**) the midnight sun. I (i) _____ (**not enjoy**) it.'

'Well, I (j) _____ just _____ (**return**) from a safari in Africa. (k) _____ you _____ (**visit**) Africa yet?'

'Yes, I (l) _____ (**go**) on safari in Africa last year and I (m) _____ (**climb**) Mount Kilimanjaro. It was really boring.'

'Well,' said the other man, 'I think that you're very ill. Only the best psychiatrist can help you. Go to see Dr Greenbaum in Harley Street.'

'I am Dr Greenbaum,' answered the man sadly.

3 Grammar

Put a word from the box into each gap.

have/haven't	has/hasn't	did/didn't			
never	ever	just	yet	ago	last

a _____ you go to America _____ year?

b '_____ he_____ been to India?' 'Yes, he _____ .'

c '_____ you _____ met the Queen?' No, I _____ .'

d 'When _____ you meet your husband?' 'Ten years
    _____ .'

e I _____ _____ finished my homework. Now I can
    watch TV.

f '_____ you finished your homework _____ ?'
    'No, I _____ .'

g I _____ play tennis _____ weekend because it was
    wet.

h Kate _____ written her thank-you letters _____ .

i We _____ been to Spain, but we _____ _____
    been to Portugal.

j '_____ they moved to their new house _____ ?'
    'Yes, they moved three days _____ .'

● READING AND SPEAKING

Three amazing grandmas

You are going to read about three special old ladies.

Pre-reading task

Work in pairs.
1 What is a typical grandmother like? What do
   grandmothers look like? What do they do?
   Write down some ideas and compare them with your
   partner's.

2 Check the meaning of these words in your dictionary.

active (*adj*)	gun (*n*)
antique shop (*n*)	knit (*v*)
cardigan (*n*)	military (*adj*)
cockroach (*n*)	regret (*v*)
civilian (*adj*)	stocking (*n*)
(do) exercises (*n*)	toy (*n*)

Reading

Divide into three groups.

Group A   Read about Dorothy Moriarty.
Group B   Read about Kitty Currie.
Group C   Read about Alice Hyde.

Answer the questions in the Comprehension Check.

THE FIRST MISS WORLD

Alice Hyde is ninety-seven years old and she always watches the Miss World competition on TV. She likes to remember the year 1911, when she became the very first Miss World. 'It was wonderful. My picture was in the best magazines and on postcards. I received hundreds of letters. A lot of men wanted to marry me! Best of all, Charlie Chaplin wrote from America and invited me to Hollywood. I really wanted to go there and be a film star, but my parents said no.'

Instead, in 1912, Alice married Charlie Hyde, a boy from her home town in the north of England. They had five children, four sons and a daughter. When Charlie retired, they moved to Spain and they lived there until Charlie died. Alice came back to England and bought an antique shop, where she worked until last year. 'I've had a wonderful life. I've travelled. I've lived abroad. I've never been to Hollywood but I don't regret that. I've known true love. My Charlie was the best husband in the world! I'm still healthy and active. I feel much younger than ninety-seven. I've just done my exercises and I'm going to Spain for my summer holiday!'

MY GRANDMA'S A BANK ROBBER!

Kitty Currie is everyone's favourite grandma. She is sixty-eight years old, has snow-white hair and always wears a pink cardigan and carries a big handbag. She likes knitting and looking after her five lovely grandsons. But she's not looking after them at the moment. Kitty Currie has gone to prison! Two months ago, Kitty, who lives in the village of Bovdon in Devon, robbed a bank! She took her grandson's toy gun, put a stocking over her face, and walked into Barclays Bank. She pointed the gun at the cashier and asked for some money. The cashier gave her £20. Kitty smiled, said 'Thank you very much,' and left. The cashier called the police, and they caught Kitty in the next street. The money, the gun, and the stocking were all in her bag.

Kitty says, 'I got married when I was sixteen. All my life I've looked after my home and my children. I've got a lovely husband and I've had a happy life but I've never done anything really exciting. I've never been abroad. I've never even had a job. Now I'm famous. I've been on TV and in the newspapers! But I'm not going to rob another bank!'

102 and she's a writer!

Dorothy Moriarty is Britain's oldest writer. She is 102 years old and has just written her first book, *The Memoirs of a Nurse*. In it she describes her life as a nurse at University College Hospital, London, in the early part of this century. At that time civilian hospitals had very little money. They were dirty and nurses worked seventy hours a week and earned £8 a year. Dorothy says, 'There were cockroaches everywhere. Nobody worried about our hospitals. All the

DOROTHY
The Memoirs of a Nurse

'Deserves to become a classic ... a totally absorbing personal odyssey'
Nursing Times

Dorothy Moriarty

money went to the military hospitals, and the newspapers were full of stories of Florence Nightingale and her soldiers. We decided to do something. We started the Royal College of Nursing and cut our working week from seventy to forty-eight hours. This was much better.'

After the First World War Dorothy went to work in Egypt, where she met her husband, Oliver. They married in 1922, but her family life was not always happy. Oliver had a drink problem and finally died. 'I've had a difficult life, but it's been very interesting, and I've always had the love of my children and grandchildren!'

Dorothy has started planning her next book. She says that with her long life she has lots of ideas!

Comprehension check

a How old is she?
b Why is she special?
c Has she ever had a job?
d When did she get married?
e Has she ever lived abroad?
f Have there been any big problems in her life?
g Which words from the vocabulary list on page 102 were in your text?

Check your answers with your group.

Speaking

1 Find someone from both of the other groups. Discuss the answers again and tell each other about your old lady.

2 Read the other two texts quickly. Are the following statements about all three ladies true (✔) or false (✗)?

a Alice Hyde is the oldest. ✗
b They are all widows.
c They have all been famous at some time in their lives.
d Dorothy and Alice have both written books about their lives.
e In the First World War military hospitals got more money than other hospitals.
f Kitty Currie robbed the bank because she was bored with her life.
g Charlie Chaplin wanted to marry Alice.
h Kitty and Alice both have five children.
i They all have plans for the future.

Discussion

1 Who do you think has had ...
... the happiest life?
... the most difficult life?
... the most interesting life?

2 What do you know about the lives of your grandmothers? Tell the class about them.

● VOCABULARY AND PRONUNCIATION

Odd one out

1 Which word is the odd one out? Why? Check the meaning of new words in your dictionary.

a waitress	grandmother	nephew	widow
b socks	gloves	tights	stockings
c flew	sailed	drove ·	rode
d doctor	patient	customer	nurse
e telephone	photocopier	fax machine	letter
f T-shirt	jeans	shorts	trousers
g taken	done	known	wrote
h face	foot	head	neck
i amazing	wonderful	boring	marvellous
j is	has	does	plays
k cat	kitten	puppy	lamb

2 Here are some of the words in Exercise 1 in phonetics. Practise saying the words.

a /glʌvz/   d /dʒi:nz/   g /əmeɪzɪŋ/   j /nɜ:s/
b /taɪts/   e /ʃɔːts/   h /wɪdəʊ/   k /pʌpɪ/
c /peɪʃnt/   f /fʊt/   i /nefju:/   l /traʊzəz/

3 Put one of the words from Exercise 1 into each gap.

a Have you seen my _____ ? My hands are really cold!
b Mary Moss has written ten novels. She _____ *Love in the Sun* two years ago.
c I have three nieces and one _____ .
d John thought the film was marvellous but I thought it was _____ .
e I haven't seen my grandmother recently. I think I'll send her a _____ .
f Our _____ has had four kittens!
g That _____ has tried on every dress in the shop and she doesn't like any of them!
h John has just bought a guitar. He _____ it all the time.
i Ruth hates flying so she _____ to New York.
j Bobby has hurt his _____ because he kicked the ball so hard.
k When I was in London I bought a _____ with *I had tea with the Queen* on the front!

● EVERYDAY ENGLISH

Telephoning

1 **T 82a** Listen to three British telephone tones.

Which one means 'You can dial'?
Which one means 'The number is ringing'?
Which one means 'The number is engaged'?

Are the tones the same or different in your country?

2 Complete the three telephone conversations. Use the phrases from the box.

> No, it isn't. I'll just get her.
> Can I take a message?
> Great! See you on Sunday at ten. Bye!
> Never mind. Perhaps next time. Bye!
> This is Jo speaking.
> I'll ring back later.
> I'm having a party on Saturday. Can you come?
> Can I speak to the manager, please?

a
A Hello. 276694.
B Hello. Can I speak to Jo, please?
A _____ .
B Oh! Hi, Jo. This is Pat. I'm just ringing to check that Sunday is still OK for tennis.
A Yes. That's fine.
B _____ .
A Bye!

b
A Hello. Chesswood 4576.
B Hello. Is that Liz?
A _____ .
C Hello. Liz here.
B Hi, Liz. It's Tom. Listen! _____ ?
C Oh sorry, Tom. I can't. I'm going to my cousin's wedding.
B _____ .
C Bye!

c

A Hello. Barclays Bank, Chesswood.

B Hello.

A _____?

A Hold on. I'll put you through ... I'm afraid Mr Smith isn't in his office.

_____?

B Don't worry.

_____.

A All right. Goodbye.

B Goodbye.

T 82b Listen and check. In pairs, memorize and practise saying one of the conversations.

3 When you do not know someone's telephone number, you can ring Directory Enquiries. You ring 192 for numbers in Britain and 153 for international numbers. Here are the names and addresses of some people you want to call.

Janet Duncan
42 Collier Lane
HARROGATE
Yorkshire
Tel._____

Ian Macdonald
21 Bridge Street
PERTH
Scotland
Tel._____

Donna Vale
278 Tower Road
TORONTO
Canada
Tel._____
Fax._____

T 82c Listen to the operator and answer her questions. Find Janet Duncan's telephone number.

Operator Directory Enquiries. Which town, please?

You _____ .

Operator Can I have the surname, please?

You _____ .

Operator And the initial?

You _____ .

Operator What's the address?

You _____ .

Operator Thank you. The number you want is

_____ .

Work in pairs. Take turns to be the operator. Find out the telephone and fax numbers of the other people. Your teacher will give the operators the numbers.

GRAMMAR SUMMARY

Present Perfect

Positive and negative

I You We They	have	(not)	been	to the States.
He She It	has			

Question

Where	have	I you we they	been?
	has	she he it	

Yes/No questions
Have you been to Russia?

Short answers
Yes, I have.
No, I haven't.

Present Perfect and Past Simple

We use the Present Perfect to refer to an indefinite time in the past.

He's travelled all over the world.
They've just arrived home.

We use the Past Simple to refer to a definite time in the past.

I left	last night. yesterday. in 1990. at three o'clock. on Monday.

Present Perfect + *yet* and *just*

I haven't done it **yet** (but I'm going to).
I have **just** done it (a short time before now).

Prepositions

She works **for** a big company.
Hamlet is a play **by** Shakespeare.
She was bored **with** life.
She wrote **about** her life as a nurse.
Don't worry **about** me.
Can I speak **to** Jo, please?

Study the Word List for this unit on page 126.

UNIT 15

Verb patterns – *say* and *tell* – Problems with officials

Thank you and goodbye

PRESENTATION (1)

Verb patterns

1   Read the thank-you letter.

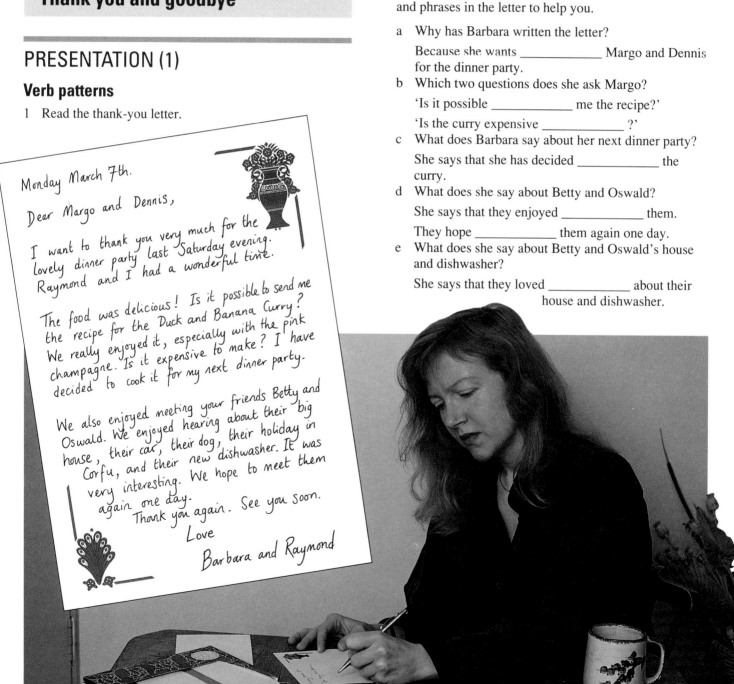

Monday March 7th.

Dear Margo and Dennis,

I want to thank you very much for the lovely dinner party last Saturday evening. Raymond and I had a wonderful time.

The food was delicious! Is it possible to send me the recipe for the Duck and Banana Curry? We really enjoyed it, especially with the pink champagne. Is it expensive to make? I have decided to cook it for my next dinner party.

We also enjoyed meeting your friends Betty and Oswald. We enjoyed hearing about their big house, their car, their dog, their holiday in Corfu, and their new dishwasher. It was very interesting. We hope to meet them again one day.
Thank you again. See you soon.
Love
Barbara and Raymond

2   Complete the answers to the questions. Use the words and phrases in the letter to help you.

a   Why has Barbara written the letter?

Because she wants _____ Margo and Dennis for the dinner party.

b   Which two questions does she ask Margo?

'Is it possible _____ me the recipe?'

'Is the curry expensive _____ ?'

c   What does Barbara say about her next dinner party?

She says that she has decided _____ the curry.

d   What does she say about Betty and Oswald?

She says that they enjoyed _____ them.

They hope _____ them again one day.

e   What does she say about Betty and Oswald's house and dishwasher?

She says that they loved _____ about their house and dishwasher.

1 We use the infinitive after many adjectives.

It was **expensive to decorate** the house.
It's **easy to learn** English.

2 We use the infinitive after some verbs.

He **wants to learn** Japanese.
I'**d like to come.**
We **decided to go** to Spain.

3 We use the *-ing* form after some verbs.

I **enjoy learning** English.
He has **finished doing** his homework.
I **like swimming.**

There is a list of verb patterns on Page 127.
Unfortunately, there are no rules!

Practice

1 Grammar

1 Read the letter again and <u>underline</u> the examples of infinitives and *-ing* forms.

2 Complete the sentences with verbs from the box in the infinitive or *-ing* form. Use the list of verb patterns on Page 127 to help you.

| drive | paint | play | fly | meet | learn |
| visit | ride | buy | rain | talk | post |

a Do you think English is difficult _____ ?

b My mother has promised _____ me a new coat for my birthday.

c How do you do? It's very nice _____ you.

d John hates _____ , but I love planes.

e I need _____ to somebody about my problem.

f We stopped _____ tennis because it started _____ .

g I don't like _____ big cars, I prefer _____ my bike.

h Bob's finished _____ the bathroom doors.

i Did you enjoy _____ the British Museum?

j Please don't forget _____ my letter.

PRESENTATION (2)

say and *tell*

T 83 Listen and complete the conversation between Barbara and a friend of hers, Alice, about the dinner party.

Alice Hi, Barbara! Did you and Raymond enjoy Margo's dinner party?

Barbara No, we _____ . It _____ !

Alice What about the food?

Barbara Oh, the food _____ ! We _____ it.

We _____ Duck and Banana Curry!

Alice Duck and what?! Ugh!

Barbara I know. I _____ duck and Ray _____ bananas!

Alice And their friends? Tell me about their friends. Were they nice?

Barbara Oh, Alice! They were friendly, but they were so _____ ! They talked for three hours about their _____ and their _____ and their _____ ! And they _____

_____ one question about us. We _____ very little, only 'Yes?' and 'No!'

Alice Oh dear! What a terrible evening!

Notice how we use *say* and *tell*.

In the letter Barbara **said (that)** the dinner party was lovely.
She **said (that)** they had a wonderful time
She **told Alice (that)** it was awful.
She **told her (that)** they didn't enjoy it.

● Grammar questions

– How do we use *say*?
– How do we use *tell*?
– Is it correct or incorrect to use *that* after *say* and *tell*?

107

Practice

1 Speaking

Work in pairs. Compare Barbara's letter and her conversation with Alice. Tell your partner about some of the differences. Talk about:

the food
the friends
the friends' conversation

> In the letter she said that the party was wonderful, but she told Alice that it was awful.

2 Writing and speaking

Write the dialogue again, but this time about a *good* dinner party. Act your dialogue for the class. Then the class makes some sentences with *say* and *tell*.

> She said the dinner party was interesting.

> He told us that the food was wonderful.

3 Correcting the mistakes

Each sentence has a mistake. Find it and correct it!

a I started smoke when I was sixteen years old.
b We'd like you coming for dinner.
c She said me the restaurant was next to the cinema.
d Jeremy have never told me about his trip to Paris.
e It's difficult for me learn Portuguese.
f I've been to the post office for buy some stamps.
g Do you want meeting the manager?
h Money can't to buy love.

● VOCABULARY

Multi-word verbs

1 Look at the dictionary extract.

> **take something off** remove a piece of clothing: *He came in and took off his coat.*

In English many verbs can add a preposition or adverb. Sometimes the meaning of the verb is literal, as in *He took off his coat.*

Look at the second dictionary extract.

> **take off** leave the ground and start to fly: *The aeroplane took off an hour late.*

Sometimes the meaning of the verb is idiomatic, as in *The plane took off.*

2 Use the multi-word verbs in the dictionary extracts in Exercise 1 and below to complete the sentences below. Put the verbs in the correct tense and form.

> **break down** (a) go wrong and stop working: *We are late because the car broke down.*
> **break down** (b) start to cry: *He broke down when he heard that his horse was dead.*

> **go out with someone** have someone as a boyfriend or girlfriend: *Paula is going out with Martin.*

> **get on with someone** work or live in a friendly way with someone: *Are you getting on with your new neighbours?*

> **get up** stand up; get out of bed: *It's time to get up, children!*

> **look after** take care of someone or something: *A nurse looks after sick people in a hospital.*

> **give something up** stop doing, using, or eating something: *I'm fat. I'm going to give up sugar and potatoes!*

> **turn off** stop something: *Turn off the light.*

> **turn on** start something: *Turn on the television.*

a My neighbours are away on holiday, so I

_____ their cat.

b The plane is delayed. It _____ yet.

c Please can you _____ the radio. That music is too loud.

d My husband wants _____ smoking, but he can't.

e Have you heard? Rita _____ with Rick. They met at Ann's party.

f '_____ you _____ well with your husband's parents?' 'No, I don't.'

g The journey took ten hours because our car

_____ on the motorway.

h Mary _____ when Roger told her that he was in love with another girl.

● READING AND LISTENING

Leaving home

Pre-reading task

Work in small groups. Discuss the following questions.

1 In your country, when do children usually stop living with their parents and leave home?
2 How old are they? Why do they leave home?
3 What are the good things and bad things about leaving home?

Reading

Read the letter. Who has written it? When? Why?

Comprehension check

Are the following statements true (✔) or false (✗)?

a Paula is inviting her parents to her wedding.
b Paula's parents think that they know what is best for Paula.
c They like Martin because he is a car salesman.
d Paula's parents are very rich.
e They bought a lot of things for her when she was a little girl.
f Paula is leaving home because she doesn't love her parents.
g Paula has a lot of brothers and sisters.
h Paula is not going to write to her parents again.

Wednesday 10th June, 4am

Dear Mum and Dad,
        I'm really sorry, but I'm leaving home. When you read this I will be far away. Don't try to find me. Martin and I are getting married next Saturday.
        I know you have never liked Martin. You didn't want me to go out with him because you said that he was just a car salesman and he wasn't good enough for me. I know that you have always wanted the best for me. I know that Martin is best for me. I love him very much indeed.
        When I was a little girl, you always gave me everything I wanted - toys, clothes, an expensive education. I know it was difficult to do this. It was a struggle because we didn't have much money, but you wanted to plan my life for me. You tried to choose my friends, my job, even my clothes. Now I am going to do what I want to do, not what you tell me to do. I want to be independent.
        I love you both very much and I am your only child, so it isn't easy to leave. I hope you can forgive me and learn to love Martin. I'd love us all to get on well together.
        Look after each other. I promise to write again soon. Paula

Listening

You are going to read and listen to a Beatles' song called *She's Leaving Home*.

1 Read the words of the first verse and choose the best word in the brackets to fill in each gap. Check the meaning of new words in your dictionary.

2 **T 84** Listen to the first verse and the chorus and check your answers. Then do the same with the other verses.

She's Leaving HOME

Wednesday morning at five o'clock as the day _____ (*begins/starts*),
Silently closing the bedroom _____ (*door/window*)
Leaving the _____ (*letter/note*) that she hoped would say more
She goes downstairs to the _____ (*dining room/kitchen*)
_____ (*Clutching/Holding*) her handkerchief
Quietly turning the backdoor key
Stepping outside she is _____ (*free/independent*).

She
We gave her most of our lives.
is leaving
Sacrificed most of our lives.
home.
We gave her everything money could buy.
She's leaving home after living alone for so many years.

Father _____ (*sleeps/snores*) as his wife gets into her dressing gown,
Picks up the _____ (*cat/letter*) that's lying there
Standing alone at the top of the stairs
She breaks down and _____ (*cries/shouts*) to her husband,
'Daddy, our baby's _____ (*gone/left*).
Why would she treat us so thoughtlessly?
How could she do this to _____ (*me/us*)?'

She
We never thought of ourselves.
is leaving
Never a thought of ourselves.
home.
We struggled hard all our lives to get by.
She's leaving home after living alone for so many years.

Friday morning at nine o'clock she is far away
Waiting to keep the appointment she _____ (*had/made*)
Meeting a man from the _____ (*car/motor*) trade.

She
What did we do that was wrong?
is having
We didn't know it was wrong.
fun.
Fun is the one thing that money can't buy.
Something inside that was always denied for so many years.
She's leaving home. Bye bye.

● EVERYDAY ENGLISH

Problems with officials

1 Have you ever had problems with officials or people who work in post offices, banks, shops, airports, railway stations, or schools, for example? Tell a partner and then the others in the class about the problems.

2 The following sentences come from four conversations with officials. Who do you think is speaking and where do you think they are?

a You have to fill in a customs form when you send a parcel overseas.

b I bought it last week and it's too small.

c Have you got a passport or a driving licence?

d You have to give us the receipt. We can't change anything without a receipt.

e What's the purpose of your visit?

f You have to show identification with cheques over £100.

g Have you filled in a customs form?

h You have to give us an address. You can't enter the country without an address!

> *Have/has to* expresses strong obligation.
>
> Policemen **have to** wear uniforms.

3 Read the conversations and put the letter of the correct sentence into each gap.

1 A Can I help you?
  B Yes. Can I change this jumper please? _____
  A Have you got the receipt?
  B No. I'm sorry, I've lost it.
  A Oh dear! _____
  B But ... !

2 A Can I send this parcel to Greece, please?
  B Yes, of course. That's £3.50. Thank you. _____
  A Customs form? What customs form?
  B _____
  A Can you give me a form then, please?
  B No, I don't have any. They're over there on that table.
  A Sorry? Where?
  B Over there. They're the green forms.

3 A That's £104.50 altogether. How do you want to pay?
  B Can I pay by cheque?
  A Yes, but have you got any identification? _____
  B Oh dear! Let me see. I've got a photo of me and my aunt at the seaside.
  A No, no, no. _____
  B No, I haven't.
  A Then I'm afraid we can't take your cheque.
  B But ... !

4 A _____
  B Oh, I'm going to study English and have a holiday.
  A And how long are you staying?
  B For a month.
  A And where are you going to stay? What's your address?
  B I'm not sure. The language school is going to find me somewhere to stay.
  A Mmm! _____
  B But ... !

T 85 Listen and check.

4 Work in pairs. Think of a problem you have had with officials. Act it for the class.

GRAMMAR SUMMARY

Verb patterns

There are different verb patterns when one verb follows another verb.

Verb + infinitive

I want	to go	home.
We'd like	to have	a holiday.
We've decided	to get	married!
I hope	to see	you again soon.

Verb + -ing

He enjoys/loves/likes	sailing.
It's stopped/started	raining.

There is a list of verb patterns on page 127.

Adjective + infinitive

It was nice	to meet	you.
It's easy	to make	mistakes.
It's difficult	to understand	what he's saying.

say and *tell*

She He	said (that)	she enjoyed the party. I was wrong.

I She	told	them me	(that)	their English was good. she wanted to go home.

NOT ~~She said me~~ she enjoyed the party.
  ~~He told~~ their English was good.

Prepositions

I want to talk to you **about** something.
Tell me **about** their friends.
I have a problem **with** people in the post office.

Study the Word List for this unit on page 126.

STOP AND CHECK

1 Correcting the mistakes

There is a mistake in each sentence. Find it and correct it!

Example
We ~~was~~ in Paris last year.   *We were in Paris last year.*

a   Why you want to learn Portuguese?
b   She hasn't never been to Madrid.
c   I've wrote to her three times and she hasn't answered yet.
d   We'd like invite you to dinner at our house.
e   How many times you been to Greece?
f   I have just finished do my homework.
g   We've met two years ago in New York.
h   Say me when you want to stop for lunch.
i   What sort books do you like reading?
j   Did you ever been to Ireland?

10

2 Questions and tenses

Ask questions about the statements.

Example
John went to New York.   When *did he go*?

a Anna's tired.	Why _____ ?
b I don't go to work by car.	How ____ you _____ ?
c This pen isn't mine.	Whose _____ ?
d I met a famous actress.	Who ____ you _____ ?
e Sarah's bought a new car.	What sort _____ ?
f We saw Bill yesterday.	Where ____ you _____ ?
g Sue's watching television.	What _____ ?
h They're going on holiday.	Where _____ ?
i Peter's left the party.	Why _____ ?
j She drank a lot of wine.	How much _____ ?

20

3 Past Simple and Present Perfect

Underline the correct tense, the Past Simple or the Present Perfect.

Example
I *saw*/have seen Jill yesterday.

a   I *met*/*have met* Anna ten years ago.
b   My sister *did never go*/*has never been* to France.
c   I'm sorry. I *didn't finish*/*haven't finished* my work yet.
d   I *ate*/*have eaten* a lot of ice-cream when I was a child.
e   They *climbed*/*have climbed* Everest in 1953.

5

4 Adverb or adjective?

Underline the correct form.

Example
I'm driving *careful*/*carefully* because it is raining.

a   Our village is always very *quiet*/*quietly*. Nothing happens.
b   Please speak more *slow*/*slowly*. I can't understand you.
c   She's a very *good*/*well* driver.
d   He doesn't drive very *good*/*well*.
e   My grandparents are very strong and *healthy*/*healthily* for their age.

5

5 Infinitive or *-ing*?

Put the verb in brackets in the correct form, infinitive or *-ing*.

Example
I'd like ____to go____ (go) to Greece next year.

a   Both my husband and I enjoy _____ (cook) very much.
b   Our new neighbours are difficult _____ (get) on with.
c   We've decided _____ (move) to the countryside.
d   Have you finished _____ (paint) the kitchen yet?
e   My uncle needs _____ (see) a doctor about his leg.

10

6 Word order

Put the words into the correct order.

Example
letter you yet have the written?
Have you written the letter yet?

a many got you how cousins have?

_____

b Rome they just have in arrived

_____

c smoking Jane up gave ago years three

_____

d quickly road along man the walked the

_____

e by play a have Shakespeare seen ever you?

_____

f has Mary party decided to to the go?

_____

g says English learn easy is teacher my that to

_____

h meeting did parents Bob's you enjoy?

_____

i people going many invite party how are to
to your you?

_____

j us they their car told about new

_____

10

7 Auxiliaries

1 Put one of the following auxiliary verbs into the gaps.

am/is/are	do/does/did	have/has

Example
I _am_ listening to music.

a Look at those children! They _____ smoking
cigarettes!

b _____ your daughter speak French well?

c _____ you learn German when you were at school?

d _____ Ben ever been to India?

e We _____ never played volleyball.

f I _____ going to give up smoking soon.

g _____ Mark and Jane live near you?

h _____ John going to phone you tomorrow?

i When _____ you learn to drive? A long time ago?

j _____ you written to thank Sue and Bill yet?

10

8 Vocabulary – word groups

Put the following words into the correct columns.

detective story jumbo jet engaged title head
horror story neck platform nose journey passenger
hands helicopter dial take off station face ringing
timetable characters train mouth dictionary arrival
departure operator biography call return ticket foot

Travel	Parts of the body	Telephoning	Books

20

9 Prepositions

Put a preposition from the box into each gap.

about in out of by on for to from

a I'm reading a book _____ the history of France.

b *Oliver Twist* is a book _____ Charles Dickens.

c Is it far _____ your house to the station?

d Is Mexico City the biggest city _____ the world?

e Jane's worried _____ her exam.

f What's _____ television tonight?

g Are you interested _____ politics?

h She works _____ a big company.

i Can I speak _____ you for a moment?

j He drove _____ the garage and down
the street.

10

Total 100

TRANSLATE

Translate the sentences into your language. Translate the
ideas, not word by word.

1 Tim drives carefully. Tim's a careful driver.

_____

2 Have you ever been to China? I went to China last year.

_____

3 He hasn't finished his homework yet.

_____

4 I've just finished my homework.

_____

5 I want to go home.

_____

6 I enjoy reading.

_____

Tapescript section

UNIT 1

Tapescript 1a

A Hello. My name's Jenny. What's your name?
B Anna.
A Where are you from, Anna?
B I'm from New York.

Tapescript 1b

A Hello. My name's Thomas. What's your name?
B Johann.
A Where are you from, Johann?
B I'm from Berlin. Where are you from?
A I'm from Oxford.

Tapescript 2

My name's Mayumi Kimura, and I'm a student. I'm 19 years old. I'm not married. I have two brothers and a sister. I live in a flat in Osaka, Japan. I want to learn English because it's an international language.

Tapescript 3

France	Spain	Greece	
England	Egypt	Russia	
Brazil	Japan		
Germany	Mexico	Hungary	Italy

Tapescript 4

1 He's from Spain.
2 I'm sixteen.
3 Her name's Pat.
4 They're from Britain.
5 Where's she from?
6 He's a teacher in France.

Tapescript 5

a A Hello, Mary. How are you?
  B Fine, thank you. And you?
  A I'm OK, thanks.

b A Hi, Dave. How are you?
  B Not bad, thanks. And you?
  A Very well. How are the children?
  B They're fine.

c A Goodbye, Chris.
  B Goodbye, Anne. Have a nice evening.
  A Thanks, Chris. See you tomorrow.

Tapescript 6

a stamp   a bag   a map   a key
an apple   a postcard   a ticket   a notebook
an orange   a letter   a suitcase   a camera
a dictionary   an envelope   a newspaper
a magazine

Tapescript 7a

a	h	j	k		
b	c	d	e	g	p	t	v
f	l	m	n	s	x	z
i	y				
o					
q	u	w			
r					

Tapescript 7b

The alphabet song

a	b	c	d	e	f	g	h	i	j	k	l
m	n	o	p								
l	m	n	o	p	q	r	s	t			
l	m	n	o	p	q	r	s	t			
u	v	w	x	y	z						

That is the English alphabet.

Tapescript 7c

name	N - A - M - E
sister	S - I - S - T - E - R
flat	F - L - A - T
student	S - T - U - D - E - N - T
doctor	D - O - C - T - O - R
house	H - O - U - S - E
letter	L - E - double T - E - R
married	M - A - double R - I - E - D
apple	A - double P - L - E
job	J - O - B

Tapescript 7d

A How do you spell your first name?
B J - A - M - E - S.
A How do you spell your surname?
B H - A - double R - I - S - O - N.
A James Harrison.
B That's right.

UNIT 2

Tapescript 8

Numbers
5   20   16   32   50   12

Phone numbers
791463   859 6 double 2   503 971
010 double 3 1 46 58 93 94

Tapescript 9

A What's her surname?
B Hopkins.
A What's her first name?
B Mary.
A Where's she from?
B England.
A What's her job?
B She's a journalist.

A What's her address?
B 35, North Street, Bristol.
A What's her phone number?
B 0272 478 2209.
A How old is she?
B Twenty-three.
A Is she married?
B No, she isn't.

Tapescript 10

This is a photo of Martin, his wife, and his children. His wife's name is Jennifer. She's a dentist. His daughter's name is Alison. She's twenty-three and she's a hairdresser. His son's name is Andy. He's nineteen and he's a student. Alison's boyfriend is a travel agent. His name is Joe.

Tapescript 11

a It's big.
b It's small.
c She's old.
d She's young.
e They're expensive.
f They're cheap.
g It's horrible.
h It's lovely.
i It's easy.
j It's difficult.
k They're old.
l They're new.
m They're hot.
n They're cold.
o It's right.
p It's wrong.

Tapescript 12a

Paola's letter to David (see page 16)

Tapescript 12b

P = Paola   K = Kurt

1 P Hello. My name's Paola.
  K Hello, Paola. I'm Kurt.
  P Where are you from?
  K I'm from Switzerland. And you? Where are you from?
  P I'm from Rome.
  K Ah! I'm from Zurich.
  P Zurich is very beautiful.
  K Yes, it is.

T = ticket seller

2 P A ticket to Green Park, please.
  T Two pounds fifty.
  P One ... two ... and fifty p.
  T Thank you. Here's your ticket.
  P Thanks.

B = Peter Briscall   C = class

3 B Good morning!
  C Good morning!
    Good morning, Peter!
    Hello!
  B How are you today?
  C Fine.
    OK.
  B How are you, Paola?
  P I'm fine thank you, Peter. And you?
  B Very well! Now, the lesson today is ...

C = assistant in café   K = Kurt

4 C Yes?
  P A coffee, please.
  C Black or white?
  P Sorry?
  C Black or white? Milk?
  P Ah! Black, please. No milk.
  C Sixty p, please.
  P Thanks.
  P Urgh!! It's horrible!
  K English coffee is very bad!

C = Catherine   T = Thomas

5 C Is your teacher good, Paola?
  P Pardon?
  C Your teacher. At the school of English.
  P Ah! Yes! Peter.
  C Is he OK?
  P Yes. He's very nice. He's funny.
  T What's your dad's job, Paola?
  P Pardon? I ...
  T Your dad. What's his job?
  P My dad ...?
  C Say father, Thomas, not dad.
  T Ah, OK. What's your father's job, Paola?
  P Now I understand. My father's job, yes.
    Um ... He's a doctor, yes.
  T Ah, right!

Tapescript 13a

sandwiches	
a ham sandwich	£1.50
a cheese sandwich	£1.30
a tuna sandwich	£1.70
a chicken sandwich	£2.00
a piece of pizza	90p
a hamburger	£2.50
an ice-cream	80p
a cup of tea	
a cup of coffee	

a Coke
an orange juice
a mineral water

A How much is a cup of tea?
B 50p.
A How much is a cup of coffee?
B 70p.
A How much is a Coke?
B 60p.
A How much is an orange juice?
B 60p.
A How much is a mineral water?
B 80p.

Tapescript 13b

a A Hello.
  B Hello. Can I have a ham sandwich, please?
  A Here you are. Anything else?
  B No, thanks.
  A One pound fifty, please.
  B Thanks.
  A Thank you.
b A Hi.
  B Hello. Can I have a cheese sandwich, please?
  A Anything to drink?
  B Yes. A cup of tea, please.
  A OK. Here you are.
  B How much is that?
  A One pound eighty, please.
  B Thanks.
c A Good morning.
  B Morning.
  A Can I have a hamburger and a cup of coffee, please?
  B OK. Here you are.
  A Thanks. How much is that?
  B Three pounds twenty.
  A One, two, three pounds ... twenty p.
  B Thanks.
  A Thank you.

UNIT 3

Tapescript 14

Sister Mary
Hans Huser
(see page 19)

Tapescript 15a

A Where does Sister Mary come from?
B Ireland.
A What does she do?
B She's a teacher.
A Does she speak French?
B Yes, she does.
A Does she speak German?
B No, she doesn't.

Tapescript 15b

a A Where does Hans come from?
  B Switzerland.
b A What does he do?
  B He's a ski-instructor.
c A Does he speak French and German?
  B Yes, he does.
d A Does he speak Spanish?
  B No, he doesn't.

Tapescript 16a

1 Georges comes from Paris.
2 Georges lives in London.
3 He works in the centre of Paris.
4 In his free time he plays tennis.
5 Keiko comes from China.
6 She lives in Washington.
7 She speaks French and German.
8 She's married to an American.
9 Mark comes from England.
10 He works in Liverpool.
11 He speaks Italian.
12 In his free time he goes walking.

Tapescript 16b

1 She likes her job.
2 She loves walking.
3 She's married.
4 Does he have three children?
5 Where does he go?
6 She watches the television.

Tapescript 17

a A Good morning, sir. Can I see your ticket?
  B Yes, of course. Here you are.
  A Thank you. Maidstone next stop.
  B Thank you.
b A Good morning, boys and girls.
  B Good morning, Mr Garret.
  A Can I have your homework, please?
  B It's on your desk, Mr Garret.
  A Thank you.
c A Goodbye, Frank. Have a good journey!
  B Thank you very much.
  A See you next Monday.
  B Yes, of course. Goodbye!
d A Excuse me. Is this seat free?
  B Yes, it is.
  A Thank you. It's cold this evening.
  B It certainly is. And the sea's very black!
e A Hello darling! Are you tired?
  B Yes, I am. And cold.
  A Sit down and have a glass of wine.
  B Mmmm! Thank you. I'm hungry, too.

Tapescript 18a

It's five o'clock.   It's eight o'clock.   It's half past five.   It's half past eleven.
It's quarter past five.   It's quarter past two.   It's quarter to six.   It's quarter to nine.
It's five past five.   It's ten past five.   It's twenty past five.   It's twenty-five past five.
It's twenty-five to six.   It's twenty to six.   It's ten to six.   It's five to six.

Tapescript 18b

A Excuse me. Can you tell me the time, please?
B Yes, of course. It's six o' clock.
A Thanks.

A Excuse me. Can you tell me the time, please?
B I'm sorry. I don't know. I don't have a watch.

UNIT 4

Tapescript 19a

On Fridays I come home from the BBC at about 2.00 in the afternoon and I just relax. On Friday evenings I don't go out, but sometimes a friend comes for dinner. He or she brings the wine and I cook the meal. I love cooking! We listen to music or we just chat.
On Saturday mornings I get up at 9.00 and I go shopping. Then in the evenings I sometimes go to the theatre or the opera with a friend – I love opera! Then we eat in my favourite Chinese restaurant.
On Sunday... Oh, on Sunday mornings I stay in bed late, I don't get up until 11.00! Sometimes in the afternoon I visit my sister. She lives in the country and has two children. I like playing with my niece and nephew, but I leave early because I go to bed at 8.00 on Sunday evenings!

Tapescript 19b

A Do you go out on Friday afternoons?
B No, I don't.
A What do you do?
B I just relax.
A Do you stay at home on Friday evenings?
B Yes, I do.
A What do you do?
B I cook dinner for friends.

Tapescript 20

1 What does he do on Sundays?
2 I stay at home on Thursday evenings.
3 He lives here.
4 I eat a lot.
5 Where do you go on Saturday evenings?
6 She likes cars.

Tapescript 21a

Mr and Mrs Forrester have a son and a daughter. The son lives at home, and the daughter is a student at university. Mr Forrester is a journalist. He works for *The Times*. He writes articles about restaurants. 'I love food!' he says.

Tapescript 21b

'Every spring the children go skiing, so my wife and I go to Paris on holiday. We stay in a hotel near the River Seine. We have breakfast in the hotel, but we have lunch in a restaurant. French food is delicious! We walk a lot, but sometimes we go by taxi. After four days we don't want to go home and go back to work.'

Tapescript 22a

Al Wheeler
Manuela da Silva
Toshi Suzuki
(see page 29)

Tapescript 22b

M = Manuela J = Jane F = Manuela's friends
P = Portuguese man
1 M Hello, everybody! This is my friend Jane, from England.
   F Hi!
     Hello!
     Hello, Jane!
   J Hello. Pleased to meet you.
   M Sit down here, Jane.
   J Thanks.
   P Do you like this music, Jane?
   J Mm. Is it American?
   P No, it's Brazilian jazz!
   M Come and have a drink, Jane ...

T = Toshi J = Ann Jones
2 T Mrs Jones! How do you do?
   J How do you do?

T Please come in. You're from our office in London, aren't you?
J Yes, that's right.
T Welcome to Tokyo! Do you like our headquarters here?
J Yes. It's very big. How many people work here?
T About six thousand people. Do you want to see our offices? ...

A = Al   M = Mick (Scottish)

3 A What do you want to do today, Mick?
M Ooh, I don't know. What do you ...
A Well, do you like fishing?
M Yes. I sometimes go fishing in a river near my house in Scotland.
A Well, here it's different. This is a very big country. I go fishing on a lake. It's a hundred kilometres long!
M A hundred kilometres!
A Yeah! There are fish this big! Are you interested? Do you want to go?
M OK!
A Right. You want a fishing line ...

Tapescript 23

a A Excuse me!
  B Yes?
  A Do you have a light?
  B I'm sorry. I don't smoke.
  A That's OK.

b A I'm sorry I'm late. The traffic is bad today.
  B Don't worry. Come and sit down. We're on page 25.

c A Can I open the window? It's very hot in here.
  B Really? I'm quite cold.
  A OK. It doesn't matter.

d G Excuse me!
  H Can I help you?
  G Can I have a film for my camera?
  H How many exposures?
  G Pardon?
  H How many exposures?
  G What does *exposures* mean?
  H How many pictures? 24? 36?
  G Ah! Now I understand! 36, please.

UNIT 5
Tapescript 24

A Is there a stereo?   A Are there any books?
B Yes, there is.   B Yes, there are.
A Is there a clock?   A Are there any magazines?
B No, there isn't.   B No, there aren't.

Tapescript 25
Picture A

There are four pictures on the walls and a mirror. There are three people in the room, a man, a woman, and a girl. There's a lovely fire and the cat is in front of the fire, sleeping. There's a lamp near the window, and a clock on the wall near the mirror. There's a photo on the television and there are some newspapers on the floor near the television. There's a glass of beer on the table in front of the man. The television isn't on.

Picture B

There are two people in the room. There's a man on the sofa and a woman next to him. The cat's in front of the fire. There are four pictures on the walls.

There are two plants, one on the left of the fire and one on the right. On the table in front of the man there are some cups and some books and on the table next to the sofa there is a telephone.

Tapescript 26

It's a modern kitchen, nice and clean with a lot of cupboards. There's a washing machine, a fridge and a cooker, but there isn't a dishwasher. There are some lovely pictures on the walls, but there aren't any photographs. There's a radio near the cooker. There are some flowers, but there aren't any plants. On the table there are some apples and oranges. Ah! And there are some cups and plates next to the sink.

Tapescript 27

What's in my bag? Well, there's a newpaper – a French newspaper – and there's my dictionary. I have some pens, three, I think. There's a photo of my wife and a photo of my childen. I have my notebook for vocabulary, of course. I write words in that every day. I have some keys, and that's all! I don't have any stamps and I don't have a bus ticket. Oh, and I have a letter, from my bank manager. He wants my money!

Tapescript 28
Anne-Marie

I live in a house in the country in Provence in the south of France. It's an old farmhouse, about five hundred years old, with very thick walls, so it's warm in winter and cool in summer, but it's difficult to look after because it's so old. There are three bedrooms, two quite big and one small, and they have wonderful views over the countryside. I have a garden where I grow flowers and vegetables. I live with my animals! I have two dogs and eight cats.

Harry

Where I live things are big. I live in Texas – that's the second biggest state in the USA – and I live with my wife and our four children. We have ten cars because we all like driving. Sometimes we drive 150 kilometres to go to a restaurant! Our house is three years old, and it's kind of big. There are fourteen or fifteen bedrooms, I don't know exactly, and outside there are two swimming pools and ... a golf course ... and some grass for my plane to land on.

Dave and Maggie

Maggie We have a small house in an area of Dublin called Donnybrook. It's quite a small house. There's a living room and a kitchen downstairs, and then two small bedrooms upstairs, but it's big enough for us. There's my husband and me, and our son, Thomas.
Dave The houses around here are about a hundred years old and people are very friendly. People don't want to move away, they want to live near their family, so my parents are very close…
Maggie ... and my mother lives next door! We have a small garden where Thomas plays, and I go out and have a chat with my mother!

Thanos

I live in a flat on the fourth floor. I live alone. There's a kitchen where I cook and eat, a living room with a balcony, and two small bedrooms. I live in Athina – you say Athens in English – but not in the centre of town because there are too many cars. It's a nice area. The shops aren't too far, and the flat is comfortable. It's about five years old, which I like. I don't like old buildings.

Tapescript 29

a A Excuse me! Is there a chemist's near here?
  B Yes. It's over there.
  A Thanks.

b A Excuse me! Is there a sports club near here?
  B Yes. It's in Queen Street. Take the second street on the right.
  A Thanks.

c A Excuse me! Is there a newsagent's near here?
  B Yes. There's one in Church Street next to the bank and there's one in Park Lane opposite the swimming pool.
  A Is that one far?
  B No. Just two minutes, that's all.

d A Is there a cinema near here?
  B Take the first left, and it's on the left, opposite the flower shop.
  A Thanks a lot.

UNIT 6
Tapescript 30a

a A Can you speak Japanese?
  B No, I can't.
b I can't hear you. The line's bad.
c A Can you use a word processor?
  B Yes, I can.
d I can't spell your name.
e Cats can see in the dark.
f She can type fifty words a minute.

Tapescript 30b

a I can type, but I can't spell.
b He can sing and he can dance.
c A Can you cook?
  B Yes, I can.
d They can ski, but they can't swim.
e We can read and we can write.
f A Can she drive?
  B No, she can't.

Tapescript 31
Sarah

Well, there are a lot of things I can't do! I can't draw and I can't drive a car, but I want to have lessons. I can ... I can type and I can use a word processor, because I have one at work and I use it all the time. What about sports? Mm. Well, I certainly can't ski, but I'm quite good at tennis, yes, I can play tennis. Well, I usually win when I play with my friends. And I can swim, of course. And I can cook. I think I'm a very good, well, no, just good ... a good cook! Now, then ... languages. I can speak French and German, I don't know any Italian at all, and I know about five words in Spanish – *adios, mañana, paella* – no, I can't speak Spanish! And I can't play any musical instruments, not the piano, the guitar, or anything.

Tapescript 32

A What day was it yesterday?
B It was Thursday.
A Where were you yesterday?
B I was at school.
A Were you at home yesterday?
B Yes, I was.
A The restaurant was cheap. But the food wasn't very good.

A Could you play the piano when you were six?
B No, I couldn't.

Tapescript 33

Sue Were you at Eve's party last Saturday?
Bill Yes, I was.
Sue Was it good?
Bill Well, it was OK.
Sue Were there many people?
Bill Yes, there were.
Sue Was Tom there?
Bill No, he wasn't. And where were you?
Sue Oh ... I couldn't go because I was at Adam's party! It was brilliant!

Tapescript 34a

This is flight information for today, 24 June. British Airways flight BA 516 to Geneva at gate 14, last call. Flight BA 516 to Geneva, last call, gate 14. Scandinavian Airlines flight SK 832 to Frankfurt at gate 7, last call. Flight SK 832 to Frankfurt, last call, gate 7. Air France flight AF 472 to Amsterdam is delayed thirty minutes. Flight AF 472 to Amsterdam, delayed thirty minutes. Lufthansa flight LH 309 to Miami, now boarding at gate 32. Flight LH 309 to Miami now boarding at gate 32. Virgin flight VS 876 to New York, now boarding at gate 20. Flight VS 876, now boarding at gate 20. Passengers are reminded to keep their luggage with them at all times. Thank you.

Tapescript 34b

At the airport
(see page 45)

Tapescript 34c

a Was it Gate 4 or 14?
b Can I see your passport, please?
c Smoking or non-smoking?
d Can I have your tray please, madam?
e Excuse me. I think that's my suitcase.
f Welcome to England! Was your flight good?

UNIT 7

Tapescript 35a

Text B
Ellen's father died in the war in 1915 and her mother died a year later. Ellen was twelve years old. Immediately she started work as a housemaid with a rich family in London.

Tapescript 35b

Text C
She worked from 5.30 in the morning until 9.00 at night. She cleaned all the rooms in the house before breakfast. She earned £25 a year.
In 1921 she moved to another family. She liked her new job because she looked after the children. There were five children, four sons and one daughter. She loved them, especially the baby, Robert. She stayed with that family for twenty years. Ellen never married. She just looked after other people's children until she retired when she was seventy years old.

Tapescript 36a

a I was only twelve years old when my mother died and I started work.
b I was always tired in my first job because I worked very long hours.
c I started work at 5.30 in the morning and I finished at 9.00 in the evening.
d Now I live in a village, but in 1920 I lived in London.
e Now I look after my five cats. In the 1920s I looked after five children.
f I loved all the children, but I loved Robert especially.
g Robert's over seventy now and I still see him. He visited me just last month.

Tapescript 36b

worked	lived	died	started	loved
finished	looked	visited	cleaned	liked
stayed	moved			

Tapescript 37

Where was she born?
When did she die?
When did her father die?
When did she marry Prince Albert?
Where did they live?
How many children did they have?

Tapescript 38

had	came	worked	went
left	hated	got	gave
became	wrote	changed	won
lost	found	bought	sold

Tapescript 39

What can I remember? Well, I left school in 1982. I was unemployed for two years, but then I found a job in an office. I sold computer software to businesses.
Suddenly computers were everywhere! Banks, hotels, hospitals, schools, homes. My Mum and Dad bought a video recorder in 1985, and my little brother got a computer video game for his birthday in 1986.
Near the end of the 1980s things got worse and in 1990 I lost my job.
Now, sport. Well, in 1980 the United States didn't go to the Olympics in Moscow, and in 1984 the USSR didn't go to the Olympics in Los Angeles, but they both went to Seoul in 1988.
Argentina won the World Cup in 1986, and Germany won it in 1990.
What about politics? Well, Mrs Thatcher was our Prime Minister for the whole of the 1980s. Reagan became the US president in 1981, Gorbachev gave the world *glasnost* and *perestroika*, and the Berlin Wall came down in 1989. Then all sorts of things changed.

Tapescript 40a

a	walk	d	writer	g	work	j	half
b	listen	e	autumn	h	short	k	foreign
c	know	f	farm	i	high	l	daughter

Tapescript 40b

a	talk	f	white
b	born	g	knife
c	bought	h	wrong
d	world	i	cupboard
e	answer	j	Christmas

Tapescript 41a

a A Ugh! Work again! I hate Mondays!
   B Me too. Did you have a nice weekend?
   A Yes. It was wonderful.

b Happy birthday to you.
   Happy birthday to you.
   Happy birthday, dear Katie.
   Happy birthday to you.

c A How many Easter eggs did you get?
   B Six. What about you?
   A Five. I had them all on Easter morning before lunch.
   B Did you?
   A And then I was sick!
   B Ugh!

d A Congratulations!
   B Oh ... thank you very much.
   A When's the happy day?
   B Pardon?
   A Your wedding day. When is it?
   B Oh! We're not sure yet. Some time in June, probably.

e A Hello! Merry Christmas, everyone!
   B Merry Christmas! Come in, come in. It's so cold outside.

f A Wonderful! It's Friday!
   B Yes. Have a nice weekend!
   A Same to you.

Tapescript 41b

a Did you have a nice weekend?
b Happy birthday!
c Merry Christmas!
d Have a nice weekend!
e Congratulations!

UNIT 8

Tapescript 42

The hamburger
An American chef from Connecticut, Louis Lassen, made and sold the first hamburgers in 1895. He called them hamburgers because sailors from Hamburg in Germany gave him the recipe. Students from Yale University and businessmen loved them and bought them. Kenneth Lassen, Louis' grandson still sells hamburgers in Connecticut.

Television
A Scotsman, John Logie Baird, transmitted the first television picture on 25 October, 1925. The first person on television was a boy who worked in the office next to Baird's workroom in London.
In 1927 Baird sent pictures from London to Glasgow. In 1928 he sent pictures to New York and also produced the first colour TV pictures.

The ball-point pen
A Hungarian, Laszlo Biro, made the first ball-point pen in 1938. In 1944 the British Army bought thirty thousand because soldiers could write with them outside in the rain. At the end of the war 'Biros' quickly became very popular all over the world. In 1948 a shop in New York sold ten thousand on one day.

Tapescript 43

A Did you know that Marco Polo brought spaghetti back from China?
B Really? He didn't! That's incredible!
A Well, it's true!

A Did you know that Napoleon was afraid of cats?
B He wasn't! I don't believe it!
A Well, it's true!

Tapescript 44

On 1 June 1992 a French burglar broke into a house in Paris. He went into the living room and stole two pictures. Then he went into the kitchen. He opened the fridge and saw some cheese. He was hungry, so he ate all the cheese. Next he saw two bottles of champagne. He was very thirsty, so he drank both bottles. Then he felt sleepy. He went upstairs for a rest, but he was tired and he fell asleep. When he woke up the next morning, there were four policemen around the bed.

Tapescript 45

Wendy Mint

Well, it was five years ago. A Sunday evening five years ago. I was in the bath and the radio was on. Er ... I always listen to pop music in the bath. Suddenly I heard this voice, the disc jockey's voice. It was beautiful, really beautiful. Warm and friendly. I thought, 'Oh! What a lovely voice!' I think I fell in love then, with his voice. Well, I listened to the end of the programme and I heard his name, Oliver Mint. I loved the name, too.

Well, er ... usually I'm quite shy, but this time I wasn't. I went to the telephone and I rang the radio station. I couldn't believe it! Suddenly there was his voice on the telephone! And we talked and talked, for about half an hour. And he said, 'Where do you live?' so I told him, and then he said, 'Can we meet?' And I said 'Yes, please!' So we met in an Italian restaurant the next evening. I was so nervous, but it was wonderful! We got married a month later and now we have a lovely baby boy. He's nearly two!

Trevor Richards

Well, I have a baker's shop. I make all the bread and cakes for it. And one day ... it was a very hot day in summer, er ... the summer of 1976, and it was lunchtime and er ... this beautiful girl came into the shop. She was with some friends and I could hear that they weren't English, but they spoke English very well and er ... they all bought sandwiches and went to the park. Well, I couldn't forget her. The way she smiled, the way she laughed, her blue, blue eyes. I waited and watched every lunchtime but she didn't come back into the shop.

Then suddenly, there she was again, and so I said, 'Hello again. You're still in England, then?' And she said, 'Yes. But this is my last day. I go back to Sweden tomorrow.' And she smiled. Now, usually I'm shy, but I took a small pink cake and I wrote *I love you* on it. And when she asked for a chicken sandwich, I looked into the blue, blue eyes and I gave her the cake! She laughed and said, 'I didn't know English men were so romantic!' Well, after that she went back to Sweden, but we wrote letters and in 1978 we got married. Now we work together in the shop and we have three children.

Tapescript 46a

first   second   third   fourth   fifth
sixth   tenth   twelfth   thirteenth
sixteenth   seventeenth   twentieth
twenty-first   thirtieth   thirty-first

Tapescript 46b

the first of April   April the first
the second of March   March the second
the seventh of September   September the seventeenth
the nineteenth of November   November the nineteenth

the twenty-third of June   June the twenty-third

the fifteenth of July, nineteen sixty-seven
the twenty-ninth of February, nineteen seventy-six
the nineteenth of December, nineteen eighty-three
the third of October, nineteen seventy
the thirty-first of May, nineteen ninety-three

Tapescript 46c

1   The fourth of January
2   May the seventh, nineteen twenty-two
3   The thirtieth of August, nineteen sixty-five
4   A   It was Friday. I know it was Friday!
      B   No, it wasn't. It was Saturday!
      A   No. I remember. It was Friday the thirteenth. The thirteenth of October!
5   A   Oh no! I forgot your birthday.
      B   It doesn't matter, really.
      A   It was last Sunday, the second. June the second. Oh I am sorry!
6   A   Hey! Did you know this? Shakespeare was born and died on the same day!
      B   That's not possible!
      A   Yes, it is. He was born on April the twenty-third, fifteen sixty-four and he died on April the twenty-third, sixteen sixteen!

UNIT 9

Tapescript 47

A   I don't like tea.
B   Oh, I do. Well, sometimes. But coffee's horrible.
A   Yeah.
B   I don't like wine, either.
A   My dad does, and my mum. They have it every day.
B   I quite like apple juice, but it can be really sweet and yuk.
A   I love beer! When my dad has some, I always take some.
B   Milk, I like milk.
A   Me, too, especially on cereal.
B   Water's just water. It's boring.
A   I like bread, but only if there's nothing else.
B   Mmm! I love bread and cheese.
A   I hate cheese. But I adore ice-cream. Mmm! Any ice-cream! All ice-cream! Yummy!
B   So do I. And chocolate. Lovely chocolate!
A   Mmm, chocolate! I quite like rice, but not a lot.
B   Me, too. But I like fruit.
A   Yeah, I like fruit, especially strawberries and apples.
B   Oranges are boring, but bananas are OK.
A   I like bananas with a bit of milk and sugar.
B   Oh, yuk! That's disgusting!
A   No, it isn't. ... I don't like eggs at all.
B   What about the rest? Biscuits, yes. Sandwiches, no. Tomatoes, yuk.
BOTH   Hamburgers, YES!

Tapescript 48

a   A   I'm thirsty.
      B   Would you like some tea?
      A   No, thanks.
      B   Would you like some apple juice?
      B   Oh, yes, please!
b   A   I'm hungry. Is there anything to eat?
      B   Would you like a biscuit?
      A   No, thanks. I'd like a sandwich.
      B   Cheese? Ham?
      A   Cheese *and* ham, please!

Tapescript 49a

1   Good afternoon. Can I help you?
2   Who's your favourite writer?
3   What would you like for Christmas?
4   Do you like animals?
5   Here's the wine list, sir.
6   Have some cream with your strawberries!

Tapescript 49b

1   A   Good afternoon. Can I help you?
      B   Yes. I'd like some fruit, please.
2   A   Who's your favourite writer?
      B   I like books by John le Carré.
3   A   What would you like for Christmas?
      B   I'd like a new bike.
4   A   Do you like animals?
      B   I like cats, but I don't like dogs.
5   A   Here's the wine list, sir.
      B   We'd like a bottle of French red wine.
6   A   Have some cream with your strawberries!
      B   No, thanks. I don't like cream.

Tapescript 50

A   Morning.
B   Good morning.
A   How can I help you?
B   I'd like some orange juice, please.
A   Er ... sorry. There's apple juice, but no orange juice.
B   Oh! What's that? Isn't that orange juice?
A   Oh, yes. So it is! My eyes! There you are.
B   Thank you. And some potatoes, please.
A   A bag like this?
B   Yes, fine. Now, some milk.
A   Sorry. I sold the last bottle just two minutes ago.
B   Oh, dear! What about some coffee?
A   Yes. There you are.
B   Thanks. Orange juice, potatoes, milk, coffee ... A kilo of apples, please.
A   I don't sell apples.
B   Really? That's strange. What about cheese? Do you have any cheese?
A   No, I don't sell cheese, either.
B   No cheese? That's incredible! OK. Now, I want some pizza, but I'm sure you don't sell pizza, do you?
A   Yes, sir. Pizza with mushrooms, pizza with cheese and ham, pizza with sausage, and pizza with tomatoes.
B   Wow! Can I have some ... pizza with cheese and ham, please?
A   Sorry, sir. Usually I have pizza, but not on Thursdays. Today's Thursday.
B   I see. I don't suppose you have any bread.
A   You're right.
B   Pardon?
A   You're right. There isn't any bread.
B   Tell me. Do you do a lot of business?
A   Oh, yes, sir. The shop's open all the time.
B   What do people buy?
A   All the things you can see.
B   Well, that's all for me. How much?
A   One pound twenty, please.
B   Thank you. Goodbye.
A   See you again soon, sir.
B   (to himself)   I don't think so.

Tapescript 51

a   A   Have another cream cake, my dear. They're delicious!
      B   I couldn't. I'm full.
      A   Oh, go on!

B   Well, all right. Just one more. That chocolate one.

b   A   Yes, please. Who's next?
    B   Hello. Can I have a chicken and salad sandwich in a brown roll, please?
    A   Salt and pepper?
    B   Yes, please.
    A   Anything else?
    B   Yes. An apple and a mineral water.
    A   Two, three ... three pounds forty.
    B   Thanks.

M = Mum T = Tom L = Lily

c   M   Tom! Lily! You're late. It's 8.30!
    T   I know, I know. I'm ready.
    M   Where's Lily?
    T   In the bathroom, I think.
    M   Still? Lily? Lily?
    L   Yes, Mum?
    M   Come on! It's 8.30.
    L   OK.
    M   Are you ready, Tom?
    T   Yes, Mum.
    M   Don't yes Mum me.
    T   No, Mum.
    M   Right, Lily, are you ready?
    L   Where's my school bag?
    M   I don't know. It's *your* bag.
    T   Here it is.
    M   Right. See you later. Give me a kiss.
    ALL Bye! See you!

d   A   Yes, please.
    B   Hello. Can I order a take-away, please?
    A   Yes, sir. What would you like?
    B   A chicken curry ... not too hot.
    A   Yes, sir.
    B   And some rice. That's all..
    A   Thank you, sir. About fifteen minutes. Is that OK?
    B   That's fine, thanks.

M = Mum D = Dad T = Tom L = Lily

e   D   Come on! It's ready.
    L   Pardon?
    D   It's ready. Dinner's on the table.
    L   OK.
    T   Mm! It smells good! What is it?
    D   Spaghetti Bolognese. Come and sit down.
    M   How was school today?
    T   OK.
    M   Were you late?
    L   No. Well, a little.

Same family + G = Grandmother

f   G   Mm. That beef was lovely, my dear.
    M   Thank you, Mother.
    D   Some more wine, Mum.
    G   No, thank you, James. One glass is enough for me. Really, Jane, I don't know how you make your gravy, but it's always so delicious!
    M   You say that every time, Mother, and I tell you how I cook it every time. It's always the same way. Meat juices and vegetable juices. Now, Mother, what about some dessert? There's fruit salad or apple pie and cream. What would you like?
    G   Well, just a little, then.
    M   Which one?
    G   Both, of course.

Tapescript 52

A   Good evening. Can I help you?
B   Yes, please. Could I have a room for the night?
A   Certainly. A single room or a double?
B   Single, please.
A   Would you like a room with a shower or a bath?

B   A shower. How much is the room?
A   £72 for the room and breakfast. Would you like an evening meal?
B   No, thanks. Just breakfast. Can I pay by credit card?
A   Yes, of course. We take Visa and Access. Could you sign the register, please?
B   Yes, sure. Do you want my address, too?
A   No. Just a signature. Do you have any luggage?
B   Just this one bag.
A   Here's your key. Your room number is 311. I hope you enjoy your stay.
B   Thanks.

UNIT 10
Tapescript 53

The country is cheaper than the city.
The country is safer than the city.
The city is noisier than the country.
The country is healthier than the city.
The city is more expensive than the country.
The city is more interesting than the country.
The city is better than the country.

Tapescript 54

a   A   The country is quieter than the city.
    B   Yes, that's true. The city is much noisier.
b   A   New York is safer than London.
    B   No, it isn't. New York is much more dangerous.
c   A   The streets of New York are cleaner than the streets of Paris.
    B   No, they aren't. They're much dirtier.
d   A   Paris is bigger than Madrid.
    B   No, it isn't. It's much smaller.
e   A   Madrid is more expensive than Rome.
    B   No, it isn't. Madrid is much cheaper.
f   A   The buildings in Rome are more modern than the buildings in New York.
    B   No, they aren't. They're much older.
g   A   The Underground in London is better than the Metro in Paris.
    B   No, it isn't! The Underground is much worse.

Tapescript 55

F   Why did you leave? You had a good job in London.
A   Yes, but I've got a better job here.
F   And you had a beautiful flat in London.
A   Well, I've got a house here.
F   Really? How many bedrooms has it got?
A   Three. And it's got a garden. It's nicer than my flat and it's cheaper. Everything is much cheaper here.
F   But you haven't got any friends!
A   I've got a lot of friends here. Everybody is very friendly. People are much friendlier than in London.
F   But the country's so boring!
A   No it isn't. It's much more interesting than London. Seaton has got shops, cinemas, theatres, and parks. And the air is cleaner and the streets are safer.
F   OK. OK. Everything is wonderful! So when can I visit you?

Tapescript 56

a   Seaview is the most expensive house.
b   Park House is the most modern house.
c   Seaview is the biggest house.

d   Seaview has got the biggest garden.
e   Park House is the nearest to the town centre.
f   Park House is the farthest from the sea.

Tapescript 57a

a   A   The Ritz is a very expensive hotel.
    B   Yes, it's the most expensive hotel in London.
b   A   Hambledon is a very pretty village.
    B   Yes, it's the prettiest village in England.
c   A   Everest is a very high mountain.
    B   Yes, it's the highest mountain in the world.
d   A   Meryl Streep is a very popular actress.
    B   Yes, she's the most popular actress in America.
e   A   Mr Clark is a very funny teacher.
    B   Yes, he's the funniest teacher in our school.
f   A   Maria is a very intelligent student.
    B   Yes, she's the most intelligent student in our class.
g   A   This is a very easy exercise.
    B   Yes, it's the easiest exercise in the book.

Tapescript 57b

a   The Ritz is a very expensive hotel.
b   Hambledon is a very pretty village.
c   Everest is a very high mountain.
d   Meryl Streep is a very popular actress.
e   Mr Clark is a very funny teacher.
f   Maria is a very intelligent student.
g   This is a very easy exercise.

Tapescript 58a

farm   factory   traffic   bridge   car park
theatre   Underground   tram   concert   river

Tapescript 58b

lake   mountains   buildings   statue
village   cottage

Tapescript 59a

Oh, it was terrible! At first it was fine. I drove out of the garage, along the road, and under the bridge. Then I drove past the pub, up the hill, and down the hill. Everything was still OK. But then I drove over the river – and – and – I turned *left* not *right* and I went through the hedge, and into the lake! Oh, it was terrible!

Tapescript 59b

Go out of the school and turn left. Walk along Station Road past the railway station and the bank. Turn left again at the traffic lights and walk over the bridge and up the hill. Turn right into Park Avenue. My house is the first on the left. It's number fifty. It takes ten minutes.

UNIT 11
Tapescript 60

P = Peter M = Mary

P   Gosh! All these people, and I don't know any of them!
M   Don't worry! First things first. What would you like to drink?
P   A glass of wine, please. Thank you. Could you tell me one or two names?
M   Of course. Right. Can you see that man over there, sitting at the table? His name's Paul and he's really nice. He's a musician and he works in LA.

P Sorry, where?
M Los Angeles.
P Uh huh.
M And he's talking to Kathy. She's on the other side of the table. She's wearing a red and white T-shirt. Kathy's very interesting. She has an art gallery in London, she's incredibly rich, and she lives in a beautiful house. Married, unfortunately for you.
P Yes.
M And then on Kathy's right there's Suzie. She's drinking some wine. She's one of my oldest friends. We were at school together.
P And what does she do?
M She's a writer, actually.
P Oh! What does she write?
M She writes children's stories. Not very successful ones, but never mind. Now, she's talking to Alex. Alex is smoking a cigar, and Alex travels all over the world. He's a film producer.
P And who are the children?
M They're Suzie's girls, Laura and Ellie. They go to St Mary's School. Do you know it?
P Yes, I do.
M And they're eating crisps and dropping them all over the carpet, aren't you?

Tapescript 61

a A Excuse me! Is this your ball?
  B No, it isn't mine. It's his.

b A Is this yours?
  C No, it isn't mine. It's hers.

c A Excuse me! Is this your ball?
  D No, it isn't mine. I think it's theirs.

d A Hello. Is this yours?
  F No, it isn't ours. It's the dog's!

Tapescript 62

a Who's on the phone?
b I'm going to the pub. Who's coming?
c There's a ten-pound note here. Whose is it?
d This is a good book. Who's reading it?
e Wow! Look at that sports car. Whose is it?
f I found these on the floor. Whose clothes are they?
g Who's that standing near the door? That man with glasses.
h Who's your favourite football team?

Tapescript 63

bread	head
steak	wake
lamb	ham
lose	shoes
sign	wine
half	laugh
soap	hope
when	again
near	beer
suit	boot
wait	late
heart	part
meat	feet
dead	said
hair	wear
war	door
ball	Paul
list	kissed

Tapescript 64

Wonderful tonight by Eric Clapton

It's late in the evening
She's wondering what clothes to wear.
She puts on her make-up,
Then brushes her long blond hair.
And then she asks me,
'Do I look all right?'
And I say 'Yes,
You look wonderful tonight.'

We go to a party
And everyone turns to see
This beautiful lady
That's walking around with me.
And then she asks me,
'Do you feel all right?'
And I say 'Yes,
I feel wonderful tonight.'

I feel wonderful
Because I see
The lovelight in your eyes.
And the wonder of it all
Is that you just don't realize
How much I love you.

It's time to go home now
And I've got an aching head.
So I give her the car keys,
She helps me to bed.
And then I tell her
As I turn out the light,
I say 'My darling,
You were wonderful tonight.'

Tapescript 65

a A Can I help you?
  B No, thanks. I'm just looking.

b A Can I help you?
  B Yes, I'm looking for a jumper.
  A What colour are you looking for?
  B Blue.
  A What size are you?
  B Medium.
  A What about this one?
  B No, I don't like the colour.
  A This one's a bit darker.
  B Mm, that's nice.
  B Can I try it on?
  A Yes, the changing rooms are over there.

c A Is it the right size?
  B It's a bit too big.

d A Is it the right size?
  B Yes, it feels fine.

e B Have you got something bigger?
  A That's the last we've got, I'm afraid.
  B I'll leave it, thanks.

f B How much is it?
  A £19.99.
  B I'll have it, please.
  A Thank you. How would you like to pay?
  B By credit card.

UNIT 12

Tapescript 66

Gemma

When I grow up I'm going to be a ballet dancer. I love dancing, I go dancing three times a week. I'm going to travel all over the world and I'm going to learn French and Russian because I want to dance

in Paris and Moscow. I'm not going to marry until I'm 35 and then I'm going to have two children. I'd like first a girl and then a boy – but maybe I can't plan that! I'm going to work until I'm 75. I'm going to teach dancing and I'm going to open a dance school. I like planning my future – it's very exciting!

Miss Black

When I retire – well – first – er, two things – I'm going to learn Russian – I can already speak French, Italian, and German and I want to learn another language – and I'm going to learn to drive. I never had time to learn when I was younger. Then I'm going to buy a car and a tent and travel all over the world. I'm not going to wear boring clothes, I'm tired of blouses and skirts – I'm going to wear jeans and tracksuits all the time. And when I come home from my travels I'm going to write a book and become a TV star and tell everyone about the places I visited and the people I met.

Tapescript 67a

A What's she going to be?
B A ballet dancer.
A What's she going to do?
B Travel all over the world.

Tapescript 67b

A Why is she going to learn French and Russian?
B Because she wants to dance in Paris and Moscow.
A When is she going to marry?
B Not until she's thirty-five.
A How many children is she going to have?
B Two.
A How long is she going to work?
B Until she's seventy-five.
A What is she going to teach?
B Dancing.

Tapescript 68

a Take an umbrella. It's going to rain.
b Hurry up! We're going to miss the bus!
c I'm very worried about this exam. I know I'm going to fail.
d Jack is studying very hard. I know he's going to pass.
e Careful! You're going to drop the plates!
f Look at all that wine and food! They're going to have a party.
g There's my sister and her boyfriend. Yuk! They're going to kiss.
h A Oh dear! I'm going to sneeze. Aaatishoo!
  B Bless you!

Tapescript 69

B = Miss Black A = Arthur

B First I'm going to Holland.
A Why?
B To see the tulips, of course!
A Oh yes! How wonderful! Where are you going after that?
B Well, then I'm going to Norway to see the midnight sun.

Tapescript 70

A What's the weather like today?
B It's cold and snowing.
A What was it like yesterday?
B Oh, it was cold and cloudy.

Tapescript 71

A It's a lovely day! What shall we do?
B Let's play tennis!

A It's raining again! What shall we do?
B Let's stay at home and watch a video.

Tapescript 72

A It's a lovely day! What shall we do?
B Let's play tennis!
A Oh, no! It's too hot to play tennis.
B Well, let's go to the beach.
A OK. I'll get my swimming costume.

A It's raining again! What shall we do?
B Let's stay at home and watch a video.
A Oh no! We watched a video last night.
B Well, let's go to the cinema.
A OK. What's on at the Odeon cinema?

UNIT 13

Tapescript 73

1 A When did the Berlin Wall come down?
  B 1989.
2 A When did the first American walk on the moon?
  B 1969.
3 A Where are the Andes mountains?
  B In South America.
4 A Who did the actress Elizabeth Taylor marry twice?
  B Richard Burton.
5 A Who won the 100 metres in the Seoul Olympics?
  B Carl Lewis.
6 A How many countries are there in the European Community?
  B Twelve.
7 A How much does an African elephant weigh?
  B Five to seven tonnes.
8 A How fast does Concorde fly?
  B 2,500 kilometres an hour.
9 A How far is it from London to New York?
  B Six thousand kilometres.
10 A How old was Charlie Chaplin when he died?
   B Eighty-eight.
11 A What languages do Swiss people speak?
   B German, French, Italian, and Romansch.
12 A What did Columbus discover in 1492?
   B America.
13 A What sort of music did Elvis Presley play?
   B Rock 'n' roll.
14 A What happens at the end of the story *Cinderella*?
   B She marries the prince.
15 A What happened in Chernobyl in 1986?
   B There was a nuclear explosion.
16 A Why do birds migrate?
   B Because the winter is cold.
17 A Which newspaper does Queen Elizabeth read?
   B *The Times*.
18 A Which language has the most words?
   B English.

Tapescript 74

1 Why do you want to go?
2 Where does she work?
3 She works in a bank.
4 Who won the match?
5 Did she marry him?
6 How old is she?
7 Johnny Page played the guitar.

8 Where did you go last night?

Tapescript 75

It was about two o'clock in the morning, and ... and suddenly I woke up. I heard a noise. I got out of bed and went slowly downstairs. There was a light in the living room. I listened very carefully. I could hear two men speaking quietly. 'Burglars!' I thought. 'Two of them!' Well, I was really frightened, so I went back upstairs, and immediately phoned the police from my bedroom. The police arrived quickly. They opened the front door with a special key and went into the living room. Then they came upstairs. 'It's all right now, sir,' they explained. 'We turned the television off for you!'

Tapescript 76

A What's the title of the book?
B It's called *The Monkey's Paw*.
A What sort of story is it?
B It's a horror story.
A Who are the main characters?
B Old Mr and Mrs White and their son, Herbert.
A What's it about?
B A monkey's paw which is magic. It can give people three wishes, but the wishes don't bring happiness.
A What happens in the end?
B The son dies in an accident at work.
A Did you enjoy it?
B Yes, I did. It was very interesting.
A Do you recommend it?
B Yes, I do.

Tapescript 77

The Girl with Green Eyes
(see page 96)

Tapescript 78a

This is a British Rail talking timetable, giving train times from London King's Cross to Newcastle, Monday to Friday. For weekend train times, phone 071 276 2477. Here are the departure times from King's Cross and the arival times in Newcastle.
0700 arriving 1005
0840 arriving 1130
0950 arriving 1245
1130 arriving 1437
1200 arriving 1455
1245 ...

Tapescript 78b

A Good morning. Can you tell me the times of trains back from Newcastle, please?
B Afternoon, evening? When do you want to come back?
A About 5 o'clock this afternoon.
B About 5 o'clock. Right. Let's have a look. There's a train that leaves at 4.45, and there's another one at 5.25.
A And what time do they get in?
B Back at King's Cross at 7.15 and 8.20.
A Thanks a lot.

Tapescript 78c

A Hello. I'd like a ticket to Newcastle, please.
B Single or return?
A Return, please.
B Day return or period return?
A I want to come back this evening, so a day return.
B How do you want to pay?

A Cash, please.
B Forty-eight pounds fifty, please.
A Twenty, forty, sixty pounds.
B Here's your change and your ticket.
A Thank you.

Tapescript 78d

This is a British Rail announcement. The train from Edinburgh arrives on platform eight at 0830. Edinburgh train, platform eight, 0830.
The train from Hertford arrives on platform six at 0835. Hertford train, platform six, 0835.
The train from Newcastle arrives on platform fifteen at 0845. The train is forty minutes late. Newcastle train, platform fifteen, 0845. Forty minutes late.
The train from Darlington arrives on platform nine at 0855. Darlington train, platform nine, 0855.
The train to Peterborough is on platform twelve, departs 0825. The train to Peterborough, platform twelve, 0825.
The train to Newcastle is on platform seventeen, departs 0840. The train to Newcastle, platform seventeen, 0840.
The train to York is on platform five, departs 0900. The train to York, platform five, 0900.

UNIT 14

Tapescript 79a

A I've been to England. I haven't been to Scotland.
B I've been to the United States. I've never been to Mexico.
C I haven't been to *any* of the countries!

Tapescript 79b

A Have you ever been to Ireland?
B No, I haven't.
A Have you ever been to Scotland?
B Yes, I have.
A When did you go?
B Two years ago.

Tapescript 80

Yes, I've lived in a foreign country. In Japan, actually. I lived in Osaka for a year. I really enjoyed it. I loved the food! Now, then. Have I worked for a big company? It depends what you mean by big. I've worked in a factory, and I've worked in an office, but they weren't very big companies. I've never stayed in an expensive hotel, but I'd love to one day. A big room, breakfast in bed, it'd be lovely!
I've been in a jumbo jet. I went in one when I flew to Japan. The plane stopped in Moscow. The flight was about twelve or thirteen hours! Cooking. Mmm. Well, I can't cook very well, but once when I was a boy scout I cooked for us all. There were about thirty of us, and I made beans on toast. It was delicious because everyone was so hungry.
I've never met anyone famous, and I don't really want to. Mm, I've only ever seen one Shakespeare play, and that was Hamlet. I saw it while I was at school. We studied it for an exam.
I've driven a tractor. When I was seventeen, I worked on a farm for a few months. I've been to hospital a few times. When I was six, I broke my leg, and when I was twenty-two I had a car accident, and I was in hospital for a couple of weeks. And I have never, ever, in my whole life, never won a competition.

Tapescript 81

L = Lilian F = Father

L We're having a lovely time, Dad.

F I'm sure there's a lot to do!

L There is! We've been for a walk in Central Park. It's so big! Everything here is big. And we've climbed the Empire State Building. The view was fantastic. We haven't been to Greenwich Village yet, and we haven't been to Chinatown, either. We're going to do that tomorrow.

F Have you seen the Statue of Liberty yet?

L Oh, yes, we have. We've just had a helicopter tour of the city, and we flew really close to it.

F What about a show? Have you seen a show on Broadway yet?

L No, we haven't. We're going to one on our last night here, but we haven't decided what to see yet.

Tapescript 82a

Three telephone tones

1 engaged

2 dialling tone

3 ringing

Tapescript 82b

a A Hello. 276694.
   B Hello. Can I speak to Jo, please?
   A This is Jo speaking.
   B Oh! Hi, Jo. This is Pat. I'm just ringing to check that Sunday is still OK for tennis.
   A Yes, that's fine.
   B Great! See you on Sunday at 10. Bye!
   A Bye!

b A Hello. Chesswood 4576.
   B Hello. Is that Liz?
   A No, it isn't. I'll just get her.
   C Hello. Liz here.
   B Hi, Liz. It's Tom. Listen! I'm having a party on Saturday. Can you come?
   C Oh, sorry, Tom. I can't. I'm going to my cousin's wedding.
   B Never mind. Perhaps next time. Bye!
   C Bye.

c A Hello. Barclays Bank, Chesswood.
   B Hello. Can I speak to the manager, please?
   A Hold on. I'll put you through ... I'm afraid Mr Smith isn't in his office. Can I take a message?
   B Don't worry. I'll ring back later.
   A All right. Goodbye.
   B Goodbye.

Tapescript 82c

Directory Enquiries. Which town, please?

Can I have the surname, please?

And the initial?

What's the address?

Thank you. The number you want is 0423 287221.

UNIT 15

Tapescript 83

A Hi Barbara! Did you and Raymond enjoy Margo's dinner party?

B No, we didn't. It was awful!

A What about the food?

B Oh, the food was disgusting! We hated it. We had Duck and Banana Curry!

A Duck and what?! Ugh!

B I know. I don't like duck and Ray doesn't like bananas!

A And their friends? Tell me about their friends. Were they nice?

B Oh, Alice! They were friendly, but they were so boring! They talked for three hours about their house and their dog and their dishwasher! And they didn't ask one question about us. We said very little, only 'Yes?' and 'No!'

A Oh dear! What a terrible evening!

Tapescript 84

She's leaving home by the Beatles

Wednesday morning at five o'clock as the day begins,
Silently closing the bedroom door
Leaving the note that she hoped would say more
She goes downstairs to the kitchen
Clutching her handkerchief
Quietly turning the backdoor key
Stepping outside she is free.

She
We gave her most of our lives
is leaving
Sacrificed most of our lives
home.
We gave her everything money could buy.
She's leaving home after living alone for so many years.

Father snores as his wife gets into her dressing gown,
Picks up the letter that's lying there
Standing alone at the top of the stairs
She breaks down and cries to her husband,
'Daddy, our baby's gone.
Why would she treat us so thoughtlessly?
How could she do this to me?'

She
We never thought of ourselves
is leaving
Never a thought of ourselves
home.
We struggled hard all our lives to get by.
She's leaving home after living alone for so many years.

Friday morning at nine o'clock she is far away
Waiting to keep the appointment she made
Meeting a man from the motor trade.

She
What did we do that was wrong?
is having
We didn't know it was wrong.
fun.
Fun is the one thing that money can't buy.
Something inside that was always denied for so many years.
She's leaving home. Bye bye.

Tapescript 85

1 A Can I help you?
   B Yes. Can I change this jumper please? I bought it last week and it's too small.
   A Have you got the receipt?
   B No. I'm sorry, I've lost it.
   A Oh dear! You have to give us the receipt. We can't change anything without a receipt.
   B But ... !

2 A Can I send this parcel to Greece, please?
   B Yes, of course. That's £3.50. Thank you. Have you filled in the customs form?
   A Customs form? What customs form?

   B You have to fill in a customs form when you send a parcel overseas.
   A Can you give me a form then, please?
   B No, I don't have any. They're over there on that table.
   A Sorry? Where?
   B Over there. They're the green forms.

3 A That's £104.50 altogether. How do you want to pay?
   B Can I pay by cheque?
   A Yes, but have you got any identification? You have to show identification with cheques over £100.
   B Oh dear! Let me see. I've got a photo of me and my aunt at the seaside.
   A No, no, no. Have you got a passport or a driving licence?
   B No, I haven't.
   A Then I'm afraid we can't take your cheque.
   B But ... !

4 A What's the purpose of your visit?
   B Oh, I'm going to study English and have a holiday.
   A And how long are you staying?
   B For a month.
   A And where are you going to stay? What's your address?
   B I'm not sure. The language school is going to find me somewhere to stay.
   A Mmm! You have to give us an address. You can't enter the country without an address!
   B But ... !

Word list

Here is a list of some of the words from the units of *Headway Elementary*.
Write the translation.

adj = adjective
adv = adverb
conj = conjunction
opp = opposite
pl = plural
prep = preposition
pron = pronoun
pp = past participle
n = noun
v = verb

UNIT 1

and (*conj*) /ənd/
apple (*n*) /æpl/
bag (*n*) /bæg/
brother (*n*) /brʌðə(r)/
camera (*n*) /kæmrə/
child (*n*) (*pl* children) /tʃaɪld/
country (*n*) /kʌntrɪ/
daughter (*n*) /dɔːtə(r)/
dictionary (*n*) /dɪkʃənrɪ/
doctor (*n*) /dɒktə(r)/
envelope (*n*) /envələup/
evening (*n*) /iːvnɪŋ/
first (*adj*) /fɜːst/
flat (*n*) /flæt/
have (*v*) /hæv/
house (*n*) /haʊs/
international (*adj*) /ɪntənæʃənl/
job (*n*) /dʒɒb/
key (*n*) /kiː/
language (*n*) /læŋgwɪdʒ/
learn (*v*) /lɜːn/
letter (*n*) /letə(r)/
live (*v*) /lɪv/
magazine (*n*) /mægəziːn/
map (*n*) /mæp/
married (*adj*) /mærɪd/
name (*n*) /neɪm/
newspaper (*n*) /njuːspeɪpə(r)/
notebook (*n*) /nəʊtbʊk/
orange (*n*) /ɒrɪndʒ/
people (*n*) /piːpl/
postcard (*n*) /pəʊstkɑːd/
sister (*n*) /sɪstə(r)/
son (*n*) /sʌn/
south (*n*) /saʊθ/
stamp (*n*) /stæmp/
student (*n*) /stjuːdənt/
suitcase (*n*) /suːtkeɪs/
surname (*n*) /sɜːneɪm/

teacher (*n*) /tiːtʃə(r)/
thank you/thanks /θæŋk juː, θæŋks/
ticket (*n*) /tɪkɪt/
want (*v*) /wɒnt/

UNIT 2

address (*n*) /ədres/
aunt (*n*) /ɑːnt/
beautiful (*adj*) /bjuːtɪfl/
big (*adj*) /bɪg/
book (*n*) /bʊk/
boyfriend (*n*) /bɔɪfrend/
cheap (*adj*) /tʃiːp/
cheese (*n*) /tʃiːz/
chicken (*n*) /tʃɪkɪn/
coffee (*n*) /kɒfɪ/
cold (*adj*) /kəʊld/
cup (*n*) /kʌp/
difficult (*adj*) /dɪfɪkəlt/
drink (*v*) /drɪŋk/
easy (*adj*) /iːzɪ/
expensive (*adj*) /ɪkspensɪv/
family (*n*) /fæməlɪ/
father (*n*) /fɑːðə(r)/
food (*n*) /fuːd/
friendly (*adj*) /frendlɪ/
good (*adj*) /gʊd/
grandfather (*n*) /grændfɑːðə(r)/
grandmother (*n*) /grændmʌðə(r)/
ham (*n*) /hæm/
happy (*adj*) /hæpɪ/
holiday (*n*) /hɒlɪdeɪ/
home (*n*) (at home) /həʊm/
horrible (*adj*) /hɒrəbl/
hot (*adj*) /hɒt/
husband (*n*) /hʌzbənd/
ice-cream (*n*) /aɪs kriːm/
lovely (*adj*) /lʌvlɪ/
milk (*n*) /mɪlk/
mineral water (*n*) /mɪnərəl wɔːtə(r)/
morning (*n*) /mɔːnɪŋ/
mother (*n*) /mʌðə(r)/
nephew (*n*) /nefjuː/
new (*adj*) /njuː/
nice (*adj*) /naɪs/
niece (*n*) /niːs/
old (*adj*) /əʊld/
or (*conj*) /ɔː(r)/
orange juice (*n*) /ɒrɪndʒ dʒuːs/
parents (*n*) /peərənts/
park (*n*) /pɑːk/
phone number (*n*) /fəʊn nʌmbə(r)/
photo (*n*) /fəʊtəʊ/
right (*adj*) (*opp* wrong) /raɪt/
sandwich (*n*) /sænwɪdʒ/
small (*adj*) /smɔːl/

tea (*n*) /tiː/
today (*adv*) /tədeɪ/
town (*n*) /taʊn/
uncle (*n*) /ʌŋkl/
understand (*v*) /ʌndəstænd/
weather (*n*) /weðə(r)/
wife (*n*) /waɪf/
work (*n*) (at work) /wɜːk/
write (*v*) /raɪt/
wrong (*adj*) /rɒŋ/
young (*adj*) /jʌŋ/

UNIT 3

actor (*n*) /æktə(r)/
afternoon (*n*) /ɑːftənuːn/
arrive (*v*) /əraɪv/
baker (*n*) /beɪkə(r)/
because (*conj*) /bɪkɒz/
bread (*n*) /bred/
but (*conj*) /bʌt/
car (*n*) /kɑː(r)/
catch (*v*) (catch a train) /kætʃ/
certainly (*adv*) /sɜːtənlɪ/
come (*v*) /kʌm/
cost (*v*) /kɒst/
drive (*v*) /draɪv/
evening (*n*) /iːvnɪŋ/
film (*n*) /fɪlm/
fly (*v*) /flaɪ/
football (*n*) /fʊtbɔːl/
fortunately (*adv*) /fɔːtʃənətlɪ/
go (*v*) /gəʊ/
hairdresser (*n*) /heədresə(r)/
half (*n*) /hɑːf/
hospital (*n*) /hɒspɪtl/
hour (*n*) /aʊə(r)/
interpreter (*n*) /ɪntɜːprɪtə(r)/
journalist (*n*) /dʒɜːnəlɪst/
journey (*n*) /dʒɜːnɪ/
leave (*v*) /liːv/
like (*v*) /laɪk/
look after (*v*) /lʊk ɑːftə(r)/
love (*v*) /lʌv/
make (*v*) /meɪk/
mechanic (*n*) /məkænɪk/
mend (*v*) /mend/
mountain (*n*) /maʊntɪn/
nurse (*n*) /nɜːs/
pilot (*n*) /paɪlət/
plane (*n*) /pleɪn/
play (*v*) /pleɪ/
receptionist (*n*) /rɪsepʃənɪst/
sea (*n*) /siː/
see (*v*) /siː/
sell (*v*) /sel/

shop (*n*) /ʃɒp/
shop assistant (*n*) /ʃɒp əsɪstənt/
singer (*n*) /sɪŋə(r)/
speak (*v*) /spiːk/
summer (*n*) /sʌmə(r)/
take (*v*) /teɪk/
taxi-driver (*n*) /tæksɪ draɪvə(r)/
teach (*v*) /tiːtʃ/
tired (*adj*) /taɪəd/
train (*n*) /treɪn/
village (*n*) /vɪlɪdʒ/
walk (*v*) /wɔːk/
week (*n*) /wiːk/
winter (*n*) /wɪntə(r)/

UNIT 4

autumn (*n*) /ɔːtəm/
bad (*adj*) /bæd/
baseball (*n*) /beɪsbɔːl/
beach (*n*) /biːtʃ/
bed (*n*) /bed/
bring (*v*) /brɪŋ/
brown (*adj*) /braʊn/
cards (*n*) (play cards) /kɑːdz/
chat (*v*) /tʃæt/
colour (*n*) /kʌlə(r)/
computer (*n*) /kəmpjuːtə(r)/
cook (*v*) /kʊk/
crossword (*n*) /krɒswɜːd/
dance (*v*) /dɑːns/
dinner (*n*) /dɪnə(r)/
eat (*v*) /iːt/
exciting (*adj*) /ɪksaɪtɪŋ/
exercise (*n*) (do exercise) /eksəsaɪz/
favourite (*adj*) /feɪvərɪt/
fish (*n*) /fɪʃ/
flower (*n*) /flaʊə(r)/
friend (*n*) /frend/
game (*n*) /geɪm/
get up (*v*) /get ʌp/
go shopping (*v*) /gəʊ ʃɒpɪŋ/
go swimming (*v*) /gəʊ swɪmɪŋ/
here (*adv*) /hɪə(r)/
hobby (*n*) /hɒbɪ/
ice-skating (*n*) /aɪs skeɪtɪŋ/
interesting (*adj*) /ɪntrəstɪŋ/
interview (*v*) /ɪntəvjuː/
know (*v*) /nəʊ/
late (*adv*) /leɪt/
listen to (*v*) /lɪsən tuː, tə/
long (*adj*) /lɒŋ/
meet (*v*) /miːt/
month (*n*) /mʌnθ/
near (*prep*) /nɪə(r)/
never (*adv*) /nevə(r)/

office (n) /ɒfɪs/
often (adv) /ɒfn, ɒftən/
painting (n) /peɪntɪŋ/
pub (n) /pʌb/

red (adj) /red/
relax (v) /rɪlæks/
river (n) /rɪvə(r)/

sailing (n) /seɪlɪŋ/
short (adj) /ʃɔ:t/
smoke (v) /sməʊk/
sometimes (adv)
  /sʌmtaɪmz/
song (n) /sɒŋ/
spring (n) /sprɪŋ/
start (v) /sta:t/
stay (v) /steɪ/
suddenly (adv) /sʌdənlɪ/
summer (n) /sʌmə(r)/
sunbathe (v) /sʌnbeɪð/

take photographs (v)
  /teɪk fəʊtəgra:fs/
traffic (n) /træfɪk/
tree (n) /tri:/

usually (adv) /ju:ʒəlɪ/

visit (v) /vɪzɪt/
volleyball (n) /vɒlibɔ:l/

watch (v) /wɒtʃ/
wet (adj) /wet/
windsurf (v) /wɪndsɜ:f/

yellow (adj) /jeləʊ/

UNIT 5

also (adj) /ɔ:lsəʊ/
armchair (n)
  /a:mtʃeə(r)/

bath (n) /ba:θ/
bathroom (n)
  /ba:θru:m/
bedroom (n)
  /bedru:m/
behind (prep) /bɪhaɪnd/

carpet (n) /ka:pɪt/
chemist's (n) /kemɪsts/
clean (adj) /kli:n/
clock (n) /klɒk/
clothes (n) /kləʊðz/
cooker (n) /kʊkə(r)/
cupboard (n) /kʌbəd/

desk (n) /desk/
dishwasher (n)
  /dɪʃwɒʃə(r)/
dog (n) /dɒg/
during (prep) /djʊərɪŋ/

everybody (pron)
  /evrɪbɒdɪ/

famous (adj) /feɪməs/
fire (n) /faɪə(r)/
fridge (n) /frɪdʒ/

garden (n) /ga:dn/

important (adj)
  /ɪmpɔ:tənt/
in front of (prep)
  /ɪn frʌnt əv/

king (n) /kɪŋ/
kitchen (n) /kɪtʃɪn/

lamp (n) /læmp/
left (adv) (opp right) /left/
library (n) /laɪbrərɪ/
like (prep) /laɪk/
living room (n) /lɪvɪŋ ru:m/

meal (n) /mi:l/
mirror (n) /mɪrə(r)/
modern (adj) /mɒdn/

news (n) /nju:z/
newsagent's (n)
  /nju:zeɪdʒənts/
next to (prep)
  /nekst tu:, tə/

on (prep) /ɒn/
other (adj) /ʌðə(r)/

palace (n) /pælɪs/
pen (n) /pen/
picture (n) /pɪktʃə(r)/
place (n) /pleɪs/
plant (n) /pla:nt/
plate (n) /pleɪt/
police station (n)
  /pəli:s steɪʃn/
politician (n) /pɒlətɪʃn/
post box (n)
  /pəʊst bɒx/
post office (n)
  /pəʊst ɒfɪs/

radio (n) /reɪdɪəʊ/
right (adv) (opp left) /raɪt/

sleep (v) /sli:p/
sofa (n) /səʊfə(r)/
stereo (n) /sterɪəʊ/
swimming pool (n)
  /swɪmɪŋ pu:l/

table (n) /teɪbl/
talk (v) /tɔ:k/
toilet (n) /tɔɪlət/

wall (n) /wɔ:l/
washing machine (n)
  /wɒʃɪŋ məʃi:n/
while (conj) /waɪl/
whole (adj) /həʊl/
window (n) /wɪndəʊ/

UNIT 6

again (adv) /əgen, əgeɪn/
arrival hall (n)
  /əraɪvəl hɔ:l/

baggage reclaim (n)
  /bægɪdʒ ri:kleɪm/
bike (n) /baɪk/
black (adj) /blæk/
boarding pass (n)
  /bɔ:dɪŋ pa:s/
boring (adj) /bɔ:rɪŋ/
(be) born (v) /bɔ:n/
brilliant (adj) /brɪlɪənt/

champion (n)
  /tʃæmpɪən/
check (v) /tʃek/
check-in desk (n)
  /tʃek ɪn desk/
cheque (n) /tʃek/
chess (n) /tʃes/
count (v) /kaʊnt/

conversation (n)
  /kɒnvəseɪʃn/
dark (adj) /da:k/
delayed (pp) (be delayed)
  /dɪleɪd/
departure lounge (n)
  /dɪpa:tʃə laʊndʒ/
destination (n)
  /destɪneɪʃn/
different (adj) /dɪfrənt/
draw (v) /drɔ:/

eye (n) /aɪ/

flight (n) /flaɪt/
fluently (adv) /flu:əntlɪ/

gate (n) (airport) /geɪt/
genius (n) /dʒi:nɪəs/

hand luggage (n)
  /hænd lʌgɪdʒ/
hear (v) /hɪə(r)/

land (v) /lænd/
last (adj) (last month/year)
  /la:st/
lunch (n) /lʌntʃ/

match (n) (football) /mætʃ/
meat (n) /mi:t/
medicine (n) (study medicine)
  /medsn/

nose (n) /nəʊz/
now (adv) /naʊ/

party (n) /pa:tɪ/
passport control (n)
  /pa:spɔ:t kəntrəʊl/
piano (n) /pɪænəʊ/
player (n) /pleɪə(r)/
practise (v) /præktɪs/

ride (v) /raɪd/

safety belt (n) /seɪftɪ belt/
smell (v) /smel/
study (v) /stʌdɪ/

teenager (n) /ti:neɪdʒə(r)/
think (v) /θɪŋk/
translate (v) /trænzleɪt/
tray (n) /treɪ/
type (v) /taɪp/

under (prep) (under 18 years old)
  /ʌndə(r)/
until (conj) (not until)
  /ʌntɪl/
use (v) /ju:z/

wear (v) /weə(r)/

year (n) /jɪə(r)/
yesterday (adv) /jestədeɪ/

UNIT 7

abroad (adv) /əbrɔ:d/

baby (n) /beɪbɪ/
become (v) /bɪkʌm/
before (prep) /bɪfɔ:(r)/
borrow (v) /bɒrəʊ/
bottle (n) /bɒtl/
buy (v) /baɪ/

change (v) /tʃeɪndʒ/
character (n)
  /kærɪktə(r)/

Christmas (n) /krɪsməs/
clean (v) /kli:n/
clerk (n) /kla:k/

debt (n) /det/
description (n)
  /dɪskrɪpʃn/
die (v) /daɪ/

earn (v) /ɜ:n/
Easter (n) /i:stə(r)/
enjoy (v) /ɪndʒɔɪ/
especially (adv)
  /ɪspeʃlɪ/
experience (n)
  /ɪkspɪərɪəns/

factory (n) /fæktərɪ/
find (v) /faɪnd/
finish (v) /fɪnɪʃ/

get (v) (= receive, become)
  /get/
give (v) /gɪv/
great (adj) (writer) /greɪt/

hard (adj) (life) /ha:d/
hate (v) /heɪt/

immediately (adv)
  /ɪmi:dɪətlɪ/

kiss (v) /kɪs/

later (adv) /leɪtə(r)/
life (n) /laɪf/
lose (v) /lu:z/

marry (v) /mærɪ/
move (v) /mu:v/

night (n) /naɪt/
novel (n) /nɒvəl/
novelist (n) /nɒvəlɪst/

over (prep) (over 90 years old)
  /əʊvə(r)/

past (n) /pa:st/
politics (n) /pɒlətɪks/
poor (adj) /pʊə(r), pɔ:(r)/
popular (adj) /pɒpjʊlə(r)/
present (n) /prezənt/
pretty (adj) /prɪtɪ/
prison (n) /prɪzn/
probably (adv) /prɒbəblɪ/

real (adj) /rɪəl/
remember (v) /rɪmembə(r)/
retire (v) /rɪtaɪə(r)/
rich (adj) /rɪtʃ/

sell (v) /sel/
send (v) /send/
software (n) /sɒftweə(r)/
spend (v) /spend/
still (adv) /stɪl/
successful (adj) /səksesfəl/
suddenly (adv) /sʌdənlɪ/

tomorrow (adv) /təmɒrəʊ/

unemployed (adj)
  /ʌnɪmplɔɪd/

video recorder (n) /vɪdɪəʊ
  rɪkɔ:də(r)/

war (n) /wɔ:(r)/
wedding (n) /wedɪŋ/
win (v) /wɪn/
wonderful (adj) /wʌndəfəl/

UNIT 8

actress (*n*) /ˈæktrəs/
afraid (*adj*) (afraid of)
  /əˈfreɪd əv/
alive (*adj*) /əˈlaɪv/
angry (*adj*) /ˈæŋgrɪ/
around (*prep*) /əˈraʊnd/
asleep (*adj*) /əˈsliːp/
baker (*n*) /ˈbeɪkə(r)/
believe (*v*) /bɪˈliːv/
birthday (*n*) /ˈbɜːθdeɪ/
biscuit (*n*) /ˈbɪskɪt/
blue (*adj*) /bluː/
burglar (*n*) /ˈbɜːglə(r)/
businessman/woman (*n*)
  /ˈbɪznɪsmən,
  ˈbɪznɪswʊmən/
cake (*n*) /keɪk/
call (*v*) (name) /kɔːl/
call (*n*) (telephone) /kɔːl/
century (*n*) /ˈsentʃərɪ/
chef (*n*) /ʃef/
couple (*n*) /ˈkʌpl/
cousin (*n*) /ˈkʌzən/
date (*n*) /deɪt/
disc jockey (*n*)
  /ˈdɪsk dʒɒkɪ/
engaged (*v*) (get engaged)
  /ɪnˈgeɪdʒd/
exam (*n*) /ɪgˈzæm/
fall asleep (*v*)
  /fɔːl əˈsliːp/
fall in love (*v*)
  /fɔːl ɪn lʌv/
feel (*v*) /fiːl/
hair (*n*) /heə(r)/
hamburger (*n*)
  /ˈhæmbɜːgə(r)/
hard (*adv*) (work hard)
  /hɑːd/
hungry (*adj*) /ˈhʌŋgrɪ/
incredible (*adj*) /ɪnˈkredəbl/
jeans (*n*) /dʒiːnz/
joke (*n*) /dʒəʊk/
laugh (*v*) /lɑːf, læf/
nervous (*adj*) /ˈnɜːvəs/
pink (*adj*) /pɪŋk/
policeman (*n*) /pəˈliːsmən/
produce (*v*) /prəˈdʒuːs/
quickly (*adv*) /ˈkwɪklɪ/
rain (*n*) /reɪn/
really (*adv*) /ˈrɪəlɪ/
recipe (*n*) /ˈresəpɪ/
record (*n*) (music)
  /ˈrekɔːd/
rest (*n*) (have a rest)
  /rest/
ring (*v*) (telephone) /rɪŋ/
romantic (*adj*)
  /rəʊˈmæntɪk/
sailor (*n*) /ˈseɪlə(r)/
same (*adj*) /seɪm/
say (*v*) /seɪ/
season (*n*) /ˈsiːzn/
shy (*adj*) /ʃaɪ/

sleepy (*adj*) /ˈsliːpɪ/
smile (*v*) /smaɪl/
snow (*v*) /snəʊ/
soldier (*n*) /ˈsəʊldʒə(r)/
steal (*v*) /stiːl/
tell (*v*) /tel/
together (*adv*) /təˈgeðə(r)/
travel (*v*) /ˈtrævl/
typewriter (*n*)
  /ˈtaɪpraɪtə(r)/
upstairs (*adv*) /ʌpˈsteəz/
voice (*n*) /vɔɪs/
wake up (*v*) /weɪk ʌp/
wait (*v*) /weɪt/
warm (*adj*) /wɔːm/

UNIT 9

aspirin (*n*) /ˈæsprɪn/
beef (*n*) /biːf/
beer (*n*) /bɪə(r)/
between (*prep*)
  /bɪˈtwiːn/
bill (*n*) (restaurant)
  /bɪl/
box (*n*) (box of matches)
  /bɒks/
can (*n*) (can of beer)
  /kæn/
cereal (*n*) /ˈsɪərɪəl/
chewing gum (*n*)
  /ˈtʃuːɪŋ gʌm/
chocolate (*n*) /ˈtʃɒklət/
cigarette (*n*) /sɪgəˈret/
city (*n*) /ˈsɪtɪ/
conditioner (*n*)
  /kənˈdɪʃənə(r)/
cream (*n*) /kriːm/
credit card (*n*)
  /ˈkredɪt kɑːd/
crisps (*n*) (food) /krɪsps/
double (*adj*) (double room)
  /ˈdʌbl/
file (*n*) (for paper) /faɪl/
fruit (*n*) /fruːt/
full (*adj*) /fʊl/
glue (*n*) /gluː/
grape (*n*) /greɪp/
gravy (*n*) /ˈgreɪvɪ/
hankie (*n*) /ˈhæŋkɪ/
honey (*n*) /ˈhʌnɪ/
ice (*n*) /aɪs/
jam (*n*) /dʒæm/
lamb (*n*) /læm/
list (*n*) /lɪst/
luggage (*n*) /ˈlʌgɪdʒ/
marmalade (*n*)
  /ˈmɑːməleɪd/
match (*n*) (for a cigarette)
  /mætʃ/
meal (*n*) /miːl/
menu (*n*) /ˈmenjuː/
mushroom (*n*)
  /ˈmʌʃruːm/
note (*n*) (money) /nəʊt/

order (*v*) (a meal)
  /ˈɔːdə(r)/
packet (*n*) /ˈpækɪt/
paint (*n*) /peɪnt/
pay (*v*) /peɪ/
petrol (*n*) /ˈpetrəl/
phone card (*n*)
  /ˈfəʊn kɑːd/
phone call (*n*)
  /ˈfəʊn kɔːl/
pork (*n*) /pɔːk/
potato (*n*) /pəˈteɪtəʊ/
prefer (*v*) /prɪˈfɜː(r)/
quick (*adj*) /kwɪk/
ready (*adj*) /ˈredɪ/
recommend (*v*)
  /rekəˈmend/
rice (*n*) /raɪs/
roll (*n*) /rəʊl/
salad (*n*) /ˈsæləd/
sauce (*n*) /sɔːs/
sausage (*n*) /ˈsɒsɪdʒ/
shirt (*n*) /ʃɜːt/
sign (*v*) (sign the register)
  /saɪn/
single (*adj*) (single room)
  /ˈsɪŋgl/
sit (*v*) /sɪt/
snack (*n*) /snæk/
soup (*n*) /suːp/
steak (*n*) /steɪk/
strawberry (*n*) /ˈstrɔːbrɪ/
tomato (*n*) /təˈmɑːtəʊ/
toothpaste (*n*)
  /ˈtuːθpeɪst/
vegetable (*n*) /ˈvedʒtəbl/
yoghurt (*n*) /ˈjɒgət/

UNIT 10

bridge (*n*) /brɪdʒ/
building (*n*) /ˈbɪldɪŋ/
car park (*n*) /ˈkɑː pɑːk/
castle (*n*) /ˈkɑːsl/
concert (*n*) /ˈkɒnsət/
cottage (*n*) /ˈkɒtɪdʒ/
cross (*v*) /krɒs/
cultural (*adj*) /ˈkʌltʃərəl/
dangerous (*adj*)
  /ˈdeɪndʒərəs/
dirty (*adj*) /ˈdɜːtɪ/
divide (*v*)
  /dɪˈvaɪd/
driving lesson (*n*)
  /ˈdraɪvɪŋ lesn/
east (*n*) /iːst/
end (*v*) /end/
excitement (*n*)
  /ɪkˈsaɪtmənt/
factory (*n*) /ˈfæktərɪ/
fast (*adj*) /fɑːst/
festival (*n*) /ˈfestəvl/
field (*n*) /fiːld/
fight (*v*) /faɪt/
free (*v*) (free oneself)
  /friː/

fresh air (*n*)
  /freʃ eə(r)/
healthy (*adj*) /ˈhelθɪ/
hedge (*n*) /hedʒ/
hill (*n*) /hɪl/
independence (*n*)
  /ɪndɪˈpendəns/
independent (*adj*)
  /ɪndɪˈpendənt/
intelligent (*adj*)
  /ɪnˈtelɪdʒənt/
join (*v*) /dʒɔɪn/
lake (*n*) /leɪk/
leader (*n*) /ˈliːdə(r)/
noisy (*adj*) /ˈnɔɪzɪ/
peace (*n*) /piːs/
pollution (*n*) /pəˈluːʃn/
population (*n*)
  /pɒpjʊˈleɪʃn/
public (*adj*) /ˈpʌblɪk/
quiet (*adj*) /ˈkwaɪət/
railway station (*n*)
  /ˈreɪlweɪ steɪʃn/
river bank (*n*)
  /ˈrɪvə bæŋk/
rose (*n*) /rəʊz/
ruin (*n*) /ˈruːɪn/
rule (*n*) /ruːl/
safe (*adj*) /seɪf/
slow (*adj*) /sləʊ/
spa (*n*) /spɑː/
square (*n*) /skweə(r)/
statue (*n*) /ˈstætʃuː/
town hall (*n*)
  /taʊn hɔːl/
traffic lights (*n*)
  /ˈtræfɪk laɪts/
tram (*n*) /træm/
transport (*n*) /ˈtrænspɔːt/
underground (*n*)
  /ˈʌndəgraʊnd/
unfriendly (*adj*)
  /ʌnˈfrendlɪ/
unhealthy (*adj*) /ʌnˈhelθɪ/
unusual (*adj*) /ʌnˈjuːʒʊəl/
view (*n*) /vjuː/
west (*n*) /west/
wood (*n*) /wʊd/

UNIT 11

afraid (*adj*) (I'm afraid =
  I'm sorry) /əˈfreɪd/
anniversary (*n*)
  /ænɪˈvɜːsərɪ/
beard (*n*) /bɪəd/
blond (*adj*) /blɒnd/
boot (*n*) /buːt/
brush (*v*) (hairbrush) /brʌʃ/
changing room (*n*)
  /ˈtʃeɪndʒɪŋ ruːm/
colourful (*adj*) /ˈkʌləfl/
dark (*adj*) /dɑːk/
darling (*n*) /ˈdɑːlɪŋ/
dead (*adj*) /ded/

dress (n) /dres/
earring (n) /ɪərɪŋ/
fair (adj) /feə(r)/
fault (n) /fɒlt/
floor (n) /flɔː(r)/
glasses (n) /glɑːsɪz/
good-looking (adj)
 /gʊd lʊkɪŋ/
grey (adj) /greɪ/
handsome (adj) /hænsəm/
heart (n) /hɑːt/
jacket (n) /dʒækɪt/
jumper (n) /dʒʌmpə(r)/
make-up (n) /meɪk ʌp/
medium (adj) /miːdɪəm/
mess (n) /mes/
moustache (n) /məstɑːʃ/
photocopier (n)
 /fəʊtəʊkɒpɪə(r)/
pink (adj) /pɪŋk/
realize (v) /rɪəlaɪz/
run (n) /rʌn/
shoe (n) /ʃuː/
short (adj) /ʃɔːt/
sign (n) /saɪn/
size (n) /saɪz/
skirt (n) /skɜːt/
slim (adj) /slɪm/
suit (n) /suːt/
T-shirt (n) /tiː ʃɜːt/
tall (adj) /tɔːl/
tie (n) /taɪ/
trainers (n) /treɪnəz/
trousers (n) /traʊzəz/
try on (v) (clothes)
 /traɪ ɒn/

UNIT 12

channel (n) (TV) /tʃænl/
choose (v) /tʃuːz/
climb (v) /klaɪm/
cloudy (adj) /klaʊdɪ/
comfortable (adj)
 /kʌmftəbl/
competition (n)
 /kɒmpətɪʃn/
drop (v) /drɒp/
dry (adj) /draɪ/
fail (v) (fail an exam)
 /feɪl/
foggy (adj) /fɒgɪ/
follow (v) /fɒləʊ/
future (n) /fjuːtʃə(r)/
guitar (n) /gɪtɑː(r)/
heavy (adj) /hevɪ/
lion (n) /laɪən/
member (n) /membə(r)/
midnight (n) /mɪdnaɪt/
miss (v) (miss the bus)
 /mɪs/
motor racing (n)
 /məʊtə reɪsɪŋ/
open (v) /əʊpən/

pass (v) (pass an exam)
 /pɑːs/
plan (n) /plæn/
prepare (v) /prɪpeə(r)/
programme (n) (TV)
 /prəʊgræm/
rock (n) /rɒk/
rope (n) /rəʊp/
route (n) /ruːt/
side (n) /saɪd/
star (n) (= a famous person)
 /stɑː(r)/
sneeze (v) /sniːz/
sunny (adj) /sʌnɪ/
tent (n) /tent/
touch (v) /tʌtʃ/
tracksuit (n) /træksuːt/
try (v) /traɪ/
umbrella (n) /ʌmbrelə/
video (n) /vɪdɪəʊ/
wash (v) /wɒʃ/
windy (adj) /wɪndɪ/
without (prep) /wɪðaʊt/
worried (adj) /wʌrɪd/

UNIT 13

accident (n) /æksɪdənt/
bored (adj) /bɔːd/
carefully (adv) /keəfəlɪ/
change (n) (= money)
 /tʃeɪndʒ/
clearly (adv) /klɪəlɪ/
cook (n) /kʊk/
death (n) /deθ/
deep (adj) /diːp/
discover (v) /dɪskʌvə(r)/
downstairs (adv)
 /daʊnsteəz/
end (n) /end/
explain (v) /ɪkspleɪn/
fat (adj) /fæt/
frightened (adj)
 /fraɪtənd/
happiness (n) /hæpɪnəs/
hat (n) /hæt/
head (n) /hed/
hide (v) /haɪd/
history (n) /hɪstrɪ/
hole (n) /həʊl/
horror story (n)
 /hɒrə stɔːrɪ/
magic (adj) /mædʒɪk/
migrate (v) /maɪgreɪt/
monkey (n) /mʌŋkɪ/
moon (n) /muːn/
need (v) /niːd/
noise (n) /nɔɪz/
platform (n) /plætfɔːm/
put (v) /pʊt/
return (n) (ticket) /rɪtɜːn/
scream (v) /skriːm/
silently (adv) /saɪləntlɪ/
single (n) (ticket) /sɪŋgl/
sky (n) /skaɪ/

sound (n) /saʊnd/
special (adj) /speʃl/
stand up (v) /stænd ʌp/
timetable (n) /taɪmteɪbl/
title (n) /taɪtl/
turn off (v) (the TV)
 /tɜːn ɒf/
weigh (v) /weɪ/
wish (n) /wɪʃ/

UNIT 14

active (adj) /æktɪv/
amazing (adj) /əmeɪzɪŋ/
company (n) /kʌmpənɪ/
customer (n)
 /kʌstəmə(r)/
cut (v) /kʌt/
dial (v) /daɪəl/
engaged (pp) (telephone)
 /ɪngeɪdʒd/
exercises (n) (do exercises)
 /eksəsaɪzɪz/
face (n) /feɪs/
fax machine (n)
 /fæks məʃiːn/
foot (n) /fʊt/
glove (n) /glʌv/
gun (n) /gʌn/
handbag (n) /hændbæg/
hurt (v) /hɜːt/
just (adv) /dʒʌst/
kitten (n) /kɪtən/
lamb (n) (=baby sheep)
 /læm/
manager (n) /mænɪdʒə(r)/
marvellous (adj)
 /mɑːvələs/
message (n) /mesɪdʒ/
neck (n) /nek/
operator (n) (telephone)
 /ɒpəreɪtə(r)/
patient (n) (hospital)
 /peɪʃənt/
point (v) /pɔɪnt/
psychiatrist (n)
 /saɪkaɪətrɪst/
puppy (n) /pʌpɪ/
rob (v) /rɒb/
shorts (n) /ʃɔːts/
show (n) /ʃəʊ/
sock (n) /sɒk/
stockings (n)
 /stɒkɪŋz/
telephone directory (n)
 /telɪfəʊn daɪrektərɪ,
 dɪrektərɪ/
tights (n) /taɪts/
toy (n) /tɔɪ/
tractor (n) /træktə(r)/
waitress (n) /weɪtrəs/
washing-up (n) (do the
 washing-up)
 /wɒʃɪŋ ʌp/

widow (n) /wɪdəʊ/
yet (adv) /jet/

UNIT 15

alone (adv) /ələʊn/
appointment (n) /əpɔɪntmənt/
begin (v) /bɪgɪn/
break down (v) (car)
 /breɪk daʊn/
coat (n) /kəʊt/
cry (v) /kraɪ/
customs (n) (airport)
 /kʌstəmz/
decide (v) /dɪsaɪd/
delicious (adj) /dɪlɪʃəs/
door (n) /dɔː(r)/
dressing gown (n)
 /dresɪŋ gaʊn/
driving licence (n)
 /draɪvɪŋ laɪsəns/
education (n) /edʒʊkeɪʃn/
enter (v) /entə(r)/
fill in (v) (fill in a form)
 /fɪl ɪn/
forget (v) /fəget/
forgive (v) /fəgɪv/
form (n) /fɔːm/
fun (n) /fʌn/
get on (v) (get on with someone)
 /get ɒn/
get up (v) (get up in the morning)
 /get ʌp/
give up (v) (give up smoking)
 /gɪv ʌp/
go out (v) (go out with someone)
 /gəʊ aʊt/
handkerchief (n)
 /hæŋkətʃiːf/
hope (v) /həʊp/
identification (n)
 /aɪdentɪfɪkeɪʃn/
neighbour (n) /neɪbə(r)/
official (n) /əfɪʃl/
parcel (n) /pɑːsl/
possible (adj) /pɒsəbl/
post (v) /pəʊst/
problem (n) /prɒbləm/
promise (v) /prɒmɪs/
receipt (n) /rɪsiːt/
salesman (n) /seɪlzmən/
seaside (n) /siːsaɪd/
shout (v) /ʃaʊt/
show (v) /ʃəʊ/
snore (v) /snɔː(r)/
stairs (n) /steəz/
take off (v) (coat)
 /teɪk ɒf/
take off (v) (plane)
 /teɪk ɒf/
trip (n) /trɪp/
turn on (v) (TV)
 /tɜːn ɒn/
uniform (n) /juːnɪfɔːm/

Appendix 1

IRREGULAR VERBS

Base form	Past Simple	Past Participle
be	was/were	been
become	became	become
begin	began	begun
break	broke	broken
bring	brought	brought
build	built	built
buy	bought	bought
can	could	been able
catch	caught	caught
choose	chose	chosen
come	came	come
cost	cost	cost
cut	cut	cut
do	did	done
drink	drank	drunk
drive	drove	driven
eat	ate	eaten
fall	fell	fallen
feel	felt	felt
fight	fought	fought
find	found	found
fly	flew	flown
forget	forgot	forgotten
get	got	got
give	gave	given
go	went	gone/been
grow	grew	grown
have	had	had
hear	heard	heard
hit	hit	hit
keep	kept	kept
know	knew	known
learn	learnt/learned	learnt/learned
leave	left	left
lose	lost	lost
make	made	made
meet	met	met
pay	paid	paid
put	put	put
read /ri:d/	read /red/	read /red/
ride	rode	ridden
run	ran	run
say	said	said
see	saw	seen
sell	sold	sold
send	sent	sent
shut	shut	shut
sing	sang	sung
sit	sat	sat
sleep	slept	slept
speak	spoke	spoken
spend	spent	spent
stand	stood	stood
steal	stole	stolen
swim	swam	swum
take	took	taken
tell	told	told
think	thought	thought
understand	understood	understood
wake	woke	woken
wear	wore	worn
win	won	won
write	wrote	written

Appendix 2

VERB PATTERNS

Verb + *-ing*	
like love enjoy hate finish stop	swimming cooking

Verb + *to* + infinitive	
choose decide forget promise need help hope try want would like would love	to go to work

Note

Have to for obligation is followed by the infinitive.

I have to go now. Goodbye.

Verb + *-ing* or *to* + infintive	
begin start	raining/to rain

Modal auxiliary verbs	
can could shall will would	go arrive

Acknowledgements

The authors would like to thank all the staff at Oxford University Press, especially the editor of this book, Sylvia Wheeldon, for their help, encouragement, and dedication thoughout the writing of the series. We are deeply indebted to them.

The publishers and authors are very grateful to the following teachers and institutions for reading and/or piloting the manuscript, and for providing invaluable comment and feedback on the course:

Jirina Babáková
Briony Beaven
Gary Gibson
Jane Hazelton
Anne Heller
Rosa Lenzuen
Cristina Nogueira
Giuseppe Ruggeri
Jeremy Page

The British School, Rome
Centre d'Etude des Langues, Troyes
Dilko English Centre, Istanbul
The English Centre, Istanbul
Formalangues, Paris
Lingua Sec S.A., Madrid
Rio Cultura, Rio de Janeiro

The publishers would like to thank the following for their permission to reproduce photographs and copyright material:
J Allan Cash Photo Library
Allsport / Michael King / Steve Powell
Barnaby's Picture Library / Alan Smith
Anthony Blake Photo Library
Bridgeman Art Library / Giraudon
Colorific! / Steve Benbow / Robert Garvey / David Burnett / Patrick Ward / J.P.Nacivet / Dilip Mehta / Alon Reininger / Jeff Slocomb
James Davis Photo Library
Dickens House, London
Philip Dunn Photo Library
Mary Evans Picture Library
Ronald Grant Archive / Robert Harding Picture Library
Jeff Holt / The New Haven Register
Hulton Deutsch Collection
Image Bank / Dann Coffey
Impact Photo Library / Alan Blair / John Arthur / Brian Harris / Steve Moss
Life File / Emma Lee / Tim Johnson / Tim Fisher / Nicola Sutton
Popperfoto
Quadrant Picture Library
Reed Consumer Books / Andrew Whittock
Retrograph Archive
The Royal Collection / Her Majesty Queen Elizabeth II
Shilland and Co Ltd
Frank Spooner / Gamma
Telegraph Colour Library / J.Sims / J.C.Davies
John Thompson Picture Library / Sally Anne Thompson / R Willbie
Topham Picture Source / UPPA
TRIP / T.S.Morse / T.M.J.Fisher / Juliet Highet / Helene Rogers / Dave Saunders / NASA / M Feeley / A Tjany Rjadno
Valentines of Dundee
John Walmsley Photo Library

Songs
'Wonderful Tonight': words and music by Eric Clapton, © 1977 and 1992 Eric Clapton
'She's Leaving Home': © 1968 by Northern Songs. All rights controlled and administered by MCA Music Ltd under licence from Northern Songs.

Location photography by:
Emily Anderson
Philip Dunn
Rob Judges
Mark Mason

David Simson / DAS Photo
TRIP / T.S. Morse / M Feeley / A Tjagny Rjadno
John Walmsley

Studio photography by: Emily Anderson, Mark Mason, John Walmsley

Illustrations by:
Kiran Ahmed / Maggie Mundy Agency
Shirley Barker / Artist Partners
Ken Binder / Satchel Illustrators
Chris Chaisty
Nicki Elson
Michael Hill
David Loftus
Sarah MacDonald
Fiona McVicar / The Inkshed
Oxford Illustrators
Nigel Paige
Rachel Ross

Thanks to the following for their time and assistance:
Andrew Bean at the Dickens House Museum
Cherwell School, Oxford
The Ironbridge Gorge Museum, Telford
Oasis Trading, Oxford
Oxford Scientific
BBC Radio Oxford
The Swan School of English, Oxford

Wortschatz: chronologisch

Diese Wortschatzliste ist pro Unit chronologisch geordnet. Alle Wörter und Ausdrücke werden so übersetzt, wie sie im Text- und Übungszusammenhang erscheinen. Die Beispielsätze in der dritten Spalte weisen auf Wörter und Ausdrücke (gekennzeichnet durch ~) hin, die besondere Aufmerksamkeit verdienen, und zeigen, wie diese Wörter angewendet werden.

Unit 1

PRESENTATION 1
hello [hə'ləʊ]	Hallo	
what [wɒt]	was	"~ 's your name?" – "Johann."
where [weə]	wo, woher	"~ are you from?" – "I'm from Oxford."

PRESENTATION 2
and [ənd]	und	
doctor ['dɒktə]	Arzt/Ärztin	
married ['mærɪd]	verheiratet	Manuel and Carla are ~.
to have [həv]	haben	
child, children (pl) [tʃaɪld 'tʃɪldrən]	Kind, Kinder (Pl.)	I have three ~.
to live [lɪv]	leben, wohnen	I ~ in Berlin.
house [haʊs]	Haus	
south [saʊθ]	Süden	Munich is in the ~ of Germany.
to want [wɒnt]	wollen	I ~ to learn English.
to learn [lɜːn]	lernen	
job [dʒɒb]	Beruf	"What is your ~?" – "I'm a doctor."
student ['stjuːdənt]	Student/in	
year [jɪə]	Jahr	I am 19 ~s old.
old [əʊld]	alt	
brother ['brʌðə]	Bruder	
sister ['sɪstə]	Schwester	
flat [flæt]	Wohnung	
because [bɪ'kɒz]	weil	I'm at the VHS ~ I want to learn English.
language ['læŋgwɪdʒ]	Sprache	

PRESENTATION 3
this [ðɪs]	dies, das	~ is Johann.
teacher ['tiːtʃɪ]	Lehrer/in	
daughter ['dɔːtə]	Tochter	
son [sʌn]	Sohn	
surname ['sɜːneɪm]	Nachname	My ~ is Hübner.

LISTENING AND SPEAKING
fine [faɪn]	gut	"How are you?" – "~, thanks. And you?"
thank you, thanks ['θæŋkjʊ, θæŋks]	danke	
how [haʊ]	wie	~ do you spell 'key'? "~ are you?" –
bad [bæd]	schlecht	"Not ~, thanks. And you?" –
very well [verɪ 'wel]	sehr gut	"~, thank you."
goodbye [gʊd'baɪ]	auf Wiedersehen	
nice [naɪs]	schön, nett	Have a ~ evening.
evening ['iːvnɪŋ]	Abend	
to see [siː]	sehen	~ you tomorrow.
tomorrow [tə'mɒrəʊ]	morgen	

VOCABULARY AND PRONUNCIATION
stamp [stæmp]	Briefmarke	
bag [bæg]	Tasche	
map [mæp]	Stadtplan	
key [kiː]	Schlüssel	
apple ['æpl]	Apfel	
postcard ['pəʊstkɑːd]	Postkarte	
ticket ['tɪkɪt]	Fahrkarte	
notebook ['nəʊtbʊk]	Notizbuch	
orange ['ɒrɪndʒ]	Apfelsine	
letter ['letə]	Brief	
suitcase ['suːtkeɪs]	Koffer	
camera ['kæmrə]	Fotoapparat	
dictionary ['dɪkʃənrɪ]	Wörterbuch	
envelope ['envələʊp]	Briefumschlag	
newspaper ['njuːspeɪpə]	Zeitung	
magazine [mægə'ziːn]	Zeitschrift	
book [bʊk]	Buch	
Wednesday ['wenzdɪ]	Mittwoch	

EVERYDAY ENGLISH
to spell [spel]	buchstabieren	"How do you ~ 'apple'?" – "A-double p-l-e."
double ['dʌbl]	doppelt	
first name [fɜːst 'neɪm]	Vorname	My ~ is Johann.
right [raɪt]	richtig	That's ~.
to know [nəʊ]	wissen, kennen	I don't ~.

Unit 2

PRESENTATION 1
country ['kʌntrɪ]	Land	
journalist ['dʒɜːnəlɪst]	Journalist/in	
address [ə'dres]	Adresse	
street [striːt]	Straße	
phone number ['fəʊn nʌmbə]	Telefonnummer	
age [eɪdʒ]	Alter	
no [nəʊ]	nein	
yes [jes]	ja	
taxi driver ['tæksɪ draɪvə]	Taxifahrer/in	
shop assistant ['ʃɒp əsɪstənt]	Verkäufer/in	
policeman [pə'liːsmən]	Polizist	
class [klɑːs]	Klasse	
Monday ['mʌndɪ]	Montag	
today [tə'deɪ]	heute	We are at school ~.
home [həʊm]	zu Hause	I am at ~.
parents ['peərənts]	Eltern	
work [wɜːk]	Arbeit	I am at ~.
champagne [ʃæm'peɪn]	Champagner	
drink [drɪŋk]	Getränk	

PRESENTATION 2
photo ['fəʊtəʊ]	Foto	
wife [waɪf]	Ehefrau	
dentist ['dentɪst]	Zahnarzt/ärztin	She is a ~.
hairdresser ['heədresə]	Friseur/in	
boyfriend ['bɔɪfrend]	Freund	
travel agent ['trævl eɪdʒənt]	Reisebürokaufmann/frau	
who [huː]	wer	"~ is David?" – "He is Paola's penfriend."

mother ['mʌðə]	Mutter		
husband ['hʌzbənd]	Ehemann		
father ['fɑːðə]	Vater		
uncle ['ʌŋkl]	Onkel		
aunt [ɑːnt]	Tante		
nephew ['nevjuː]	Neffe		
niece [niːs]	Nichte		
grandfather ['grændfɑːðə]	Großvater		
grandmother ['grændmʌðə]	Großmutter		
engineer [endʒɪ'nɪə]	Ingenieur/in		

VOCABULARY

difficult ['dɪfɪkəlt]	schwierig	*opp* easy
expensive [ɪk'spensɪv]	teuer	*opp* cheap
old [əʊld]	alt	*opp* young; new
hot [hɒt]	heiß	*opp* cold
horrible ['hɒrəbl]	schrecklich	*opp* lovely
cold [kəʊld]	kalt	*opp* hot
cheap [tʃiːp]	billig	*opp* expensive
new [njuː]	neu	*opp* old
lovely ['lʌvlɪ]	schön	*opp* horrible
small [smɔːl]	klein	*opp* big
big [bɪg]	groß	*opp* small
easy ['iːzɪ]	leicht, einfach	*opp* difficult
young [jʌŋ]	jung	*opp* old
wrong [rɒŋ]	falsch	*opp* right

READING AND LISTENING

dear [dɪə]	liebe/r	*~ John,*
		Thank you for your letter ...
school [skuːl]	Schule	
with [wɪð, wɪθ]	mit, bei	*Paola is ~ an English family in London.*
other ['ʌðə]	andere/s/r	*I have the ~ books at home.*
different ['dɪfrənt]	verschieden	*The children are at ~ schools.*
funny ['fʌnɪ]	lustig	
good [gʊd]	gut	
top [tɒp]	oben	*The address is at the ~ of the letter.*
family ['fæməlɪ]	Familie	
friendly ['frendlɪ]	freundlich	
but [bʌt]	aber	*It's cold today, ~ sunny.*
to understand [ʌndə'stænd]	verstehen	*English isn't easy to ~.*
interesting ['ɪntrəstɪŋ]	interessant	
weather ['weðə]	Wetter	
sunny ['sʌnɪ]	sonnig	
beautiful ['bjuːtɪfl]	schön	
all [ɔːl]	alle	*The children are ~ at home.*
centre ['sentə]	Zentrum, Mitte	*Hyde Park is in the ~ of London.*
to use [juːz]	benutzen	*It isn't easy to ~ the London Underground.*
underground ['ʌndəgraʊnd]	U-Bahn	
now [naʊ]	jetzt, gerade, nun	*Paola is in London ~.*
food [fuːd]	Essen	
coffee ['kɒfɪ]	Kaffee	
to write [raɪt]	schreiben	
soon [suːn]	bald	*Write to me ~.*
love [lʌv]	liebe Grüße	*~ Paola.*
happy ['hæpɪ]	glücklich	
holiday ['hɒlədeɪ]	Urlaub, Ferien	*We are on ~.*

EVERYDAY ENGLISH

corner ['kɔːnə]	Ecke	
ham [hæm]	Schinken	
cheese ['tʃiːz]	Käse	
tuna ['tjuːnə]	Thunfisch	
chicken ['tʃɪkɪn]	Hähnchen	
piece [piːs]	Stück, Teil	*A ~ of pizza is 90p.*
ice cream [aɪs'kriːm]	Eiskrem	
cup [kʌp]	Tasse	
tea [tiː]	Tee	
coke [kəʊk]	Coca-Cola	
orange juice [ɒrɪndʒ 'dʒuːs]	Orangensaft	
mineral water ['mɪnərəl wɔːtə]	Mineralwasser	
how much [haʊ 'mʌtʃ]	wieviel	*~ is a cheese sandwich?*
pound [paʊnd]	Pfund	*A hamburger is two ~s fifty.*
can [kæn]	können, dürfen	
please [pliːz]	bitte	*Can I have a cup of tea, ~?*
anything ['enɪθɪŋ]	(irgend)etwas	*~ to drink?*
		~ else?
to drink [drɪŋk]	trinken	
here you are [hɪə jʊ'ɑː]	bitte schön	*"Can I have a coke, please?" – "Yes, ~."*
(good) morning ['mɔːnɪŋ]	(Guten) Morgen	

Unit 3

PRESENTATION 1

to come [kʌm]	kommen	*"Where do you ~ from?" – "I ~ from Japan."*
nun [nʌn]	Nonne	
to work [wɜːk]	arbeiten	*Mark King ~s in an office.*
girl [gɜːl]	Mädchen	
to teach [tiːtʃ]	unterrichten	*She ~es in Ireland.*
to like [laɪk]	mögen, gern haben/tun	*He ~s his job.*
to love [lʌv]	lieben	*She ~s the holidays.*
green [griːn]	grün	
countryside	Landschaft	
to go walking ['wɔːkɪŋ]	spazierengehen	*I ~ in the countryside.*
free time [friː 'taɪm]	Freizeit	*I play football in my ~.*
ski instructor ['skiː ɪnstrʌktə]	Skitrainer/in, -lehrer/in	
village ['vɪlɪdʒ]	Dorf	
mountain ['maʊntɪn]	Berg	
summer ['sʌmə]	Sommer	*In ~ it is warm, but in winter it is cold.*
sports shop ['spɔːts ʃɒp]	Sportartikelgeschäft	
shop [ʃɒp]	Geschäft, Laden	
winter ['wɪntə]	Winter	
skiing ['skiːɪŋ]	Skilaufen	
to speak [spiːk]	sprechen	*He ~s French.*
to play [pleɪ]	spielen	
football ['fʊtbɔːl]	Fußball	
town [taʊn]	Stadt	
near [nɪə]	in der Nähe von	*She lives ~ the school.*
sea [siː]	Meer	
too [tuː]	auch	*Hans is nice. His wife is nice, ~.*
place of work [pleɪs əv 'wɜːk]	Arbeitsstelle	
dog [dɒg]	Hund	

interpreter [ɪn'tɜ:prɪtə]	Dolmetscher/in	
United Nations	Vereinte Nationen	*The ~ is in New York.*
[ju:'naɪtɪd neɪʃnz]		
office ['ɒfɪs]	Büro	

PRESENTATION 2

how many	wie viele	*"~ languages do you*
[haʊ 'menɪ]		*speak?" – "Two, Italian*
		and French."
to watch television	fernsehen	
[wɒtʃ 'telɪvɪʒn]		
to wash [wɒʃ]	waschen	

VOCABULARY AND PRONUNCIATION

singer ['sɪŋə]	Sänger/in	
nurse [nɜ:s]	Krankenschwester/ -pfleger	
actor ['æktə]	Schauspieler	
mechanic [mɪ'kænɪk]	Mechaniker/in	
receptionist	Herr/Dame am	
[rɪ'sepʃənɪst]	Empfang	
baker ['beɪkə]	Bäcker/in	
to make [meɪk]	machen	
bread [bred]	Brot	
to look after	sich kümmern um,	*She looks after old people.*
[lʊk 'ɑ:ftə]	sorgen für	
people ['pi:pl]	Leute	
hospital ['hɒspɪtl]	Krankenhaus	
to translate	übersetzen	
[trænz'leɪt]		
to sell [sel]	verkaufen	
thing [θɪŋ]	Ding, Sache	
to fly [flaɪ]	fliegen	*He flies a private plane.*
plane [pleɪn]	Flugzeug	
night club ['naɪt klʌb]	Nachtklub	
to cut [kʌt]	(ab)schneiden	
hair [heə]	Haar/e	*Her ~ is nice.*
to mend [mend]	reparieren	
car [kɑ:]	Auto	

READING AND LISTENING

to leave [li:v]	verlassen	*I ~ work at 5.30.*
to drive [draɪv]	fahren	*I ~ to work, I don't*
to catch [kætʃ]	nehmen	*~ the train.*
train [treɪn]	Zug	
ferry ['ferɪ]	Fähre	
to arrive [ə'raɪv]	ankommen	*I ~ at school at 8.00.*
journey ['dʒɜ:nɪ]	Reise	
to take [teɪk]	dauern	*The journey to London ~s*
		six hours.
to cost [kɒst]	kosten	
only ['əʊnlɪ]	nur	*The journey costs ~ £16.*
pence [pens]	Pence	
fortunately	glücklicherweise	*~, Mr Garret likes his job.*
['fɔ:tʃənətlɪ]		
long-distance	Langstrecken-	
[lɒŋ'dɪstəns]		
every ['evrɪ]	jede/r/s	*He goes to England ~*
		Monday.
mile [maɪl]	Meile	
afternoon [ɑ:ftə'nu:n]	Nachmittag	*We go walking in the ~.*
then [ðen]	dann	*~ we watch television in*
evening ['i:vnɪŋ]	Abend	*the ~.*
there and back	hin und zurück	
[ðeə ənd 'bæk]		
hour ['aʊə]	Stunde	
day [deɪ]	Tag	
week [wi:k]	Woche	*He works five days a ~.*

Tuesday ['tju:zdɪ]	Dienstag	*On Mondays and on ~s I*
		have an English class.
tired ['taɪəd]	müde	
to say [seɪ]	sagen	
man [mæn]	Mann	
by [baɪ]	mit	*He goes to work ~ car, and I*
		go ~ train.
why [waɪ]	warum	
what time [taɪm]	wie spät, um	*"~ does he catch the ferry?"*
	wieviel Uhr	*– " At 5.30."*
when [wen]	wann	*"~ do you want to leave?" –*
		"In the morning."
how long [lɒŋ]	wie lange	*"~ does it take to drive to*
		work?" – "Thirty minutes."
sir [sɜ:]	Herr	*Excuse me, please ~.*
of course [əf'kɔ:s]	natürlich	
next [nekst]	nächste/r/s	*See you ~ Wednesday.*
stop [stɒp]	Haltestelle	
boy [bɔɪ]	Junge	
homework	Hausaufgabe	
['həʊmwɜ:k]		
desk [desk]	Schreibtisch	
seat [si:t]	Sitzplatz	
certainly ['sɜ:tnlɪ]	sicher, gewiß	*"It is wet today." – "It ~ is."*
darling ['dɑ:lɪŋ]	Liebling	
to sit (down)	sich setzen	
[sɪt 'daʊn]		
glass [glɑ:s]	Glas	
wine [waɪn]	Wein	
hungry ['hʌŋgrɪ]	hungrig	*He is ~.*
ticket inspector	Fahrkarten-	
['tɪkɪt ɪnspektə]	kontrolleur/in	
passenger ['pæsɪndʒə]	Passagier	

EVERYDAY ENGLISH

o'clock [ə'klɒk]	Uhr	*It is seven ~.*
half [hɑ:f]	halb	*The train leaves at ~ past*
		four.
past [pɑ:st]	nach (mit Uhrzeiten)	
quarter ['kwɔ:tə]	Viertel	*The English class is at ~ past*
		ten.
to [tʊ, tə]	vor (mit Uhrzeiten)	*The Spanish class is at*
		quarter ~ eleven.
exactly [ɪg'zæktlɪ]	exakt, genau	
nearly ['nɪəlɪ]	fast	
just [dʒʌst]	gerade	*It is ~ after quarter to three.*
after ['ɑ:ftə]	nach	
excuse me	Entschuldigung,	
[ɪk'skju:z mɪ]	Verzeihung	
to tell [tel]	erzählen, sagen	
time [taɪm]	(Uhr)zeit	*"Excuse me, what ~ is it,*
		please?" –
sorry ['sɒrɪ]	es tut mir leid	*"I'm ~, I don't know."*
watch [wɒtʃ]	Armbanduhr	

Unit 4

PRESENTATION 1

to interview ['ɪntəvju:]	interviewen	
early ['ɜ:lɪ]	früh	*She catches an ~ morning*
		train.
news [nju:z]	Nachrichten	*The ~ is at 6 o'clock.*
programme	Sendung	*He likes the ~ after the news.*
['prəʊgræm]		
(to be) called	heißen	*The restaurant is ~ 'Ciao'.*
['kɔ:ld]		

world [wɜːld]	Welt	
weekday ['wiːkdeɪ]	Wochentag	
to get up [get 'ʌp]	aufstehen	I ~ at 7.00 every morning.
to start [stɑːt]	anfangen	He ~s work at 9.00.
exciting [ɪk'saɪtɪŋ]	aufregend	
to meet [miːt]	treffen, kennen- lernen	I ~ my friends in a café every Wednesday.
a lot of [ə'lɒtəv]	viele	Maria writes ~ letters.
weekend [wiːk'end]	Wochenende	I like relaxing at ~s.
to chat [tʃæt]	plaudern	
to visit ['vɪzɪt]	besuchen	He ~s his parents every week.
to relax [rɪ'læks]	sich entspannen	
to eat [iːt]	essen	
to bring [brɪŋ]	bringen	
to stay [steɪ]	bleiben	
to go [gəʊ]	gehen, fahren	
to listen ['lɪsn]	zuhören	I ~ to the early morning news programme.
to cook [kʊk]	kochen	
to go out [gəʊ 'aʊt]	ausgehen	
Friday ['fraɪdɪ]	Freitag	
about [ə'baʊt]	ungefähr	It's ~ 60 miles from his home to London.
just [dʒʌst]	nur, bloß	I ~ want to go to bed early.
sometimes ['sʌmtaɪmz]	manchmal	I ~ go out on Saturday evenings.
friend [frend]	Freund/in	
dinner ['dɪnə]	Abendessen	A friend comes for ~.
meal [miːl]	Mahlzeit, Essen	
cooking ['kʊkɪŋ]	Kochen	
music ['mjuːzɪk]	Musik	
Saturday ['sætədɪ]	Samstag	
to go shopping ['ʃɒpɪŋ]	einkaufen gehen	
theatre ['θɪətə]	Theater	At weekends I often go to the ~.
opera ['ɒprə]	Oper	I sometimes go to the ~.
favourite ['feɪvərɪt]	Lieblings-	This is my ~ restaurant.
Sunday ['sʌndɪ]	Sonntag	
bed [bed]	Bett	
late [leɪt]	spät	
until [ən'tɪl]	bis	At weekends I often sleep ~ 10 o'clock.
not until [ən'tɪl]	erst	At weekends I don't get up until 10 o'clock.
country ['kʌntrɪ]	Land	I sometimes go walking in the ~.

PRESENTATION 2

to travel ['trævl]	reisen	
to do [duː]	tun, machen	What do you ~ at weekends?
disco ['dɪskəʊ]	Diskothek	
usually ['juːʒəlɪ]	gewöhnlich	I ~ play cards on Saturday evenings.
Thursday ['θɜːzdɪ]	Donnerstag	
here [hɪə]	hier	I live in this street ~.
to read [riːd]	lesen	
cards [kɑːdz]	Karten	
to smoke [sməʊk]	rauchen	
never ['nevə]	niemals	I ~ drink wine.
not at all [nɒtə'tɔːl]	überhaupt nicht	"Do you speak French?" – "No, ~."
both [bəʊθ]	beide	Jane and I ~ like cooking.
word processor ['wɜːd prəʊsesə]	Textverarbeitungs- maschine	

PRESENTATION 3

university [juːnɪ'vɜːsətɪ]	Universität	My son is at ~.
article ['ɑːtɪkl]	Artikel	
about [ə'baʊt]	über	He writes articles ~ France.
spring [sprɪŋ]	Frühling	In ~ I usually play a lot of tennis.
river ['rɪvə]	Fluß	
breakfast ['brekfəst]	Frühstück	
to have breakfast	frühstücken	
delicious [dɪ'lɪʃəs]	köstlich, lecker	
to walk [wɔːk]	gehen, laufen	
to go back to work	mit der Arbeit wieder anfangen	I don't want to ~ next Monday.
queen [kwiːn]	Königin	
question ['kwestʃən]	Frage	
to go swimming ['swɪmɪŋ]	schwimmen gehen	
answer ['ɑːnsə]	Antwort	

VOCABULARY

to dance [dɑːns]	tanzen	
to do crosswords ['krɒswɜːdz]	Kreuzworträtsel lösen	
to take photographs ['fəʊtəgrɑːfs]	fotografieren	
to go ice-skating ['aɪsskeɪtɪŋ]	Schlittschuh laufen	"What sports do you like?" – "I like going ice-skating and sailing."
game [geɪm]	Spiel	
to go sailing ['seɪlɪŋ]	segeln	
to paint [peɪnt]	malen	"What is your hobby?" – "I love ~ing."
cinema ['sɪnəmɑː]	Kino	
to go windsurfing ['wɪndsɜːfɪŋ]	windsurfen	"What do you do on holiday?" – "We drive to the beach and ~."
to sunbathe ['sʌnbeɪð]	sich sonnen	We like sunbathing.
to go fishing ['fɪʃɪŋ]	angeln, fischen (gehen)	
really ['rɪəlɪ]	wirklich	"I like going swimming." – "Oh, ~? Where do you go?"

READING AND LISTENING

long [lɒŋ]	lang	
short [ʃɔːt]	kurz	
ice hockey ['aɪshɒkɪ]	Eishockey	
lake [leɪk]	See	
season ['siːzn]	Jahreszeit	What is your favourite ~, spring, summer, autumn or winter?
so [səʊ]	also	He lives near the office, ~ he walks to work.
autumn ['ɔːtəm]	Herbst	
north [nɔːθ]	Norden	Manchester is in the ~ of England.
colour ['kʌlə]	Farbe	
tree [triː]	Baum	
red [red]	rot	
yellow ['jeləʊ]	gelb	
brown [braʊn]	braun	
to think [θɪŋk]	denken	"Where is Johann?" – "I don't know. I ~ he is at home."
always ['ɔːlweɪz]	immer	I ~ play volleyball in the summer.

January ['dʒænjʊərɪ]	Januar	
February ['februərɪ]	Februar	
often ['ɒfn]	oft	*I ~ go to the cinema on Saturdays.*
wet [wet]	naß	
grey [greɪ]	grau	
suddenly ['sʌdnlɪ]	plötzlich	*~ it's winter and the days are short.*
beach [biːtʃ]	Strand	
export department ['ekspɔːt dɪpɑːtmənt]	Exportabteilung	
special ['speʃl]	spezial, speziell	
flower ['flaʊə]	Blume	
especially [ɪ'speʃəlɪ]	besonders, speziell	*"Do you like reading?" – "Yes, ~ on holiday."*
to sing [sɪŋ]	singen	
song [sɒŋ]	Lied	
shy [ʃaɪ]	schüchtern	
to watch [wɒtʃ]	ansehen, anschauen	

EVERYDAY ENGLISH

to have a light [laɪt]	Feuer haben	*Do you ~, please?*
traffic ['træfɪk]	Verkehr	
page [peɪdʒ]	Seite	*The text is on ~ 53.*
to worry ['wʌrɪ]	sich Sorgen machen	*Don't ~. It's OK.*
quite [kwaɪt]	ziemlich, ganz	*The new song is ~ nice.*
to open ['əʊpən]	öffnen	
window ['wɪndəʊ]	Fenster	
to matter ['mætə]	etw. ausmachen	*"I don't know his name." – "It doesn't ~."*
to help [help]	helfen	*"Hello, can I ~ you?" – "No, thank you."*
exposure [ɪk'spəʊʒə]	Belichtung	
picture ['pɪktʃə]	Bild (Foto)	
Pardon? ['pɑːdn]	Wie bitte?	
to mean [miːn]	bedeuten	*"What does 'flower' ~ in German?" – "Blume."*

Unit 5

PRESENTATION 1

room [ruːm]	Zimmer	
living room ['lɪvɪŋrʊm]	Wohnzimmer	
chair [tʃeə]	Stuhl	
picture ['pɪktʃə]	Bild	
mirror ['mɪrə]	Spiegel	
armchair ['ɑːmtʃeə]	Sessel	
telephone ['telɪfəʊn]	Telefon	
table ['teɪbl]	Tisch	
fire ['faɪə]	Feuer	
lamp [læmp]	Lampe	
plant [plɑːnt]	Pflanze	
clock [klɒk]	Uhr	
next to [nekst]	neben	*The lamp is ~ the sofa.*
in front of [frʌnt]	vor	*The sofa is ~ the window.*
behind [bɪ'haɪnd]	hinter	*The plant is ~ the telephone.*
cat [kæt]	Katze	
stop! [stɒp]	halt, halten Sie	

PRESENTATION 2

kitchen ['kɪtʃɪn]	Küche	
clean [kliːn]	sauber	
cupboard ['kʌbəd]	Schrank	
washing machine ['wɒʃɪŋ məʃiːn]	Waschmaschine	

fridge [frɪdʒ]	Kühlschrank	
cooker ['kʊkə]	Herd	
dishwasher ['dɪʃwɒʃə]	Geschirrspülmaschine	
wall [wɔːl]	Wand	
any ['enɪ]	irgendwelche	*There aren't ~ apples in the fridge.* *Are there ~ cups here?*
some [sʌm]	einige	*There are ~ cups in the cupboard.*
plate [pleɪt]	Teller	
sink [sɪŋk]	Spülbecken	
classroom ['klɑːsrʊm]	Klassenzimmer	
floor [flɔː]	Boden	
pen [pen]	Kugelschreiber	
address book [ə'dres bʊk]	Adreßbuch	

READING

building ['bɪldɪŋ]	Gebäude	*I work in a big ~.*
inside [ɪn'saɪd]	innerhalb	*The photos are ~ the envelope.*
whole [həʊl]	ganz	*The ~ world knows the Queen's address in London.*
famous ['feɪməs]	berühmt	
to grow up [grəʊ]	aufwachsen	*Kings and queens ~ in palaces.*
like [laɪk]	ähnlich wie	*There are a lot of books in the classroom. It is ~ a small library.*
to prepare [prɪ'peə]	vorbereiten	
own [əʊn]	eigene/s/r	*I have my ~ room at home.*
piper ['paɪpə]	(Dudelsack)pfeifer	
outside [aʊt'saɪd]	außerhalb	*I meet her ~ her office every Friday.*
to do the washing-up [wɒʃɪŋ'ʌp]	abspülen	
everybody ['evrɪbɒdɪ]	jeder(mann)	*He is a very nice man. ~ likes him.*
during ['djʊərɪŋ]	während	*He drinks a lot of coffee ~ the day.*
course [kɔːs]	Gang	*At home we usually eat two ~s.*
palace ['pælɪs]	Palast	
Prime Minister [praɪm 'mɪnɪstə]	Premierminister/in	
first [fɜːst]	zuerst	*Buckingham Palace, ~ built in 1703, is where the Queen lives.*
to build [bɪld]	bauen	
place [pleɪs]	Ort, Stelle	
also ['ɔːlsəʊ]	auch	*The kitchen is the place where we cook our meals. It is ~ the place where we eat.*
president ['prezɪdənt]	Präsident/in	
king [kɪŋ]	König	
politician [pɒlə'tɪʃn]	Politiker/in	
police station [pə'liːs steɪʃn]	Polizeiwache	
post office ['pəʊst ɒfɪs]	Postamt	
club [klʌb]	Verein, Klub	
swimming pool ['swɪmɪŋ puːl]	Schwimmbad	
carpet ['kɑːpɪt]	Teppich	
full-time [fʊl'taɪm]	ganztags	*He works ~.*
bath [bɑːθ]	Bad	
clothes [kləʊðz]	Kleidung	*My new ~ are in the cupboard.*

to feed [fi:d]	füttern, ernähren	
royal ['rɔɪəl]	königlich	
to sleep [sli:p]	schlafen	
bedroom ['bedrʊm]	Schlafzimmer	
egg [eg]	Ei	
to talk [tɔ:k]	reden, sich unterhalten	*He always ~s about football.*
perhaps [pə'hæps]	vielleicht	*I'm hungry. Is there any cheese, or ~ some ham?*
to invite [ɪn'vaɪt]	einladen	
white [waɪt]	weiß	
water ['wɔ:tə]	Wasser	
port [pɔ:t]	Portwein	
liqueur [lɪ'kjʊə]	Likör	
first [fɜ:st]	erste/r/s	*I like the ~ song, but I don't like the ~ one.*
second ['sekənd]	zweite/r/s	
to speak to somebody [spi:k]	mit jdm. reden, sprechen	*I want to ~ to you.*
left [left]	links	*"Excuse me, where is the baker's?" – "Take the first turning on the ~."*
right [raɪt]	rechts	*The bank is on the ~, next to the library.*
to finish (food) ['fɪnɪʃ]	aufessen	
more than [mɔ: ðən]	mehr als	*This book is ~ one hundred pages long.*
same [seɪm]	gleich	*We read the ~ newspaper.*
what sort of ...? [sɔ:t]	was für (ein/e) ...?	*~ newspaper do you read?*
to happen ['hæpən]	geschehen, passieren	*What ~s when the Queen meets the Prime Minister?*
supermarket ['su:pəmɑ:kɪt]	Supermarkt	

LISTENING AND SPEAKING

number ['nʌmbə]	Anzahl	
garden ['gɑ:dn]	Garten	
terrace ['terəs]	Terrasse	

EVERYDAY ENGLISH

to buy [baɪ]	kaufen	
cigarette [sɪgə'ret]	Zigarette	
to borrow ['bɒrəʊ]	ausleihen	*Can I ~ your book, please?*
public toilet [pʌblɪk 'tɔɪlət]	öffentliche Toilette	
bus stop ['bʌs stɒp]	Bushaltestelle	
newsagent's ['nju:zeɪdʒənts]	Zeitungsladen	
phone box ['fəʊnbɒks]	Telefonzelle	
post box ['pəʊstbɒks]	Briefkasten	
chemist's ['kemɪsts]	Apotheke	
travel agent's ['trævl eɪdʒənts]	Reisebüro	
library ['laɪbrərɪ]	Bücherei	
pub [pʌb]	Kneipe	
baker's ['beɪkəz]	Bäckerei	
over there [əʊvə 'ðeə]	da drüben	*The bus stop is ~.*
opposite ['ɒpəzɪt]	gegenüber	*He lives ~ the cinema.*
far [fɑ:]	weit	*Can we walk to the pub? Is it ~?*
what about ...? ['wɒt əbaʊt]	wie ist es mit ...?	*"Is there a post office in Park Lane?" – "Yes." – "~ a bank?"*

Unit 6

PRESENTATION 1

dark [dɑ:k]	dunkel	
to type [taɪp]	tippen	*I can ~ sixty words a minute.*
word [wɜ:d]	Wort	
to hear [hɪə]	hören	*I'm sorry, I can't ~ you.*
line [laɪn]	Leitung	*The ~ is bad.*
to draw [drɔ:]	zeichnen	
piano [pɪ'ænəʊ]	Klavier	*Can you play the ~?*
to count [kaʊnt]	zählen	
chess [tʃes]	Schach	
to smell [smel]	riechen	*The dinner ~s delicious.*
to forecast the weather ['fɔ:kɑ:st, 'weðə]	das Wetter vorhersagen	
to check [tʃek]	kontrollieren, überprüfen	*Can you ~ the spelling of 'book', please?*
spelling ['spelɪŋ]	Rechtschreibung	
conversation [kɒnvə'seɪʃn]	Unterhaltung, Gespräch	

PRESENTATION 2

yesterday ['jestədeɪ]	gestern	*It was Friday ~.*
month [mʌnθ]	Monat	
last [lɑ:st]	letzte/r/s	
could [kʊd]	könnte(n)	*~ you play chess when you were ten?*
when [wen]	als	*Could he count ~ he was two?*
this morning ['mɔ:nɪŋ]	heute früh	*Were you at work ~?*
last night [lɑ:st naɪt]	gestern Abend	*Where were you ~?*
lunchtime ['lʌntʃtaɪm]	Mittagszeit	*I was at home at ~.*
well [wel]	na ja	*~, the film wasn't bad.*
brilliant ['brɪlɪənt]	großartig	
barbecue ['bɑ:bɪkju:]	Grillparty	
match [mætʃ]	Spiel	
(to be) born [bɔ:n]	geboren (sein)	*I was ~ in London.*

READING AND SPEAKING

genius ['dʒi:nɪəs]	Genie	
player ['pleɪə]	Spieler/in	
to practise ['præktɪs]	üben	
all day [ɔ:l 'deɪ]	den ganzen Tag über	*He was in Stuttgart ~.*
different ['dɪfrənt]	anders	*He is ~ from his brother.*
to ride a bike [raɪd, baɪk]	Fahrrad fahren	
under ['ʌndə]	unter	*He is the ~-18 swimming champion of Germany.*
champion ['tʃæmpɪən]	Meister/in	
either ['aɪðə]	auch nicht	*I can't speak French and I can't speak Spanish, ~.*
still [stɪl]	trotzdem	*I can't play the piano, but I ~ like music.*
boring ['bɔ:rɪŋ]	langweilig	*I don't like playing chess. It's ~.*
to study ['stʌdɪ]	studieren	*I ~ languages at University.*
medicine ['medsɪn]	Medizin	
fluently ['flu:əntlɪ]	fließend	*He speaks French ~.*
calculus ['kælkjʊləs]	Differential- und Integralrechnung	
algebra ['ældʒɪbrə]	Algebra	
important [ɪm'pɔ:tnt]	wichtig, bedeutend	
to ask a question ['kwestʃən]	eine Frage stellen	*Can I ask you some questions?*
first of all	zunächst	*~, how are you?*

6 Wortschatz

VOCABULARY AND PRONUNCIATION

black [blæk] — schwarz
eye [aɪ] — Auge
to wear [weə] — tragen — *I usually ~ jeans at weekends.*

meat [miːt] — Fleisch
cheque [tʃek] — Scheck — *Can I pay by ~, please?*
nose [nəʊz] — Nase
sun [sʌn] — Sonne
hat [hæt] — Hut

EVERYDAY ENGLISH

flight [flaɪt] — Flug
destination [destɪ'neɪʃn] — Reiseziel
gate [geɪt] — Flugsteig
remark [rɪ'maːk] — Bemerkung
call [kɔːl] — (Auf-)Ruf
delayed [dɪ'leɪd] — verspätet — *The flight is ~.*
to board [bɔːd] — einsteigen, an Bord gehen
passport control ['paːspɔːt kəntrəʊl] — Paßkontrolle
baggage reclaim [bægɪdʒ 'riːkleɪm] — Gepäckausgabe
check-in-desk ['tʃekɪn desk] — Abfertigungs-schalter
arrival hall [ə'raɪvl hɔːl] — Empfangshalle
departure lounge [dɪ'paːtʃə laʊndʒ] — Abflughalle
again [ə'gen] — wieder — *Can you come ~ next week?*
hand luggage ['hænd lʌgɪdʒ] — Handgepäck
smoking ['sməʊkɪŋ] — Raucher — *~ or non-smoking, madam?*
non-smoking [nɒn'sməʊkɪŋ] — Nichtraucher
boarding pass ['bɔːdɪŋ paːs] — Bordkarte
tray [treɪ] — Tablett
madam ['mædəm] — gnädige Frau
to fasten ['faːsn] — befestigen — *Please ~ your seatbelts. We land in five minutes.*
seatbelt ['siːtbelt] — Sicherheitsgurt
to land [lænd] — landen
welcome ['welkəm] — Willkommen — *~ to Germany, Mrs Smith.*
never mind [nevə 'maɪnd] — schon gut — *"I don't have a pen." – "~, you can use my pen."*
safely ['seɪflɪ] — sicher, heil, wohlbehalten
outside [aʊt'saɪd] — draußen — *The children can't play ~.*

Unit 7

PRESENTATION 1

to earn [ɜːn] — verdienen — *She ~s £14,000 a year.*
to move [muːv] — umziehen
to retire [rɪ'taɪə] — sich pensionieren lassen — *She ~d last year.*
to die [daɪ] — sterben — *He ~d in 1948 when he was 75 years old.*
over ['əʊvə] — über — *My grandmother is ~ 80 years old.*
to remember [rɪ'membə] — sich erinnern — *I can ~ when Germany won the World Cup in 1990.*
life [laɪf] — Leben

past [paːst] — Vergangenheit
war [wɔː] — Krieg — *Her father died in the Second World ~.*
immediately [ɪ'miːdɪətlɪ] — sofort — *I must do my homework ~.*
housemaid ['haʊsmeɪd] — Hausmädchen
rich [rɪtʃ] — reich
to clean [kliːn] — saubermachen
before [bɪ'fɔː] — vor — *Do you want a drink ~ dinner?*
another [ə'nʌðə] — ein andere/r/s — *She moved to ~ house.*
to marry ['mærɪ] — heiraten — *They married in 1950 and had six children.*
only ['əʊnlɪ] — erst — *I was ~ ten years old when we moved to London.*
to finish work ['fɪnɪʃ wɜːk] — Feierabend machen — *He ~es work at 5.30 every day.*

PRESENTATION 2

nationality [næʃə'nælətɪ] — Nationalität — *"What ~ is she?" – "Japanese."*
subject ['sʌbdʒɪkt] — Fach, Unterrichtsfach

PRESENTATION 3

to become [bɪ'kʌm] — werden — *She became a grandmother at the age of forty-five.*
to lose [luːz] — verlieren — *I lost my key yesterday.*
to hate [heɪt] — hassen
to find [faɪnd] — finden — *My son found my key.*
to get [get] — bekommen — *I got a lot of presents for my birthday.*
to change [tʃeɪndʒ] — wechseln
to give [gɪv] — geben — *He gave me some flowers.*
to win [wɪn] — gewinnen — *We won the football match.*
politics ['pɒlətɪks] — Politik
unemployed [ʌnɪm'plɔɪd] — arbeitslos — *He is ~.*
video recorder ['vɪdɪəʊ rɪkɔːdə] — Videorecorder
birthday ['bɜːθdeɪ] — Geburtstag — *It's his ~ today. He got a book for his ~.*
to come down [kʌm 'daʊn] — fallen — *The Berlin Wall came down in 1989.*
night [naɪt] — Nacht — *He often goes out at ~.*
someone ['sʌmwʌn] — jemand — *Can ~ help me, please?*
kiss [kɪs] — Kuß
something ['sʌmθɪŋ] — etwas — *Did you eat ~ for dinner?*
present ['preznt] — Geschenk
shoe [ʃuː] — Schuh
to enjoy [ɪn'dʒɔɪ] — gefallen — *We didn't ~ our holiday last year.*

READING

writer ['raɪtə] — Schriftsteller/in
novelist ['nɒvəlɪst] — Romancier
factory ['fæktərɪ] — Fabrik
lawcourt ['lɔːkɔːt] — Gericht, Gerichtshof
clerk [klaːk] — (Büro-)Angestellte(r)
popular ['pɒpjʊlə] — beliebt — *He is a very ~ person.*
abroad [ə'brɔːd] — im/ins Ausland — *He lives ~. She goes ~ every summer.*
debt [det] — Schuld — *His father was in ~.*
experience [ɪk'spɪərɪəns] — Erfahrung — *He had a horrible ~ when he was eleven.*
successful [sək'sesfəl] — erfolgreich
prison ['prɪzn] — Gefängnis — *His father went to ~.*

clothes shop ['kləʊðz ʃɒp]	Bekleidungs-geschäft	
businessman ['bɪznɪsmən]	Geschäftsmann	
money ['mʌnɪ]	Geld	
wonderful ['wʌndəfəl]	wunderbar	
novel ['nɒvl]	Roman	
great [greɪt]	sehr gut, großartig	
real [rɪəl]	echt	
character ['kærɪktə]	Charakter, Person	
middle-class ['mɪdlklɑːs]	Mittelklasse	
lady ['leɪdɪ]	Lady, Dame	
gentleman ['dʒentlmən]	Herr	
poor [pʊə]	arm	
to spend [spend]	verbringen, ausgeben	*She spent a lot of time shopping and spent a lot of money.*
hard [hɑːd]	hart	*He works ~.*
clever ['klevə]	clever, schlau	
bottle ['bɒtl]	Flasche	
to forget [fə'get]	vergessen	*I forgot his birthday.*
short story [ʃɔːt 'stɔːrɪ]	Kurzgeschichte	
description [dɪ'skrɪpʃn]	Beschreibung	
full [fʊl]	voll	*The park was ~ of flowers.*
to stop [stɒp]	aufhören	*He never ~ped working.*

VOCABULARY AND PRONUNCIATION
farm [fɑːm]	Bauernhof	
high [haɪ]	hoch	
foreign ['fɒrən]	ausländisch	
knife [naɪf]	Messer	

EVERYDAY ENGLISH
wedding ['wedɪŋ]	Hochzeit	
Christmas ['krɪsməs]	Weihnachten	*Merry ~ everyone!* / *She always goes home for ~.*
New Year's Eve [njuː jɪəz 'iːv]	Silvester	
Easter ['iːstə]	Ostern	*She always sees her family at ~.*
Valentine's Day ['væləntaɪnz deɪ]	Valentinstag	
sick [sɪk]	krank	
custom ['kʌstəm]	Sitte	
congratulations [kəngrætʃʊ'leɪʃnz]	herzlichen Glückwunsch	*~! When is your wedding day?*
sure [ʃɔː]	sicher	
yet [jet]	noch nicht	*"When are you leaving?" – "I'm not sure ~."*
probably ['prɒbəblɪ]	wahrscheinlich	*She is ~ just late.*
everyone ['evrɪwʌn]	jeder(mann)	*~ is here.*
same to you [seɪm]	gleichfalls	*"Have a good holiday!" – "Thanks, ~."*

Unit 8

PRESENTATION 1
century ['sentʃərɪ]	Jahrhundert	
ago [ə'gəʊ]	vor	*I was on holiday two weeks ~.*
typewriter ['taɪpraɪtə]	Schreibmaschine	
record ['rekɔːd]	Schallplatte	
ball-point pen [bɔːlpɔɪnt 'pen]	Kugelschreiber	

chef [ʃef]	Küchenchef/in	
sailor ['seɪlə]	Seemann	
recipe ['resəpɪ]	Rezept	*Can I have your ~ for apple cake, please?*
to transmit [trænz'mɪt]	übermitteln	
workroom ['wɜːkrʊm]	Arbeitszimmer	
to send [send]	schicken	*I sent a letter to her last week.*
to produce [prə'djuːs]	produzieren	*The factory ~s cars.*
army ['ɑːmɪ]	Armee	
soldier ['səʊldʒə]	Soldat/in	
rain [reɪn]	Regen	*He was outside in the ~ for three hours.*
end [end]	Ende	*Can I see you at the ~ of the week?*
biro ['baɪərəʊ]	Kugelschreiber (Kuli)	
quickly ['kwɪklɪ]	schnell	*He read the book ~.*
incredible [ɪŋ'kredəbl]	unglaublich	*That's ~!*
true [truː]	genau, wahr	*"Did he really bring his dog to work?" – "Yes, it's ~."*
(to be) afraid of [ə'freɪd]	Angst haben vor	*Are you ~ the dark?*
to believe [bɪ'liːv]	glauben	*You didn't really meet the Queen in London! I don't ~ you!*

PRESENTATION 2
term [tɜːm]	Semester	
to break into [breɪk 'ɪntʊ]	einbrechen	*Someone broke into our house yesterday.*
to steal [stiːl]	stehlen	*They stole some pictures.*
to feel [fiːl]	sich fühlen	*He felt tired, so he went to bed.*
to fall [fɔːl]	fallen	
to wake up [weɪk]	aufwachen	*She woke up late.*
burglar ['bɜːglə]	Einbrecher/in	
thirsty ['θɜːstɪ]	durstig	*I'm very ~.*
sleepy ['sliːpɪ]	müde, schläfrig	
upstairs [ʌp'steəz]	(nach) oben	
rest [rest]	Ruhe	
to fall asleep [ə'sliːp]	einschlafen	*He fell asleep immediately.*

VOCABULARY AND PRONUNCIATION
banana [bə'nɑːnə]	Banane	
odd one out [ɒd wʌn 'aʊt]	'nicht passen'	*Which is the ~?*
animal ['ænɪml]	Tier	
kind [kaɪnd]	Art	*A cat is a ~ of animal.*
fruit [fruːt]	Obst, Früchte	
cake [keɪk]	Kuchen	
biscuit ['bɪskɪt]	Gebäck	
to laugh [lɑːf]	lachen	
to fall in love [lʌv]	sich verlieben	*They fell in love in 1980, and got engaged in 1981.*
to get engaged [ɪn'geɪdʒd]	sich verloben	
to get married ['mærɪd]	heiraten	*They got married in 1982.*
blue [bluː]	blau	
voice [vɔɪs]	Stimme	*He had a very loud ~.*
nervous ['nɜːvəs]	nervös	
angry ['æŋgrɪ]	böse	
cousin ['kʌzn]	Cousin/e	
joke [dʒəʊk]	Witz	*I told her a ~, but she didn't laugh.*
chocolate ['tʃɒklət]	Schokolade	
neighbour ['neɪbə]	Nachbar/in	
exam [ɪg'zæm]	Prüfung	
to break [breɪk]	brechen	*I broke a plate yesterday.*

together [tə'geðə]	zusammen	*They work ~.*
love letter [lʌv 'letə]	Liebesbrief	
to wait [weɪt]	warten	*Please ~ for me.*
to smile [smaɪl]	lächeln	
to ring [rɪŋ]	anrufen	*I rang my friend in Paris.*

EVERYDAY ENGLISH

date [deɪt]	Datum	*What's the ~ today?*
to end [end]	enden	*When does term ~?*
Independence Day [ɪndɪ'pendəns deɪ]	Unabhängigkeitstag	
public holiday [pʌblɪk 'hɒlədeɪ]	gesetzlicher Feiertag	*Tomorrow is a ~ in England.*

Unit 9

PRESENTATION 1

milk [mɪlk]	Milch	
tomato [tə'mɑ:təʊ]	Tomate	
rice [raɪs]	Reis	
grape [greɪp]	Weintraube	
strawberry ['strɔ:brɪ]	Erdbeere	
packet ['pækɪt]	Schachtel	*I would like a ~ of cigarettes, please.*
ready ['redɪ]	fertig, bereit	*Are you ~ to go now?*
to order ['ɔ:dɪ]	bestellen	*Are you ready to ~?*
steak [steɪk]	Steak	
sort [sɔ:t]	Sorte, Art	*I like all ~s of games.*
cream [kri:m]	Sahne	
air [eə]	Luft	
mushroom ['mʌʃru:m]	Pilz	
bacon ['beɪkən]	Speck	
note [nəʊt]	Geldschein	*I only have a ten pound ~, is that OK?*

PRESENTATION 2

potato [pə'teɪtəʊ]	Kartoffel	
toothpaste ['tu:θpeɪst]	Zahnpasta	
soap [səʊp]	Seife	
conditioner [kən'dɪʃənə]	Pflegespülung	
writing paper ['raɪtɪŋ peɪpə]	Schreibpapier	
glue [glu:]	Klebstoff	
paint [peɪnt]	Farbe	
file [faɪl]	Ordner	
box [bɒks]	Schachtel	*I would like a ~ of matches, please.*
match [mætʃ]	Streichholz	
phone card ['fəʊn kɑ:d]	Telefonkarte	
chewing gum ['tʃu:ɪŋ gʌm]	Kaugummi	
hanky ['hæŋkɪ]	Taschentuch	
sausage ['sɒsɪdʒ]	Wurst	
That's ..., please. [pli:z]	Das macht ..., bitte.	*"How much is that?" – "That's £2.50, please."*
pocket ['pɒkɪt]	Tasche	*Do you have a hanky in your jeans ~?*
petrol ['petrəl]	Benzin	
beer [bɪə]	Bier	
kilo ['ki:ləʊ]	Kilo	*a ~ of potatoes*
can [kæn]	Dose	
dozen ['dʌzn]	Dutzend	*I would like half a ~ eggs, please.*

READING AND LISTENING

traditional [trə'dɪʃənl]	traditionell	
nowadays ['naʊədeɪz]	heutzutage	*~ a lot of people just have toast and a cup of coffee for breakfast.*
cereal ['sɪərɪəl]	Getreideflocken	
sugar ['ʃʊgə]	Zucker	
marmalade ['mɑ:məleɪd]	(Orangen-)Marmelade	
jam [dʒæm]	Marmelade	
honey ['hʌnɪ]	Honig	
instant coffee ['ɪnstənt kɒfɪ]	Pulverkaffee	
visitor ['vɪzɪtə]	Besucher/in	
disgusting [dɪs'gʌstɪŋ]	ekelhaft	*The food in this pub is ~.*
quick [kwɪk]	schnell	*A lot of people go for a ~ drink after work.*
city ['sɪtɪ]	Stadt	
to choose [tʃu:z]	aussuchen	
roll [rəʊl]	Brötchen	*Would you like a brown or a white ~?*
salad ['sæləd]	(gemischter) Salat	
to serve [sɜ:v]	servieren, anbieten	*Pubs often ~ good food at lunchtime.*
snack [snæk]	Snack, Zwischenmahlzeit	
crisp [krɪsp]	Kartoffelchip	
afternoon tea (cream tea) [ɑ:ftə'nu:n ti:, 'kri:m ti:]	Nachmittagstee	*In Britain people often serve ~ at 5 o'clock.*
scone [skəʊn]	brötchenartiges Buttergebäck	
main [meɪn]	Haupt-	*British people usually eat their ~ meal in the evening.*
between [bɪ'twi:n]	zwischen	*The hotel serves breakfast ~ 7.00 and 9.00.*
roast [rəʊst]	gebraten	
beef [bi:f]	Rindfleisch	
lamb [læm]	Lamm	
pork [pɔ:k]	Schweinefleisch	
vegetable ['vedʒtəbl]	Gemüse	*What ~s would you like?*
gravy ['greɪvɪ]	Bratensaft	
sauce [sɔ:s]	Soße	
take-away meal ['teɪkəweɪ mi:l]	Essen außer Haus, Essen zum Mitnehmen	*Chinese and Indian ~s are very popular in England.*

EVERYDAY ENGLISH

single room ['sɪŋgl rʊm]	Einzelzimmer	
double room ['dʌbl rʊm]	Doppelzimmer	
to hope [həʊp]	hoffen	
stay [steɪ]	Aufenthalt	
shower ['ʃaʊə]	Dusche	
to pay [peɪ]	(be)zahlen	*How would you like to ~?*
credit card ['kredɪt kɑ:d]	Kreditkarte	*Can I pay by ~, please?*
to sign [saɪn]	unterschreiben	*Please ~ here.*
register ['redʒɪstə]	Gästebuch	
signature ['sɪgnətʃə]	Unterschrift	
menu ['menju:]	Speisekarte	
bill [bɪl]	Rechnung	
shirt [ʃɜ:t]	Hemd	
to wake up [weɪk]	aufwecken	*Can you wake me up at 7.00, please?*
reception desk [rɪ'sepʃn desk]	Empfang	

traveller's cheque ['trævləz tʃek]	Reisescheck	
to recommend [rekə'mend]	empfehlen	*Can you ~ a good hotel in Munich?*

Unit 10

PRESENTATION 1

fast [fɑːst]	schnell	
safe [seɪf]	sicher	
quiet ['kwaɪət]	ruhig	
healthy ['helθɪ]	gesund	
slow [sləʊ]	langsam	
unhealthy [ʌn'helθɪ]	ungesund	
unfriendly [ʌn'frendlɪ]	unfreundlich	
dirty ['dɜːtɪ]	schmutzig	
noisy ['nɔɪzɪ]	laut	
dangerous ['deɪndʒərəs]	gefährlich	

PRESENTATION 2

coast [kəʊst]	Kuste	*She lives in a village on the south ~ of England.*
everything ['evrɪθɪŋ]	alles	*~ is much quieter here.*
nothing ['nʌθɪŋ]	nichts	*"How many cars do you have?" – "Six." – "That's ~! I've got ten!"*

PRESENTATION 3

cottage ['kɒtɪdʒ]	Häuschen	
metre ['miːtə]	Meter	*The bedroom is six ~s long.*
dining room ['daɪnɪŋrʊm]	Eßzimmer	
study ['stʌdɪ]	Arbeitszimmer	
garage ['gærɑːʒ]	Garage	
kilometre ['kɪləmiːtə]	Kilometer	*Her house is two ~s from the school where she works.*
pretty ['prɪtɪ]	hübsch	
exercise ['eksəsaɪz]	Übung	
tall [tɔːl]	groß	*She is very ~.*
busy ['bɪzɪ]	beschäftigt	*I'm very ~ at work.*

VOCABULARY AND PRONUNCIATION

hill [hɪl]	Hügel	
traffic lights ['træfɪk laɪts]	Ampel	*We can go now. The ~ are green.*
field [fiːld]	Feld	
pollution [pə'luːʃn]	Verschmutzung	
fresh air [freʃ 'eə]	frische Luft	*I enjoy the ~ in the country.*
woods [wʊdz]	Wald	*We like walking in the ~.*
bridge [brɪdʒ]	Brücke	
car park ['kɑː pɑːk]	Parkplatz	
tram [træm]	Straßenbahn	*You can travel by ~ in Budapest.*
concert hall ['kɒnsət hɔːl]	Konzerthalle	
river bank ['rɪvə bæŋk]	Flußufer	
musician [mjuː'zɪʃn]	Musiker/in	

READING AND SPEAKING

population [pɒpjʊ'leɪʃn]	Bevölkerung	*The UK has a ~ of over 60 million.*
to divide [dɪ'vaɪd]	teilen	*The Berlin Wall ~d the city into two parts.*
part [pɑːt]	Teil	

west [west]	Westen	
east [iːst]	Osten	
view [vjuː]	Aussicht	*There is a good ~ of the town from the hills.*
to join [dʒɔɪn]	verbinden	*The bridge ~s the west bank and the east bank.*
history ['hɪstrɪ]	Geschichte	*1066 is an important date in the ~ of England.*
thousand ['θaʊznd]	Tausend	
cultural ['kʌltʃərəl]	kulturell	
capital ['kæpɪtl]	Hauptstadt	*Edinburgh is the ~ of Scotland.*
ruin ['ruːɪn]	Ruine	*The castle on the hill is in ~s.*
to take control [kən'trəʊl]	die Macht übernehmen	*The Communists took control of Prague in 1948.*
to try [traɪ]	versuchen	*Yesterday he tried to ride a bike for the first time.*
to free [friː]	befreien	
to pull down [pʊl 'daʊn]	stürzen, niederreißen	*They pulled down the old building next to the library.*
to fight [faɪt]	kämpfen (gegen)	*They fought hard.*
communist rule ['kɒmjʊnɪst ruːl]	kommunistische Herrschaft	
unusual [ʌn'juːʒl]	ungewöhnlich	
completely [kəm'pliːtlɪ]	völlig	
peace and quiet [piːs 'kwaɪət]	Frieden, Ruhe	*I like the ~ of the village.*
excitement [ɪk'saɪtmənt]	Spannung, Aufregung	
public transport [pʌblɪk 'trænspɔːt]	öffentlicher Verkehr	
idea [aɪ'dɪə]	Idee	*That's a good ~!*
spa [spɑː]	Heilbad	
way [weɪ]	Weg, Art und Weise	*The best ~ to see the town is by bus.*
to cross [krɒs]	überqueren, kreuzen	*The bridge ~es the river here.*
castle ['kɑːsl]	Schloß, Burg	
independent [ɪndɪ'pendənt]	unabhängig	
independence [ɪndɪ'pendəns]	Unabhängigkeit	
square [skweə]	Platz	*The ~ in the centre of Munich is called Marienplatz.*
medieval [medɪ'iːvl]	mittelalterlich	
town hall [taʊn 'hɔːl]	Rathaus	
amazing [ə'meɪzɪŋ]	erstaunlich	
astronomical clock [æstrə'nɒmɪkl klɒk]	astronomische Uhr	
atmosphere ['ætməsfɪə]	Atmosphäre	*The restaurant has a good ~.*
to get round [raʊnd]	umgehen	*What's an easy way to ~ the town?*
to walk round [wɔːk raʊnd]	einen Rundgang machen	*You can ~ the old city walls in York.*

EVERYDAY ENGLISH

along [ə'lɒŋ]	entlang	*Go ~ the main road, past the cinema, and the theatre is on the right.*
past [pɑːst]	vorbei	
through [θruː]	durch	*I often walk ~ the park.*
driving lesson ['draɪvɪŋ lesn]	Fahrstunde	
road [rəʊd]	Straße	

hedge [hedʒ]	Hecke	
railway station	Bahnhof	
['reɪlweɪ steɪʃn]		
to turn [tɜːn]	abbiegen	*Go past the chemist's and ~ left at the traffic lights.*

Unit 11

PRESENTATION 1

jumper ['dʒʌmpə]	Pullover	
jacket ['dʒækɪt]	Jackett	
trousers ['traʊzəz]	Hose	*His new ~ are very nice.*
suit [suːt]	Anzug	
tie [taɪ]	Krawatte	
trainers ['treɪnəz]	Turnschuhe	
dress [dres]	Kleid	
skirt [skɜːt]	Rock	
boot [buːt]	Stiefel	
fair [feə]	hell	*She has ~ hair.*
moustache [mə'stɑːʃ]	Schnurrbart	
beard [bɪəd]	Bart	
handsome ['hænsəm]	gutaussehend	*He is ~ and she is pretty.*
good-looking	gutaussehend	*They are both ~.*
[gʊd'lʊkɪŋ]		
slim [slɪm]	schlank	
glasses ['glɑːsɪz]	Brille	*Are my ~ here?*
to stand up	aufstehen	*He is standing up and she is sitting down.*
[stænd 'ʌp]		
to hold [həʊld]	halten	
earring ['ɪərɪŋ]	Ohrring	
all over [ɔːl 'əʊvə]	überall	*He travels ~ the world.*
cigar [sɪ'gɑː]	Zigarre	
pity ['pɪtɪ]	schade	*"I can't come to the party tomorrow." – "What a ~!"*
moment ['məʊmənt]	Augenblick	*I am waiting for Sue at the ~.*
wedding anniversary	Hochzeitstag	*It is our ~ next week.*
['wedɪŋ æni'vɜːsəri]		
to run [rʌn]	rennen	
photocopier	Fotokopierer	
['fəʊtəʊkɒpɪə]		
footballer ['fʊtbɔːlə]	Fußballspieler/in	
air stewardess	Flugbegleiterin	
[eə stjʊə'des]		
actress ['æktrɪs]	Schauspielerin	
captain ['kæptɪn]	Kapitän	
to act [ækt]	handeln	*Fiona is ~ing in a film.*

PRESENTATION 2

whose [huːz]	wessen	*"~ is this jacket?" – "It's mine."*
to cry [kraɪ]	weinen	*Why are you ~ing?*
fault [fɒlt]	Fehler, Schuld	*I didn't break the glass, it wasn't my ~.*
tonight [tə'naɪt]	heute abend	*Sue is going out ~.*
mess [mest]	Durcheinander	*Your room is in a ~ .*
racket ['rækɪt]	Schläger	
coat [kəʊt]	Mantel	

VOCABULARY AND PRONUNCIATION

sign [saɪn]	Zeichen, Schild	
head [hed]	Kopf	
heart [hɑːt]	Herz	
dead [ded]	tot	*My grandfather is ~. He died two years ago.*
foot, feet *(pl)*	Fuß, Füße *(Pl)*	
[fʊt, fiːt]		

LISTENING

to wonder ['wʌndə]	sich fragen	*I ~ why he didn't come.*
to look [lʊk]	aussehen	*She ~s lovely.*
to turn [tɜːn]	sich umdrehen	
around [ə'raʊnd]	herum	*We are taking her ~ the town on Monday.*
love [lʌv]	Liebe	
light [laɪt]	Licht	
to realize ['rɪəlaɪz]	erkennen, sich klar werden	*You don't ~ how much things cost.*
aching ['eɪkɪŋ]	schmerzend	
to turn out [tɜːn 'aʊt]	ausschalten	*Can you ~ the light, please?*
to brush [brʌʃ]	bürsten	
(to be) worried	sich Sorgen machen	*She is ~ about her exam.*
['wʌrɪd]		

EVERYDAY ENGLISH

to try on [traɪ 'ɒn]	anprobieren	*"Can I ~ this dress, please?" – "Certainly, madam."*
medium ['miːdɪəm]	Mittel-	
size [saɪz]	Größe	*What ~ are you – small or medium?*
changing room	Umkleidekabine	*Where are the ~s?*
['tʃeɪndʒɪŋ rʊm]		
to look for ['lʊk fə]	suchen	*I am looking for a new dress for the party on Saturday.*
I'm afraid [ə'freɪd]	leider	*We don't sell sandwiches, ~.*

Unit 12

PRESENTATION 1

dancer ['dɑːnsə]	Tänzer/in	
blouse [blaʊz]	Bluse	
tracksuit ['træksuːt]	Trainingsanzug	
to sneeze [sniːz]	niesen	
to pass [pɑːs]	bestehen	*I'm going to study to ~ the exam.*
to fail [feɪl]	durchfallen	*I'm going to study because I don't want to ~ the exam.*
to miss [mɪs]	verpassen	*We are going to ~ the train.*
to rain [reɪn]	regnen	
to drop [drɒp]	fallen lassen	
umbrella [ʌm'brelə]	Regenschirm	
to hurry up [hʌrɪ 'ʌp]	sich beeilen	*We must ~! We are late.*
careful ['keəfəl]	Vorsicht	*~! The plate is very hot.*
Bless you! ['bles jʊ]	Gesundheit!	*"I'm going to sneeze ... Aaattishoo!" – "~!"*

PRESENTATION 2

pyramid ['pɪrəmɪd]	Pyramide	
midnight ['mɪdnaɪt]	Mitternacht	
tulip ['tjuːlɪp]	Tulpe	
bullfight ['bʊlfaɪt]	Stierkampf	
lion ['laɪən]	Löwe	
to turn on [tɜːn 'ɒn]	einschalten, anmachen	*Can you ~ the light, please?*
door [dɔː]	Tür	
to phone [fəʊn]	anrufen	
news [njuːz]	Neuigkeiten	*There was no ~ yesterday.*

READING AND SPEAKING

cycling ['saɪklɪŋ]	Radfahren	
golf [gɒlf]	Golf	
motor racing	(Auto-)Rennen	
['məʊtə reɪsɪŋ]		

mountain climbing ['maʊntɪn klaɪmɪŋ]		*My father likes ~.*
rock [rɒk]	Fels	
rope [rəʊp]	Seil	
climber ['klaɪmə]	Kletterer/in	
bivouac ['bɪvʊæk]	Biwak	
to climb [klaɪm]	klettern	
future ['fjuːtʃə]	Zukunft	*She wants to be a rock star in the ~.*
to begin [bɪ'gɪn]	anfangen	*She began her climb very early.*
climb [klaɪm]	Klettertour	
guitar [gɪ'tɑː]	Gitarre	
without [wɪ'ðaʊt]	ohne	*He often walks to work ~ a coat in summer.*
to join [dʒɔɪn]	beitreten	*She ~ed the volleyball club.*
member ['membə]	Mitglied	*She is a ~ of the hockey club.*
competition [kɒmpə'tɪʃn]	Wettkampf	
snow [snəʊ]	Schnee	
heavy ['hevɪ]	schwer	*The snow is ~.*
to move [muːv]	sich bewegen	
side [saɪd]	Seite	
to follow ['fɒləʊ]	folgen	*I am going to ~ the route on the map.*
to touch [tʌtʃ]	berühren	
face [feɪs]	Oberfläche	*The ~ of the rock was cold and wet.*
comfortable ['kʌmftəbl]	komfortabel	
catalogue ['kætəlɒg]	Katalog	
tent [tent]	Zelt	*We are going to sleep in a ~ on holiday.*

VOCABULARY

windy ['wɪndɪ]	windig	
to snow [snəʊ]	schneien	
cloudy ['klaʊdɪ]	bewölkt	
foggy ['fɒgɪ]	neblig	
dry [draɪ]	trocken	
what's ... like?	wie ist ...?	*"What's the weather like today?" – "It's sunny."*
degree [dɪ'griː]	Grad	*"How hot is it outside?" – "20 ~s celcius."*

EVERYDAY ENGLISH

let's ... [lets]	laß(t) uns ...	*~ go out tonight.*
to get [get]	holen	*I'll ~ my coat and then we can go.*
swimming costume ['swɪmɪŋ kɒstjuːm]	Badeanzug	
channel ['tʃænl]	Programm	*The programme I want to watch is on ~ 4.*

Unit 13

PRESENTATION 1

general knowledge [dʒenrəl 'nɒlɪdʒ]	Allgemeinwissen	
moon [muːn]	Mond	
twice [twaɪs]	zweimal	*I enjoyed the film so much, I saw it ~.*
European Community [jʊərə'pɪən kə'mjuːnətɪ]	Europäische Gemeinschaft	
elephant ['elɪfənt]	Elefant	
to weigh [weɪ]	wiegen	*How much do you ~?*

tonne [tʌn]	Tonne (1000 kg)	
to discover [dɪ'skʌvə]	entdecken	
bird [bɜːd]	Vogel	
to migrate [maɪ'greɪt]	auswandern	
most [məʊst]	meiste/r/s	*Who earns the ~ money, Sue or Bill?*
to need [niːd]	brauchen	
litre ['liːtə]	Liter	
comedy duo ['kɒmədɪ djuːəʊ]	Komödiantenpaar	

PRESENTATION 2

habit ['hæbɪt]	Gewohnheit, Angewohnheit	*Eating healthily is a good ~.*
badly ['bædlɪ]	schlecht	*He speaks French ~.*
carefully ['keəfəlɪ]	sorgfältig	*She read the letter ~.*
driver ['draɪvə]	Fahrer/in	
easily ['iːzɪlɪ]	einfach	*She passed the exam ~.*
cook [kʊk]	Koch/Köchin	
quietly ['kwaɪətlɪ]	leise	*He opened the door ~.*
slowly ['sləʊlɪ]	langsam	*He isn't a fast driver. He drives ~.*
unfortunately [ʌn'fɔːtʃənɪtlɪ]	leider	*We wanted to go with them, but ~ we missed the bus.*
terrible ['terəbl]	schrecklich	
accident ['æksɪdənt]	Unfall	
typical ['tɪpɪkl]	typisch	*Bacon and eggs is a ~ English breakfast.*
test [test]	Prüfung	
to scream [skriːm]	schreien	

VOCABULARY

title ['taɪtl]	Titel	
monkey ['mʌnkɪ]	Affe	
paw [pɔː]	Pfote	
horror story ['hɒrə stɔːrɪ]	Gruselgeschichte	
magic ['mædʒɪk]	Zauber-	
wish [wɪʃ]	Wunsch	
happiness ['hæpɪnɪs]	Glück	
frightened ['fraɪtənd]	verängstigt	*I read the horror story and was very ~.*
deep [diːp]	tief	
hole [həʊl]	Loch	
to come alive [ə'laɪv]	lebendig werden	
duke [djuːk]	Herzog	
duchess ['dʌtʃɪs]	Herzogin	
to return [rɪ'tɜːn]	zurückkehren	*He ~ed to London for a week.*
silently ['saɪləntlɪ]	lautlos, schweigsam	*It was very late, so she went quickly and ~ to bed.*
middle ['mɪdl]	mittlere	*The ~ house has a nice garden.*
sound [saʊnd]	Geräusch	
sky [skaɪ]	Himmel	
to hide [haɪd]	sich verstecken	*I hid in the woods, so he couldn't find me.*
detective story [dɪ'tektɪv stɔːrɪ]	Kriminalroman	
romance [rəʊ'mæns]	Romanze	
biography [baɪ'ɒgrəfɪ]	Biographie	
adventure [əd'ventʃə]	Abenteuer	

READING AND LISTENING

journey ['dʒɜːnɪ]	Reise	
stranger ['streɪndʒə]	Fremde/r	
(to be) related [rɪ'leɪtɪd]	verwandt (sein)	*"Is Martin ~ to Alison?" – "Yes, he is her father."*

back [bæk]	Rückseite	*The picture is on the ~ of the magazine.*
to get off [get 'ɒf]	aussteigen	*You can ~ the bus at the town hall.*
carriage ['kærɪdʒ]	Wagen	*Her seat was in one of the middle ~s on the train.*
bored [bɔːd]	gelangweilt	*Sue was ~.*
to close [kləʊz]	zumachen	*The baby ~d his eyes and fell asleep.*
smile [smaɪl]	Lächeln	
mouth [maʊθ]	Mund	
to put [pʊt]	setzen, stellen, legen	*She ~ the money in her pocket.*
platform ['plætfɔːm]	Bahnsteig	*I saw him on the ~ at the railway station.*
wide [waɪd]	weit	

EVERYDAY ENGLISH

to decide [dɪ'saɪd]	entscheiden	*He was tired and ~d to go home.*
timetable ['taɪmteɪbl]	Fahrplan	
to come back [kʌm bæk]	zurückkehren	*When do you want to ~?*
to get in [get ɪn]	ankommen	*What time does the 5.15 from Edinburgh ~, please?*
day return [deɪ rɪ'tɜːn]	Tagesrückfahrkarte	
change [tʃeɪndʒ]	Wechselgeld	*"£15.20, please." – "Thank you. Here's your ~."*
single (ticket) ['sɪŋgl tɪkɪt]	Einzelfahrkarte	
return (ticket) [rɪ'tɜːn]	Rückfahrkarte	
period return [pɪərɪəd rɪ'tɜːn]	zeitlich begrenzte Rückfahrkarte	
cash [kæʃ]	Bargeld	*"How do you want to pay?" – "~, please."*
on time [ɒn 'taɪm]	pünktlich	*I hope the train is ~.*

Unit 14

PRESENTATION 1

ever ['evə]	je	*Have you ~ been to Spain?*
company ['kʌmpənɪ]	Firma	*He works for a computer ~.*
jet [dʒet]	Düsenflugzeug	
play [pleɪ]	Theaterstück	
tractor ['træktə]	Traktor	

PRESENTATION 2

helicopter ['helɪkɒptə]	Hubschrauber	
tour [tʊə]	Rundfahrt	
sad [sæd]	traurig	
marvellous ['mɑːvələs]	wunderbar	
safari [sə'fɑːrɪ]	Safari	
ill [ɪl]	krank	*He has been ~ for a long time. He's a very sick man.*
psychiatrist [saɪ'kaɪətrɪst]	Psychiater/in	
to answer ['ɑːnsə]	antworten	*"What time is it?" I asked. "It's 2 o'clock," he ~ed.*
sadly ['sædlɪ]	traurig	

READING AND SPEAKING

active ['æktɪv]	aktiv	
antique [æn'tiːk]	antik	
cardigan ['kɑːdɪgən]	Strickjacke	
cockroach ['kɒkrəʊtʃ]	Küchenschabe	

civilian [sɪ'vɪlɪən]	zivil	
to do exercises ['eksəsaɪzɪz]	üben, trainieren	*She does her exercises every day.*
gun [gʌn]	Gewehr	
to knit [nɪt]	stricken	
military ['mɪlɪtrɪ]	militärisch	
to regret [rɪ'gret]	bedauern	*I've never had a job but I don't ~ it.*
stocking ['stɒkɪŋ]	Strumpf	
toy [tɔɪ]	Spielzeug	
to receive [rɪ'siːv]	bekommen	
instead [ɪn'sted]	statt dessen	*I didn't work. ~ I looked after the children.*
robber ['rɒbə]	Räuber	
handbag ['hændbæg]	Handtasche	
to rob [rɒb]	ausrauben	
to point at [pɔɪnt]	richten auf	*He ~ed his camera at me and took a photo.*
cashier [kæ'ʃɪə]	Kassierer/in	
to catch [kætʃ]	fangen	*The police caught the robber.*
memoirs ['memwɑːz]	Erinnerungen, Memoiren	
to describe [dɪ'skraɪb]	beschreiben	
everywhere ['evrɪweə]	überall	*The room was in a mess. There were clothes ~.*
to cut [kʌt]	kürzen	*The company ~ our working week from 38 to 37 hours.*
finally ['faɪnəlɪ]	schließlich	*He ~ left at 2 o'clock.*
to plan [plæn]	planen	*I have started ~ning my next holiday.*
widow ['wɪdəʊ]	Witwe	

VOCABULARY AND PRONUNCIATION

waitress ['weɪtrɪs]	Kellnerin	
sock [sɒk]	Socken	
glove [glʌv]	Handschuh	
tights [taɪts]	Strumpfhose	*The ~ were expensive.*
customer ['kʌstəmə]	Kunde/Kundin	
fax machine ['fæks məʃiːn]	Faxgerät	
shorts [ʃɔːts]	Shorts	*Your football ~ are in the cupboard.*
face [feɪs]	Gesicht	*She wears a lot of make-up on her ~.*
neck [nek]	Hals	
kitten ['kɪtn]	Kätzchen	
puppy ['pʌpɪ]	Welpe	
recently ['riːsntlɪ]	kürzlich	*I haven't been to work ~ because I've been ill.*
to hurt [hɜːt]	verletzen	
to kick [kɪk]	kicken	

EVERYDAY ENGLISH

to dial ['daɪəl]	wählen	
to ring [rɪŋ]	klingeln	*(telephone) The number isn't ~ing.*
engaged [ɪn'geɪdʒd]	besetzt	*(telephone) It is ~.*
to take a message ['mesɪdʒ]	etw. ausrichten	*(telephone) Jo isn't here. Can I ~?*
to put somebody through [θruː]	jdn. durchstellen	*(telephone) She is in her office. I'll put you through.*
directory enquiries [dɪ'rektərɪ ɪn'kwaɪərɪz]	Telefonauskunft	*You can ring ~.*
operator ['ɒpəreɪtə]	Vermittlung	*The ~ will give you the right telephone number.*
initial [ɪ'nɪʃl]	Anfangsbuchstabe	*"What is Mrs Duncan's ~?" – "J for Janet."*

Unit 15

PRESENTATION 1

possible ['pɒsəbl]   möglich   *Is it ~ to give me her telephone number?*

duck [dʌk]   Ente

curry ['kʌrɪ]   Curry

to post [pəʊst]   mit der Post schicken   *Did you remember to ~ the letter?*

to promise ['prɒmɪs]   versprechen   *You ~d to take me out later.*

to prefer [prɪ'fɜ:]   bevorzugen   *I don't like video films, I ~ to go to the cinema.*

PRESENTATION 2

awful ['ɔ:fəl]   schrecklich, furchtbar

trip [trɪp]   Reise, Ausflug

VOCABULARY

to take off [ɒf]   ausziehen, abheben   *Mary took her coat off.*
The plane took off on time.

to break down [breɪk 'daʊn]   eine Panne haben, zusammen-brechen   *The tractor broke down.*
Sue broke down when she heard the bad news.

horse [hɔ:s]   Pferd

to go out with someone   mit jdm. gehen   *Alison is going out with Joe.*

to get on   sich verstehen   *Do you ~ with the new manager?*

to give up   aufgeben   *I'm going to ~ chocolate.*

loud [laʊd]   laut

motorway ['məʊtəweɪ]   Autobahn

READING AND LISTENING

salesman ['seɪlzmən]   Verkäufer

enough [ɪ'nʌf]   genug   *The food wasn't hot ~.*
We don't have ~ time.

indeed [ɪn'di:d]   wirklich, tatsächlich   *I want to go to London very much ~.*

education [edʒʊ'keɪʃn]   Ausbildung

struggle ['strʌgl]   Kampf

only ['əʊnlɪ]   einzig   *Paula is their ~ child.*

to forgive [fə'gɪv]   vergeben   *I'm sorry. Please ~ me.*

note [nəʊt]   Notiz, Brief

to clutch [klʌtʃ]   umklammert halten   *She left the room ~ing the letter.*

to step [step]   treten   *She ~ped inside the building.*

free [fri:]   frei

to sacrifice ['sækrɪfaɪs]   opfern

alone [ə'ləʊn]   allein   *I like living ~.*

to snore [snɔ:]   schnarchen

dressing gown ['dresɪŋ gaʊn]   Bademantel

to pick up [pɪk 'ʌp]   aufheben   *He picked up the newspaper.*

to lie [laɪ]   liegen   *The cat was lying on the sofa.*

to shout [ʃaʊt]   schreien

to treat [tri:t]   behandeln   *He ~ed his parents badly.*

thoughtlessly ['θɔ:tlɪslɪ]   gedankenlos, unüberlegt

thought [θɔ:t]   Gedanke

to struggle ['strʌgl]   kämpfen

to get by   durchkommen   *We work hard to ~.*

appointment [ə'pɔɪntmənt]   Verabredung, Termin   *"I'd like to see the manager, please." – "Do you have an ~?"*

trade [treɪd]   Handel

---

fun [fʌn]   Spaß   *Sue's party was ~.*
Have ~ at the theatre!

to deny [dɪ'naɪ]   ablehnen, leugnen   *He was denied visitors in hospital.*

EVERYDAY ENGLISH

official [ə'fɪʃl]   Beamte/Beamtin

to fill in [fɪl 'ɪn]   ausfüllen   *You have to ~ a form when you need a new driving licence.*

customs ['kʌstəmz]   Zoll

form [fɔ:m]   Formular

parcel ['pɑ:sl]   Paket

overseas [əʊvə'si:z]   (nach) Übersee   *You need a passport when you travel ~.*

driving licence ['draɪvɪŋ laɪsns]   Führerschein

receipt [rɪ'si:t]   Quittung, Bon

purpose ['pɜ:pəs]   Zweck, Absicht   *What is the ~ of your trip to the USA?*

visit ['vɪzɪt]   Besuch

to show [ʃəʊ]   zeigen

identification [aɪdentɪfɪ'keɪʃn]   Ausweis

to enter ['entə]   eintreten

altogether [ɔ:ltə'geðə]   insgesamt   *£2.50 and £1.30 – that's £3.80 ~.*

seaside ['si:saɪd]   (am) Meer   *I'm going to spend my summer holiday at the ~.*

Wortschatz: alphabetisch

Hier finden Sie alle Wörter und Ausdrücke des Buches in alphabetischer Reihenfolge. Die Ziffer am Ende jeden Eintrages zeigt, in welcher Unit das Wort zuerst vorkommt.

a lot of viele *4*
about über *4*; ungefähr *4*
abroad im/ins Ausland *7*
accident Unfall *13*
aching schmerzend *11*
to act handeln *11*
active aktiv *14*
actor Schauspieler *3*
actress Schauspielerin *11*
address Adresse *2*
address book Adreßbuch *5*
adventure Abenteuer *13*
(to be) afraid of Angst haben vor *8*
after nach *3*
afternoon Nachmittag *3*
afternoon tea Nachmittagstee *9*
again wieder *6*
age Alter *2*
ago vor *8*
air Luft *9*
air stewardess Flugbegleiterin *11*
algebra Algebra *6*
all alle *2*
all day den ganzen Tag über *6*
all over überall *11*
alone allein *15*
along entlang *10*
also auch *5*
altogether insgesamt *15*
always immer *4*
amazing erstaunlich *10*
angry böse *8*
animal Tier *8*
another ein andere/r/s *7*
answer Antwort *4*
to answer antworten *14*
antique antik *14*
any irgendwelche *5*
anything (irgend)etwas *2*
apple Apfel *1*
appointment Verabredung, Termin *15*
armchair Sessel *5*
army Armee *8*
around herum *11*
arrival hall Empfangshalle *6*
to arrive ankommen *3*
article Artikel *4*
to ask a question eine Frage stellen *6*
astronomical clock astronomische Uhr *10*
atmosphere Atmosphäre *10*
aunt Tante *2*
autumn Herbst *4*
awful schrecklich, furchtbar *15*

back Rückseite *13*
bacon Speck *9*
bad schlecht *1*
badly schlecht *13*
bag Tasche *1*

baggage reclaim Gepäckausgabe *6*
baker Bäcker/in *3*
baker's Bäckerei *5*
ball-point pen Kugelschreiber *8*
banana Banane *8*
barbecue Grillparty *6*
bath Bad *5*
beach Strand *4*
beard Bart *11*
beautiful schön *2*
because weil *1*
to become werden *7*
bed Bett *4*
bedroom Schlafzimmer *5*
beef Rindfleisch *9*
beer Bier *9*
before vor *7*
to begin anfangen *12*
behind hinter *5*
to believe glauben *8*
between zwischen *9*
big groß *2*
bill Rechnung *9*
biography Biographie *13*
bird Vogel *13*
biro Kugelschreiber (Kuli) *8*
birthday Geburtstag *7*
biscuit Gebäck *8*
bivouac Biwak *12*
black schwarz *6*
Bless you! Gesundheit! *12*
blouse Bluse *12*
blue blau *8*
to board einsteigen, an Bord gehen *6*
boarding pass Bordkarte *6*
book Buch *1*
boot Stiefel *11*
bored gelangweilt *13*
boring langweilig *6*
(to be) born geboren (sein) *6*
to borrow ausleihen *5*
both beide *4*
bottle Flasche *7*
box Schachtel *9*
boy Junge *3*
boyfriend Freund *2*
bread Brot *3*
to break brechen *8*
to break down eine Panne haben, zusammenbrechen *15*
to break into einbrechen *8*
breakfast Frühstück *4*
(to have) breakfast frühstücken *4*
bridge Brücke *10*
brilliant großartig *6*
to bring bringen *4*
brother Bruder *1*
brown braun *4*
to brush bürsten *11*
to build bauen *5*
building Gebäude *5*
bullfight Stierkampf *12*
burglar Einbrecher/in *8*
bus stop Bushaltestelle *5*
businessman Geschäftsmann *7*
busy beschäftigt *10*
but aber *2*
to buy kaufen *5*

by mit *3*
cake Kuchen *8*
calculus Differential- und Integralrechnung *6*
call (Auf-)Ruf *6*
(to be) called heißen *4*
camera Fotoapparat *1*
can können, dürfen *2*
can Dose *9*
capital Hauptstadt *10*
captain Kapitän *11*
car Auto *3*
car park Parkplatz *10*
cardigan Strickjacke *14*
cards Karten *4*
careful Vorsicht *12*
carefully sorgfältig *13*
carpet Teppich *5*
carriage Wagen *13*
cash Bargeld *13*
cashier Kassierer/in *14*
castle Schloß, Burg *10*
cat Katze *5*
catalogue Katalog *12*
to catch nehmen *3*; fangen *14*
centre Zentrum, Mitte *2*
century Jahrhundert *8*
cereal Getreideflocken *9*
certainly sicher, gewiß *3*
chair Stuhl *5*
champagne Champagner *2*
champion Meister/in *6*
change Wechselgeld *13*
to change wechseln *7*
changing room Umkleidekabine *11*
channel Programm *12*
character Charakter, Person *7*
to chat plaudern *4*
cheap billig *2*
to check kontrollieren, überprüfen *6*
check-in-desk Abfertigungsschalter *6*
cheese Käse *2*
chef Küchenchef/in *8*
chemist's Apotheke *5*
cheque Scheck *6*
chess Schach *6*
chewing gum Kaugummi *9*
chicken Hähnchen *2*
child, children (pl) Kind, Kinder *(Pl.)* *1*
chocolate Schokolade *8*
to choose aussuchen *9*
Christmas Weihnachten *7*
cigar Zigarre *11*
cigarette Zigarette *5*
cinema Kino *4*
city Stadt *9*
civilian zivil *14*
class Klasse *2*
classroom Klassenzimmer *5*
clean sauber *5*
to clean saubermachen *7*
clerk (Büro-)Angestellte(r) *7*
clever clever, schlau *7*
climb Klettertour *12*
to climb klettern *12*
climber Kletterer/in *12*
clock Uhr *5*
to close zumachen *13*
clothes Kleidung *5*

clothes shop Bekleidungsgeschäft 7
cloudy bewölkt 12
club Verein, Klub 5
to clutch umklammert halten 15
coast Küste 10
coat Mantel 11
cockroach Kückenschabe 14
coffee Kaffee 2
coke Coca-Cola 2
cold kalt 2
colour Farbe 4
to come kommen 3
to come alive lebendig werden 13
to come back zurückkehren 13
to come down fallen 7
comedy duo Komödiantenpaar 13
comfortable komfortabel 12
communist rule kommunistische Herr-
  schaft 10
company Firma 14
competition Wettkampf 12
completely völlig 10
concert hall Konzerthalle 10
conditioner Pflegespülung 9
congratulations herzlichen Glückwunsch 7
conversation Unterhaltung, Gespräch 6
cook Koch/Köchin 13
to cook kochen 4
cooker Herd 5
cooking Kochen 4
corner Ecke 2
to cost kosten 3
cottage Häuschen 10
could könnte(n) 6
to count zählen 6
country Land 2
countryside Landschaft 3
course Gang 5
cousin Cousin/e 8
cream Sahne 9
cream tea Nachmittagstee 9
credit card Kreditkarte 9
crisp Kartoffelchip 9
to cross überqueren, kreuzen 10
crossword Kreuzworträtsel 4
to cry weinen 11
cultural kulturell 10
cup Tasse 2
cupboard Schrank 5
curry Curry 15
custom Sitte 7
customer Kunde/Kundin 14
customs Zoll 15
to cut (ab)schneiden 3; kürzen 14
cycling Radfahren 12

to dance tanzen 4
dancer Tänzer/in 12
dangerous gefährlich 10
dark dunkel 6
darling Liebling 3
date Datum 8
daughter Tochter 1
day Tag 3
day return Tagesrückfahrkarte 13
dead tot 11
dear liebe/r 2
debt Schuld 7

to decide entscheiden 13
deep tief 13
degree Grad 12
delayed verspätet 6
delicious köstlich, lecker 4
dentist Zahnarzt/ärztin 2
to deny ablehnen, leugnen 15
departure lounge Abflughalle 6
to describe beschreiben 14
description Beschreibung 7
desk Schreibtisch 3
destination Reiseziel 6
detective story Kriminalroman 13
to dial wählen 14
dictionary Wörterbuch 1
to die sterben 7
different verschieden 2; anders 6
difficult schwierig 2
dining room Eßzimmer 10
dinner Abendessen 4
directory enquiries Telefonauskunft 14
dirty schmutzig 10
disco Diskothek 4
to discover entdecken 13
disgusting ekelhaft 9
dishwasher Geschirrspülmaschine 5
to divide teilen 10
to do tun, machen 4
doctor Arzt/Ärztin 1
dog Hund 3
door Tür 12
double doppelt 1
double room Doppelzimmer 9
dozen Dutzend 9
to draw zeichnen 6
dress Kleid 11
dressing gown Bademantel 15
drink Getränk 2
to drink trinken 2
to drive fahren 3
driver Fahrer/in 13
driving lesson Fahrstunde 10
driving licence Führerschein 15
to drop fallen lassen 12
dry trocken 12
duchess Herzogin 13
duck Ente 15
duke Herzog 13
during während 5

early früh 4
to earn verdienen 7
earring Ohrring 11
easily einfach 13
east Osten 10
Easter Ostern 7
easy leicht, einfach 2
to eat essen 4
education Ausbildung 15
egg Ei 5
either auch nicht 6
elephant Elefant 13
end Ende 8
to end enden 8
engaged besetzt 14
(to get) engaged sich verloben 8
engineer Ingenieur/in 2
to enjoy gefallen 7

enough genug 15
to enter eintreten 15
envelope Briefumschlag 1
especially besonders, speziell 4
European Community Europäische
  Gemeinschaft 13
evening Abend 1
ever je 14
every jede/r/s 3
everybody jeder(mann) 5
everyone jeder(mann) 7
everything alles 10
everywhere überall 14
exactly exakt, genau 3
exam Prüfung 8
excitement Spannung, Aufregung 10
exciting aufregend 4
excuse me Entschuldigung,Verzeihung 3
exercise Übung 10
(to do) exercises üben, trainieren 14
expensive teuer 2
experience Erfahrung 7
export department Exportabteilung 4
exposure Belichtung 4
eye Auge 6

face Oberfläche 12; Gesicht 14
factory Fabrik 7
to fail durchfallen 12
fair hell 11
to fall fallen 8
to fall asleep einschlafen 8
to fall in love sich verlieben 8
family Familie 2
famous berühmt 5
far weit 5
farm Bauernhof 7
fast schnell 10
to fasten befestigen 6
father Vater 2
fault Fehler, Schuld 11
favourite Lieblings- 4
fax machine Faxgerät 14
to feed füttern, ernähren 5
to feel sich fühlen 8
ferry Fähre 3
field Feld 10
to fight kämpfen (gegen) 10
file Ordner 9
to fill in ausfüllen 15
finally schließlich 14
to find finden 7
fine gut 1
to finish (food) aufessen 5
to finish work Feierabend machen 7
fire Feuer 5
first erste/r/s; zuerst 5
first name Vorname 1
first of all zunächst 6
(to go) fishing angeln, fischen (gehen) 4
flat Wohnung 1
flight Flug 6
floor Boden 5
flower Blume 4
fluently fließend 6
to fly fliegen 3
foggy neblig 12
to follow folgen 12

food Essen 2
foot, feet *(pl)* Fuß, Füße *(Pl.)* 11
football Fußball 3
footballer Fußballspieler/in 11
to forecast the weather das Wetter vorhersagen 6
foreign ausländisch 7
to forget vergessen 7
to forgive vergeben 15
form Formular 15
fortunately glücklicherweise 3
free frei 15
to free befreien 10
free time Freizeit 3
fresh air frische Luft 10
fridge Kühlschrank 5
friend Freund/in 4
friendly freundlich 2
frightened verängstigt 13
fruit Obst, Früchte 8
full voll 7
full-time ganztags 5
fun Spaß 15
funny lustig 2
future Zukunft 12

game Spiel 4
garage Garage 10
garden Garten 5
gate Flugsteig 6
general knowledge Allgemeinwissen 13
genius Genie 6
gentleman Herr 7
to get bekommen 7; holen 12
to get by durchkommen 15
to get in ankommen 13
to get off aussteigen 13
to get on sich verstehen 15
to get round umgehen 10
to get up aufstehen 4
girl Mädchen 3
to give geben 7
to give up aufgeben 15
glass Glas 3
glasses Brille 11
glove Handschuh 14
glue Klebstoff 9
to go gehen, fahren 4
to go back to work mit der Arbeit wieder anfangen 4
to go out ausgehen 4
to go out with someone mit jdm. gehen 15
golf Golf 12
good gut 2
good-looking gutaussehend 11
goodbye auf Wiedersehen 1
grandfather Großvater 2
grandmother Großmutter 2
grape Weintraube 9
gravy Bratensaft 9
great sehr gut, großartig 7
green grün 3
grey grau 4
to grow up aufwachsen 5
guitar Gitarre 12
gun Gewehr 14

habit Gewohnheit, Angewohnheit 13
hair Haar/e 3
hairdresser Friseur/in 2
half halb 3
ham Schinken 2
handbag Handtasche 14
hand luggage Handgepäck 6
handsome gutaussehend 11
hanky Taschentuch 9
to happen geschehen, passieren 5
happiness Glück 13
happy glücklich 2
hard hart 7
hat Hut 6
to hate hassen 7
to have haben 1
head Kopf 11
healthy gesund 10
to hear hören 6
heart Herz 11
heavy schwer 12
hedge Hecke 10
helicopter Hubschrauber 14
hello Hallo 1
to help helfen 4
here hier 4
here you are bitte schön 2
to hide sich verstecken 13
high hoch 7
hill Hügel 10
history Geschichte 10
to hold halten 11
hole Loch 13
holiday Urlaub, Ferien 2
home zu Hause 2
homework Hausaufgabe 3
honey Honig 9
to hope hoffen 9
horrible schrecklich 2
horror story Gruselgeschichte 13
horse Pferd 15
hospital Krankenhaus 3
hot heiß 2
hour Stunde 3
house Haus 1
housemaid Hausmädchen 7
how wie 1
how long wie lange 3
how many wie viele 3
how much wieviel 2
hungry hungrig 3
to hurry up sich beeilen 12
to hurt verletzen 14
husband Ehemann 2

I'm afraid leider 11
ice cream Eiskrem 2
ice hockey Eishockey 4
(to go) ice-skating Schlittschuh laufen 4
idea Idee 10
identification Ausweis 15
ill krank 14
immediately sofort 7
important wichtig, bedeutend 6
in front of vor 5
incredible unglaublich 8
indeed wirklich, tatsächlich 15
independence Unabhängigkeit 10

Independence Day Unabhängigkeitstag 8
independent unabhängig 10
initial Anfangsbuchstabe 14
inside innerhalb 5
instant coffee Pulverkaffee 9
instead statt dessen 14
interesting interessant 2
interpreter Dolmetscher/in 3
to interview interviewen 4
to invite einladen 5

jacket Jackett 11
jam Marmelade 9
jet Düsenflugzeug 14
job Beruf 1
to join verbinden 10; beitreten 12
joke Witz 8
journalist Journalist/in 2
journey Reise 3
jumper Pullover 11
just gerade 3; nur, bloß 4

key Schlüssel 1
to kick kicken 14
kilo Kilo 9
kilometre Kilometer 10
kind Art 8
king König 5
kiss Kuß 7
kitchen Küche 5
kitten Kätzchen 14
knife Messer 7
to knit stricken 14
to know wissen, kennen 1

lady Lady, Dame 7
lake See 4
lamb Lamm 9
lamp Lampe 5
to land landen 6
language Sprache 1
last letzte/r/s 6
last night gestern Abend 6
late spät 4
to laugh lachen 8
lawcourt Gericht, Gerichtshof 7
to learn lernen 1
to leave verlassen 3
left links 5
let's ... laß(t) uns ... 12
letter Brief 1
library Bücherei 5
to lie liegen 15
life Leben 7
light Licht 11
(to have a) light Feuer haben 4
like ähnlich wie 5
to like mögen, gern haben/tun 3
line Leitung 6
lion Löwe 12
liqueur Likör 5
to listen zuhören 4
litre Liter 13
to live leben, wohnen 1
living room Wohnzimmer 5
long lang 4
long-distance Langstrecken- 3
to look aussehen 11

to look after sich kümmern um, sorgen für *3*
to look for suchen *11*
to lose verlieren *7*
loud laut *15*
love liebe Grüße *2*; Liebe *11*
to love lieben *3*
love letter Liebesbrief *8*
lovely schön *2*
lunchtime Mittagszeit *6*

madam gnädige Frau
magazine Zeitschrift *1*
magic Zauber- *13*
main Haupt- *9*
to make machen *3*
man Mann *3*
map Stadtplan *1*
marmalade (Orangen-)Marmelade *9*
married verheiratet *1*
(to get) married heiraten *8*
to marry heiraten *7*
marvellous wunderbar *14*
match Spiel *6*; Streichholz *9*
to matter etwas ausmachen *4*
meal Mahlzeit, Essen *4*
to mean bedeuten *4*
meat Fleisch *6*
mechanic Mechaniker/in *3*
medicine Medizin *6*
medieval mittelalterlich *10*
medium Mittel- *11*
to meet treffen, kennenlernen *4*
member Mitglied *12*
memoirs Erinnerungen, Memoiren *14*
to mend reparieren *3*
menu Speisekarte *9*
mess Durcheinander *11*
metre Meter *10*
middle mittlere *13*
middle-class Mittelklasse *7*
midnight Mitternacht *12*
to migrate auswandern *13*
mile Meile *3*
military militärisch *14*
milk Milch *9*
mineral water Mineralwasser *2*
mirror Spiegel *5*
to miss verpassen *12*
moment Augenblick *11*
money Geld *7*
monkey Affe *13*
month Monat *6*
moon Mond *13*
more than mehr als *5*
(good) morning (Guten) Morgen *2*
most meiste/r/s *13*
mother Mutter *2*
motor racing (Auto-)Rennen *12*
motorway Autobahn *15*
mountain Berg *3*
mountain climbing Bergsteigen *12*
moustache Schnurrbart *11*
mouth Mund *13*
to move umziehen *7*; sich bewegen *12*
mushroom Pilz *9*
music Musik *4*
musician Musiker/in *10*

nationality Nationalität *7*
near in der Nähe von *3*
nearly fast *3*
neck Hals *14*
to need brauchen *13*
neighbour Nachbar/in *8*
nephew Neffe *2*
nervous nervös *8*
never niemals *4*
never mind schon gut *6*
new neu *2*
New Year's Eve Silvester *7*
news Nachrichten *4*; Neuigkeiten *12*
newsagent's Zeitungsladen *5*
newspaper Zeitung *1*
next nächste/r/s *3*
next to neben *5*
nice schön, nett *1*
niece Nichte *2*
night Nacht *7*
night club Nachtklub *3*
noisy laut *10*
non-smoking Nichtraucher *6*
north Norden *4*
nose Nase *6*
not at all überhaupt nicht *4*
note Geldschein *9*; Notiz, Brief *15*
notebook Notizbuch *1*
nothing nichts *10*
novel Roman *7*
novelist Romancier *7*
now jetzt, gerade, nun *2*
nowadays heutzutage *9*
number Anzahl *5*
nun Nonne *3*
nurse Krankenschwester/-pfleger *3*

o'clock Uhr *3*
odd one out 'nicht passen' *8*
of course natürlich *3*
office Büro *3*
official Beamte/Beamtin *15*
often oft *4*
old alt *1*
on time pünktlich *13*
only nur *3*; erst *7*; einzig *15*
to open öffnen *4*
opera Oper *4*
operator Vermittlung *14*
opposite gegenüber *5*
orange Apfelsine *1*
orange juice Orangensaft *2*
to order bestellen *9*
other andere/s/r *2*
outside außerhalb *5*; draußen *6*
over über *7*
over there da drüben *5*
overseas (nach) Übersee *15*
own eigene/s/r *5*

packet Schachtel *9*
page Seite *4*
paint Farbe *9*
to paint malen *4*
palace Palast *5*
parcel Paket *15*
Pardon? Wie bitte? *4*
parents Eltern *2*

part Teil *10*
to pass bestehen *12*
passenger Passagier *3*
passport control Paßkontrolle *6*
past nach (mit Uhrzeiten) *3*; Vergangenheit *7*; vorbei *10*
paw Pfote *13*
to pay (be)zahlen *9*
peace and quiet Frieden, Ruhe *10*
pen Kugelschreiber *5*
people Leute *3*
perhaps vielleicht *5*
period return zeitlich begrenzte Rückfahrkarte *13*
petrol Benzin *9*
to phone anrufen *12*
phone box Telefonzelle *5*
phone card Telefonkarte *9*
phone number Telefonnummer *2*
photo Foto *2*
photocopier Fotokopierer *11*
piano Klavier *6*
to pick up aufheben *15*
picture Bild (Foto) *4*
piece Stück, Teil *2*
piper (Dudelsack)pfeifer *5*
pity schade *11*
place Ort, Stelle *5*
place of work Arbeitsstelle *3*
to plan planen *14*
plane Flugzeug *3*
plant Pflanze *5*
plate Teller *5*
platform Bahnsteig *13*
play Theaterstück *14*
to play spielen *3*
player Spieler/in *6*
please bitte *2*
pocket Tasche *9*
to point at richten auf *14*
police station Polizeiwache *5*
policeman Polizist *2*
politician Politiker/in *5*
politics Politik *7*
pollution Verschmutzung *10*
poor arm *7*
popular beliebt *7*
population Bevölkerung *10*
pork Schweinefleisch *9*
port Portwein *5*
possible möglich *15*
to post mit der Post schicken *15*
post box Briefkasten *5*
postcard Postkarte *1*
post office Postamt *5*
potato Kartoffel *9*
pound Pfund *2*
to practise üben *6*
to prefer bevorzugen *15*
to prepare vorbereiten *5*
present Geschenk *7*
president Präsident/in *5*
pretty hübsch *10*
Prime Minister Premierminister/in *5*
prison Gefängnis *7*
probably wahrscheinlich *7*
to produce produzieren *8*
programme Sendung *4*

to promise versprechen *15*
psychiatrist Psychiater/in *14*
pub Kneipe *5*
public holiday gesetzlicher Feiertag *8*
public toilet öffentliche Toilette *5*
public transport öffentlicher Verkehr *10*
to pull down stürzen, niederreißen *10*
puppy Welpe *14*
purpose Zweck, Absicht *15*
to put setzen, stellen, legen *13*
to put somebody through jdn. durch-stellen *14*
pyramid Pyramide *12*

quarter Viertel *3*
queen Königin *4*
question Frage *4*
quick schnell *9*
quickly schnell *8*
quiet ruhig *10*
quietly leise *13*
quite ziemlich, ganz *4*

racket Schläger *11*
railway station Bahnhof *10*
rain Regen *8*
to rain regnen *12*
to read lesen *4*
ready fertig, bereit *9*
real echt *7*
to realize erkennen, sich klar werden *11*
really wirklich *4*
receipt Quittung, Bon *15*
to receive bekommen *14*
recently kürzlich *14*
reception desk Empfang *9*
receptionist Herr/Dame am Empfang *3*
recipe Rezept *8*
to recommend empfehlen *9*
record Schallplatte *8*
red rot *4*
register Gästebuch *9*
to regret bedauern *14*
(to be) related verwandt (sein) *13*
to relax sich entspannen *4*
remark Bemerkung *6*
to remember sich erinnern *7*
rest Ruhe *8*
to retire sich pensionieren lassen *7*
return (ticket) Rückfahrkarte *13*
to return zurückkehren *13*
rice Reis *9*
rich reich *7*
to ride a bike Fahrrad fahren *6*
right richtig *1*; rechts *5*
to ring anrufen *8;* klingeln *14*
river Fluß *4*
river bank Flußufer *10*
road Straße *10*
roast gebraten *9*
to rob ausrauben *14*
robber Räuber *14*
rock Fels *12*
roll Brötchen *9*
romance Romanze *13*
room Zimmer *5*
rope Seil *12*
royal königlich *5*

ruin Ruine *10*
to run rennen *11*

to sacrifice opfern *15*
sad traurig *14*
sadly traurig *14*
safari Safari *14*
safe sicher *10*
safely sicher, heil, wohlbehalten *6*
(to go) sailing segeln *4*
sailor Seemann *8*
salad (gemischter) Salat *9*
salesman Verkäufer *15*
same gleich *5*
same to you gleichfalls *7*
sauce Soße *9*
sausage Wurst *9*
to say sagen *3*
school Schule *2*
scone brötchenartiges Buttergebäck *9*
to scream schreien *13*
sea Meer *3*
seaside (am) Meer *15*
season Jahreszeit *4*
seat Sitzplatz *3*
seatbelt Sicherheitsgurt *6*
second zweite/r/s *5*
to see sehen *1*
to sell verkaufen *3*
to send schicken *8*
to serve servieren, anbieten *9*
shirt Hemd *9*
shoe Schuh *7*
shop Geschäft, Laden *3*
shop assistant Verkäufer/in *2*
(to go) shopping einkaufen gehen *4*
short kurz *4*
short story Kurzgeschichte *7*
shorts Shorts *14*
to shout schreien *15*
to show zeigen *15*
shower Dusche *9*
shy schüchtern *4*
sick krank *7*
side Seite *12*
sign Zeichen, Schild *11*
to sign unterschreiben *9*
signature Unterschrift *9*
silently lautlos, schweigsam *13*
to sing singen *4*
singer Sänger/in *3*
single (ticket) Einzelfahrkarte *13*
single room Einzelzimmer *9*
sink Spülbecken *5*
sir Herr *3*
sister Schwester *1*
to sit (down) sich setzen *3*
size Größe *11*
ski instructor Skitrainer/in, -lehrer/in *3*
skiing Skilaufen *3*
skirt Rock *11*
sky Himmel *13*
to sleep schlafen *5*
sleepy müde, schläfrig *8*
slim schlank *11*
slow langsam *10*
slowly langsam *13*
small klein *2*

to smell riechen *6*
smile Lächeln *13*
to smile lächeln *8*
to smoke rauchen *4*
smoking Raucher *6*
to sneeze niesen *12*
to snore schnarchen *15*
snow Schnee *12*
to snow schneien *12*
so also *4*
soap Seife *9*
sock Socken *14*
soldier Soldat/in *8*
some einige *5*
someone jemand *7*
something etwas *7*
sometimes manchmal *4*
son Sohn *1*
song Lied *4*
soon bald *2*
sorry es tut mir leid *3*
sort Sorte, Art *9*
sound Geräusch *13*
south Süden *1*
spa Heilbad *10*
to speak sprechen *3*
to speak to somebody mit jdm. reden *5*
special spezial, speziell *4*
to spell buchstabieren *1*
spelling Rechtschreibung *6*
to spend verbringen; ausgeben *7*
sports shop Sportartikelgeschäft *3*
spring Frühling *4*
square Platz *10*
stamp Briefmarke *1*
to stand up aufstehen *11*
to start anfangen *4*
stay Aufenthalt *9*
to stay bleiben *4*
to steal stehlen *8*
to step treten *15*
still trotzdem *6*
stocking Strumpf *14*
stop Haltestelle *3*
stop! halt, halten Sie *5*
to stop aufhören *7*
stranger Fremde/r *13*
strawberry Erdbeere *9*
street Straße *2*
struggle Kampf *15*
to struggle kämpfen *15*
student Student/in *1*
study Arbeitszimmer *10*
to study studieren *6*
subject Fach, Unterrichtsfach *7*
successful erfolgreich *7*
suddenly plötzlich *4*
sugar Zucker *9*
suit Anzug *11*
suitcase Koffer *1*
summer Sommer *3*
sun Sonne *6*
to sunbathe sich sonnen *4*
sunny sonnig *2*
supermarket Supermarkt *5*
sure sicher *7*
surname Nachname *1*
(to go) swimming schwimmen gehen *4*

swimming costume Badeanzug *12*
swimming pool Schwimmbad *5*

table Tisch *5*
to take dauern *3*
to take a message etw. ausrichten *14*
to take control die Macht übernehmen *10*
to take off abheben; ausziehen *15*
to take photographs fotografieren *4*
take-away meal Essen zum Mitnehmen *9*
to talk reden, sich unterhalten *5*
tall groß *10*
taxi driver Taxifahrer/in *2*
tea Tee *2*
to teach unterrichten *3*
teacher Lehrer/in *1*
telephone Telefon *5*
to tell erzählen, sagen *3*
tent Zelt *12*
term Semester *8*
terrace Terrasse *5*
terrible schrecklich *13*
test Prüfung *13*
thank you, thanks danke *1*
That's ..., please. Das macht ..., bitte. *9*
theatre Theater *4*
then dann *3*
there and back hin und zurück *3*
thing Ding, Sache *3*
to think denken *4*
thirsty durstig *8*
this dies, das *1*
this morning heute früh *6*
thought Gedanke *15*
thoughtlessly gedankenlos, unüberlegt *15*
thousand Tausend *10*
through durch *10*
ticket Fahrkarte *1*
ticket inspector Fahrkartenkontrolleur/in *3*
tie Krawatte *11*
tights Strumpfhose *14*
time Zeit *3*
timetable Fahrplan *13*
tired müde *3*
title Titel *13*
to vor (mit Uhrzeiten) *3*
today heute *2*
together zusammen *8*
tomato Tomate *9*
tomorrow morgen *1*
tonight heute abend *11*
tonne Tonne (1000 kg) *13*
too auch *3*
toothpaste Zahnpasta *9*
top oben *2*
to touch berühren *12*
tour Rundfahrt *14*
town Stadt *3*
town hall Rathaus *10*
toy Spielzeug *14*
tracksuit Trainingsanzug *12*
tractor Traktor *14*
trade Handel *15*
traditional traditionell *9*
traffic Verkehr *4*
traffic lights Ampel *10*
train Zug *3*
trainers Turnschuhe *11*

tram Straßenbahn *10*
to translate übersetzen *3*
to transmit übermitteln *8*
to travel reisen *4*
travel agent Reisebürokaufmann/frau *2*
travel agent's Reisebüro *5*
traveller's cheque Reisescheck *9*
tray Tablett *6*
to treat behandeln *15*
tree Baum *4*
trip Reise, Ausflug *15*
trousers Hose *11*
true genau, wahr *8*
to try versuchen *10*
to try on anprobieren *11*
tulip Tulpe *12*
tuna Thunfisch *2*
to turn abbiegen *10*; sich umdrehen *11*
to turn on einschalten, anmachen *12*
to turn out ausschalten *11*
twice zweimal *13*
to type tippen *6*
typewriter Schreibmaschine *8*
typical typisch *13*

umbrella Regenschirm *12*
uncle Onkel *2*
under unter *6*
underground U-Bahn *2*
to understand verstehen *2*
unemployed arbeitslos *7*
unfortunately leider *13*
unfriendly unfreundlich *10*
unhealthy ungesund
United Nations Vereinte Nationen *3*
university Universität *4*
until bis *4*
 not until erst *4*
unusual ungewöhnlich *10*
upstairs (nach) oben *8*
to use benutzen *2*
usually gewöhnlich *4*

Valentine's Day Valentinstag *7*
vegetable Gemüse *9*
very well sehr gut *1*
video recorder Videorecorder *7*
view Aussicht *10*
village Dorf *3*
visit Besuch *15*
to visit besuchen *4*
visitor Besucher/in *9*
voice Stimme *8*

to wait warten *8*
waitress Kellnerin *14*
to wake up aufwachen *8*; aufwecken *9*
to walk gehen, laufen *4*
(to go) walking spazierengehen *3*
to walk round einen Rundgang machen *10*
wall Wand *5*
to want wollen *1*
war Krieg *7*
to wash waschen *3*
washing machine Waschmaschine *5*
(to do the) washing-up abspülen *5*
watch Armbanduhr *3*
to watch ansehen, anschauen *4*

to watch television fernsehen *3*
water Wasser *5*
way Weg, Art und Weise *10*
to wear tragen *6*
weather Wetter *2*
wedding Hochzeit *7*
wedding anniversary Hochzeitstag *11*
week Woche *3*
weekday Wochentag *4*
weekend Wochenende *4*
to weigh wiegen *13*
welcome Willkommen *6*
well na ja *6*
west Westen *10*
wet naß *4*
what was *1*
what about ...? wie ist es mit ...? *5*
what sort of? was für (ein/e)? *5*
what time wie spät, um wieviel Uhr *3*
when wann *3*; als *6*
where wo, woher *1*
white weiß *5*
who wer *2*
whole ganz *5*
whose wessen *11*
why warum *3*
wide weit *13*
widow Witwe *14*
wife Ehefrau *2*
to win gewinnen *7*
window Fenster *4*
(to go) windsurfing windsurfen *4*
windy windig *12*
wine Wein *3*
winter Winter *3*
wish Wunsch *13*
with mit, bei *2*
without ohne *12*
to wonder sich fragen *11*
wonderful wunderbar *7*
woods Wald *10*
word Wort *6*
word processor Textverarbeitungsmaschine *4*
work Arbeit *2*
to work arbeiten *3*
workroom Arbeitszimmer *8*
world Welt *4*
(to be) worried sich Sorgen machen *11*
to worry sich Sorgen machen *4*
to write schreiben *2*
writer Schriftsteller/in *7*
writing paper Schreibpapier *9*
wrong falsch *2*

year Jahr *1*
yellow gelb *4*
yesterday gestern *6*
yet noch nicht *7*
young jung *2*